Graham Greene Studies
Volume 1, 2017

Graham Greene Birthplace Trust
University of North Georgia Press

**Editors:**

Joyce Stavick and
Jon Wise

**Editorial Board:**

**Digital Editors:**

Jon Mehlferber

**Associate Editors:**

Ethan Howard
Kayla Mehalcik

**Published by:**

University of North Georgia Press
Dahlonega, Georgia

The University of North Georgia Press is a teaching press, providing a service-learning environment for students to gain real life experiences in publishing and marketing. The entirety of the layout and design of this volume was created and executed by Ethan Howard, a student at the University of North Georgia.

Cover Photo Courtesy of Bernard Diederich

**For more information, please visit:**

http://digitalcommons.northgeorgia.edu/ggs/

Copyright © 2017 by University of North Georgia Press. All rights reserved. No part of this book may be reproduced in whole or in part without written permission from the publisher, except by reviewers who may quote brief excerpts in connection with a review in newspaper, magazine, or electronic publications; nor may any part of this book be reproduced, stored in a retrieval system, or transmitted in any form or by any means electronic, mechanical, photocopying, recording, or other without the written permission from the publisher.

Printed in the United States of America, 2017

# In Memory of David R.A. Pearce, scholar, poet, and friend

David Pearce was born in Whitstable in 1938. That Kentish coastline was, in the early war years, under threat; and for a while, as a small child, he was an evacuee in Cornwall. After school at St Edmund's, Canterbury, and then St Edmund Hall, Oxford, he taught at Stanbridge Earls, Hampshire, and then, for thirty-three years at Berkhamsted School where he was Head of English and a boarding housemaster. He was a joint-founder of the Graham Greene Birthplace Trust, and, through that, rejoiced in friends all round the world. The importance of his family life and other interests may be deduced from his poems, most recently those published in his volume, *The Street*, 2016, Mountain Arbor Press.

# Contents

| | Page No. |
|---|---|
| Introduction................................................................Joyce Stavick and Jon Wise | vii |

## Articles

| | |
|---|---|
| **Reflections**................................................................Judith Adamson | 1 |
| **Shades of Greene in Catholic Literary Modernism**................................................................Mark Bosco | 8 |
| **Figures in Greene's Carpet:** | |
|     *The Power & the Glory* to *Monsignor Quixote*................................................................Robert M. Davis | 24 |
| **Graham Greene's Books for Children**................................................................François Gallix | 39 |
| **Graham Greene & the Congo, 1959:** | |
|     Personal Memories and Background of *A Burnt-Out Case*................................................................Michel Lechat | 46 |
| **The Furthest Escape Of All:** | |
|     Darkness And Refuge In The Belgian Congo................................................................Michael Meeuwis | 56 |
| **"Memory Cheats": Deception, Recollection and the Problem of Reading in** | |
|     *The Captain and the Enemy*................................................................Frances McCormack | 82 |
| **Graham Greene in Love and War:** | |
|     French Indochina and the Making of *The Quiet American*................................................................Kevin Ruane | 97 |
| **"The Invisible Japanese Gentleman":** | |
|     Graham Greene's Literary Influence in Japan................................................................Motonori Sato | 110 |
| **"All Writers are Equal but Some Writers are More Equal than Others":** | |
|     Some Reflections on Links and Contrasts Between | |
|     Graham Greene and George Orwell................................................................Neil Sinyard | 122 |
| **Darkest Greeneland: *Brighton Rock***................................................................Cedric Watts | 133 |

## Features

| | |
|---|---|
| **Travels with Graham Greene**................................................................Bernard Diederich | 145 |
|     In Greene's Footprints, Red and Black Greenes of St. Kitts, Stolichnaya for a Bon Blan | |
| **Traveling in Greeneland**................................................................Quentin Falk | 158 |
| ***Dr. Fischer of Geneva* or There's so Much More to Christmas Crackers**................................................................David Pearce | 163 |

## Book Review

| | |
|---|---|
| **Jon Wise and Mike Hill: *The Works of Graham Greene Volume 2:*** | |
|     *The Graham Greene Archives*................................................................Judith Adamson | 178 |
| ***The Ritz***................................................................Graham Greene | 181 |

## Call for Papers
................................................................ 183

## Maps and Illustrations

| | Page No. |
|---|---|
| Map of Greene's Travel in Africa, 1959 | 60 |
| Map of Mission Stations along Greene's 1959 journey in Africa | 77 |
| Photo of Greene, Phat Diem, 1951 | 99 |
| Photo of Greene with French maintenance crew, 1951 | 100 |
| Photo of Greene with French troops, Phat Diem, 1951 | 102 |
| Photo of Bishop Le Huu Tu, 1951 | 102 |
| Note of Dedication by Tu to Greene | 102 |
| Photos of Greene at Orphanage, Phat Diem, 1951 | 107 |

## Acknowledgements:

Many people have contributed to the production of *Graham Greene Studies*; our thanks to those at the University of North Georgia who helped with editing and production: BJ Robinson, Corey Parson, Amy Beard, Jon Mehlferber, Allison Galloup, Kayla Mehalcik, Ethan Howard, and Brian Corrigan. Thanks also to members of the Graham Greene Birthplace Trust who helped with publicity and correspondence: Giles Clark and Mike Hill. Finally, our thanks to Bernard Diederich and the family of David Pearce for permission to print photos.

# Introduction

Welcome to the first volume of *Graham Greene Studies.*

*Graham Greene Studies* is an international, peer-reviewed and disseminated journal of scholarly research pertaining to the life and work of Graham Greene. It will be published biennially. The intention is to provide a forum for academic study and at the same time to appeal to as wide an audience as possible, reflecting the very active, international interest which continues to be shown in the work of this writer. The journal will establish a venue for disseminating research, book and film reviews, and other original scholarship germane to the study of Graham Greene.

The project was conceived by Professor Joyce Stavick, Department Head, English, at the University of North Georgia. Professor Stavick's successful mission to secure the go-ahead for this project is based on an on-going concern that there is at present no academic journal dedicated to this major 20th Century writer of international acclaim.

Professor Stavick's co-editor, Dr. Jonathan Wise, is a Trustee of the Graham Greene Birthplace Trust (GGBT) and co-author of a critically acclaimed, two-volume bibliography of the works of Graham Greene. The University of North Georgia's partnership with the GGBT acknowledges the contribution made by the Trust over the past eighteen years to the study of the work and the life of Greene. This has been made possible through the dedication of the Trust members who, since 1998, have organized and run an annual, four-day, international festival held in the town of Berkhamsted, UK, birthplace of Graham Greene.

Indeed, this inaugural volume is, in effect, a tribute to the achievements of the Graham Greene International Festival. The articles are drawn from a variety of past papers delivered at one or other of these events. Because of the festival's reputation, the festival organizers have been able to draw upon a rich variety of speakers: academics, peers of the British realm, celebrities, fellow writers, and other individuals from the UK and abroad who have had a connection to Greene, each of whom has contributed richly to our knowledge of the man and his work.

As editors, we freely acknowledge that we are not the first to have sought to publish a Graham Greene journal. *Dangerous Edges of Graham Greene: Journeys with Saints and Sinners* (London: Continuum, 2011), edited by Dermot Gilvary and Darren J. N. Middleton, is a fine collection of seventeen such essays. In its earlier years, the GGBT also published a series of monographs consisting of verbatim texts of key lectures. Audio and video recordings have also been made at most of the Festivals; together, these constitute a substantial resource for researchers. Details about access and further information can be obtained from the GGBT Secretary through the Trust website www.grahamgreenebt.org .

The papers which make up this first edition of the journal arrived at the editors' desks in a wide variety of formats. Circumstances demanded that some had been taken straight from the lecturers' notes; others were complete with footnotes and full bibliographies. It should be noted that this variety of approach will not occur in future editions, and contributions will conform to the guidelines referred to in the *2017 Call for Papers* advertisement printed elsewhere in this journal.

Two factors strike one immediately when examining the contents page of the inaugural volume of *Graham Greene Studies*. First, the fact that the majority of the contributors are not UK nationals is a clear reflection of the enduring international appeal of the writer. Four contributors are not writing in their native languages. Second, for a long period in the past Greene was dubbed "a Catholic writer," a description he always rejected. Interestingly, only one paper included here directly addresses this aspect of the writer's work.

Both Judith Adamson in "Reflections" and Michael Meeuwis in "The Furthest Escape of All" provide acute insights into the creative process of writing. Adamson shows through reference to a single initial incident how Greene re-cycled and adapted a private experience which much later culminated in its use in one of his most accomplished novels, *The Quiet American*. Michael Meeuwis, who has gained access to some hitherto unknown and private materials, together with the original holograph of Greene's 'Congo Journal' (which differs considerably from the published version), is able to demonstrate by example how the writer's personal experience guided the composition of *A Burnt-Out Case*, both directly and indirectly.

We must extend our gratitude to Edith Dasnoy, widow of Dr. Michel Lechat, for granting us access to the manuscript of her late husband's address at the 2006 Festival, entitled "Graham Greene and the Congo, 1959." This paper neatly complements Michael Meeuwis's pioneering study of what is a fascinating, and little explored, interlude in Greene's life.

Our determination that this selection should reflect the full spectrum of past festivals is demonstrated by the inclusion of Cedric Watts' paper from the 1999 Festival, "Darkest Greeneland: *Brighton Rock*." Watts' work has stood the test of time; his intimate knowledge of the Brighton landscape provides further evidence of Greene's mastery of "place" in his novels. Frances McCormack's 'Memory Cheats', like the essays of Meeuwis and Watts, also concentrates on a single work: Greene's last novel, *The Captain and the Enemy*, which has been mostly disregarded by critics. McCormack finds evidence to contradict this notion, analysing in depth the complexities of this challenging text that his friend Leopoldo Durán claimed "almost drove [Greene] to despair."

Kevin Ruane's "Graham Greene in Love and War," does make passing references to the text of *The Quiet American* but concentrates for the most part on chronicling Greene's experiences of Vietnam in the early 1950s as he tried to come to terms with a complicated and "unravelling" political map. It should be noted that Ruane's research is on-going, particularly with respect to Greene's friend, the rather shadowy Trevor Wilson.

Both Mark Bosco and Bob Davis examine themes in the writer's novels. Mark Bosco's "Shades of Greene in Catholic Literary Modernism" argues that Greene, in common with other Catholic and Anglo-Catholic writers of the time, found a way to counter the secular writers' contention that religion had no place in modern life or, indeed, in modernism. By contrast, Davis's 2007 lecture, "Figures in Greene's Carpet," traces a familiar theme which runs through most of the writer's novels: the pursuit of the individual through a damaged landscape. Davis concentrates on the period between the publication of *The Power and the Glory* in 1940 and *Monsignor Quixote* in 1982. Neil

Sinyard, in "All Writers are Equal but Some Writers are More Equal than Others," finds both contrasts and similarities, some quite surprising, in the work of Graham Greene and another "towering figure" of mid-20th Century English literature, George Orwell.

François Gallix and Motonori Sato delivered papers at the 2011 and 2014 Festivals which in turn examine an unremarked aspect of the writer's work and Greene's impact on two Japanese authors. Gallix, "Graham Greene's Books for Children," in addition to analysing the books the author wrote specifically for that audience, makes connections with Greene's pre-occupation with his own childhood and the books he read as a youngster. In "The Invisible Japanese Gentleman," Motonori Sato explains how Saiichi Maruya and Shusaku Endo were both influenced by Greene's style. Sato also shows how Endo, most unusually a Christian convert living in a Buddhist and Shinto culture, was helped by Greene to get published in the West.

2016 marked the 25th anniversary of the death of Graham Greene. It is inevitable that, with the passing of time, there are now fewer of those who knew the writer personally or worked with him. It is therefore fitting that we have the reminiscences of two people who fit this category. These appear in the "Features" section. Bernard Diederich was a trusted friend of Greene during the later stages of his life and, with his extensive knowledge of the region, became the writer's guide to Haiti and Central America. Quentin Falk has appeared at many festivals, where his knowledge of film in general—and films associated with Graham Greene in particular—has been greatly valued. Falk got to know the writer well during the short time when he was working on the first edition of his book *Travels in Greeneland: The Cinema of Graham Greene* (now in its 4th edition, published by the UNG Press) and later during the now famous National Film Theatre Guardian Lecture in 1984 when a reticent Greene delivered a rare public lecture that was covertly filmed.

We have also chosen to include in the Features section, "*Dr. Fischer of Geneva* or There's so Much More to Christmas Crackers," a talk delivered by David R. A. Pearce at the 2009 Festival. "Drap," as he was affectionately called by his students, was instrumental in the formation of The Trust, was Festival Director for several years, and was a school master at Berkhamsted School, Greene's *alma mater*. Festival goers could not miss his unmistakable presence typified by a splendid, resounding verbal delivery. After much deliberation, we have decided not to edit David's paper on the 1980 novella *Dr. Fischer of Geneva or The Bomb Party* beyond the standard style adopted for this journal. His public contributions at the festivals were not only knowledgeable and incisive but they were also performances. We hope that, when reading his paper, those who knew him will be able to hear his voice again. Sadly, David died as *GGS* was preparing for publication. Our thoughts are with his family, and we will miss him.

It is fitting that the last word should come from the man himself. Graham Greene was fond of the "good life" and he certainly tried to stay at, if not the best, certainly the world's most iconic hotels while on his numerous travels. This included *The Ritz Hotel* in London, which he frequented, particularly when he was domiciled in France after 1966. He wrote *The Ritz* in 1976 when he heard that the famous establishment was about to be sold. The poem was to have been published alongside the uncollected travel reports, essays and reviews which make up *Reflections* (1990). In May 1989, Professor Judith Adamson, who assisted the aging writer in preparing the book for publication, wrote to him: "Do you want 'The Ritz' added as a PS to 'Ghosts of a Possible Adventure'?" (an essay in *Reflections* about the Café Royal, another London luxury hotel). I prefer it there to placing it chronologically. And would you please check it as I had a problem reading your writing and want to be sure I got it down properly." (Adamson was working from a holograph in Greene's notoriously difficult handwriting.) Two months later, Greene replied, 'I hesitate about using THE RITZ as I still go there and Victor has retired. In actual fact things have a bit improved there. On yet third thoughts I would rather leave out THE RITZ.'

We are pleased to publish the poem for the first time.

*Joyce Stavick & Jon Wise*
December 2016

# Reflections

## Judith Adamson

### The 2014 Graham Greene International Festival

In 1987, before digitization made research in the Humanities easier, I worked my way through decades of newspapers and journals looking for essays Graham Greene only vaguely remembered having written. I was not surprised when he suggested coming to the archive to help me. That summer in Antibes we had talked about the adventure of using letters to capture the tone of someone's life and old newspapers to recreate the idiom of social interchange. Greene appreciated this now nearly obsolete method of research because it suggested his novelist's hunt for material. He knew the sensation of holding old paper, the texture of it, the smell. He loved second-hand bookshops for their mustiness and the treasure hunt they offered; "the magic world of chance and adventure," he called it, "which sometimes leads you to strange places."

We included in *Reflections* most of the essays I found, which his friend, Max Reinhardt, published in 1990. It was the last of Greene's books to appear in his lifetime, and when I came to re-edit it for Vintage in September 2014, I expected that many of the essays would be dated and have to be cut, if for no other reason than to make room for unpublished pieces I had since found. As I did not want to noticeably change the book, I was pleased to find the writing still fresh and of interest, not as archival material, but as useful comment about the present. It was not shaped by any allegiance to state or idea but by Greene's own steady gaze that debunked the hypocritical and made the wider point everywhere. And there remained the fascination of such a valuable record of what reality looked like to him before he transformed it into fiction.

That said, I was surprised by something I had not noticed before: the way Greene often recorded his private experience of public events first in a letter, then in an essay and then, more obviously, in a novel. I knew the skill with which he had recycled his work, using commissioned reports from the world's hot spots to fund his travels, then cutting the same material for journals like the *Tablet* or *London Magazine*, to bury them in *Ways of Escape*. He was a publisher too and he knew the market. But I had not realized that the process began in letters. This was a different kind of recycling, more like the gathering of an image or the reconfiguration of fragments into narrative. With Richard Greene's *Graham Greene: A Life in Letters* in hand, here is just one of the progressions I found:

On 13 October 1926 when Greene was in hospital for an appendectomy, he wrote to his fiancée, Vivienne Dayrell-Browning:

We had an awful to-do yesterday evening—the first time I've ever been in a room when someone dies. A small boy with a broken leg had had an operation and after his parents left him, the surgeon found his breathing shallow. There was a scrambling for the tail end of his life & he was gone. Absolutely unexpected .... The terrible thing was when the mother turned up about 8:45. I've never seen anyone with all their self-control gone before. She had to be supported in and she was calling out things at the top of her voice—what made it worse it was the sort of things people say on the cinema & which one had fondly imagined real life was free of—sentimental hackneyed things. "Why did you go without saying goodbye to your mother?"& "Royston, Royston" (the ridiculous name seemed to make it worse), & "What shall I do without him?" "Sister, sister, don't tell me we're parted." All in a sort of scream. It was ghastly lying in bed listening to it. Then they half carried her out. I'm afraid we're going to have another death in the ward today.... An old man of about 76, who'd been in a motor accident, head fractured, one hand smashed & both legs. Are people who write entirely & absolutely selfish, darling? Even though in a way I hated it yesterday evening—one half of me was saying how lucky it was—added experience—& I kept on catching myself trying to memorize details—Sister's face, the faces of the other men in the ward. And I felt quite excited aesthetically. It made one rather disgusted with oneself.

Forty-five years later, in 1971 in *A Sort of Life,* he rewrote the hospital scene with small variations. There he said the child's death was "our second death. The first we had barely noticed: an old man dying from cancer of the mouth." But this "second death disturbed the whole ward. The first was inevitable fate, the second was contingency." As in the 1926 letter, the boy's parents left when the child went to sleep. There was a burst of activity, and the parents returned. But in *A Sort of Life,*

"to shut out the sound of the mother's tears and cries," Greene added that all his

"companions in the ward lay with their earphones on, listening—there was nothing else for them to hear—to Children's Hour. All my companions but not myself. There is a splinter of ice in the heart of a writer. I watched and listened. This was something which one day I might need: the woman speaking, uttering the banalities she must have remembered from some women's magazine, a genuine grief that could communicate only in clichés. "My boy, my boy, why did you not wait till I came?" The father sat silent with his hat on his knees, and you could tell that even in his unhappiness he was embarrassed by the banality of his wife's words, by the scene she was so badly playing to the public ward.

When the private 1926 letter was crafted for publication by the seasoned Greene, it contained the same telling detail. With a sense of drama and irony, everyone else is listening to "Children's Hour"—nice addition that—and the effect of the child's death is heightened by its being the second one, the first only "an inevitable fate." But two things are the same: the compassionate recording of the mother's "genuine grief that could only communicate in clichés," and the self-conscious writer watching himself watch and listen with a "splinter of ice in his heart."

How did we get from the one description to the other, from what was never intended for publication to what was, from the private letter in which the young Greene was "rather disgusted" with himself as he plundered other people's lives for fictional use to the constructed public narrative in which the now famous novelist admitted to having "a splinter of ice" in his heart and enjoined us to watch him as he watched himself watch the mother play to the public ward? And where did the progression lead?

On 18 August 1939, Greene published "Bombing Raid" in *The Spectator*. He described the clothes he wore on the practice run, and "the fragile look of the huge bombers inside, all glass and aluminium, tubes coiling everywhere, a long empty tunnel like a half-built Underground leading to the rear gun, a little cramped space in front behind the cockpit for the navigator at his table and the wireless operator. In the cockpit you feel raised over the whole world, even over your plane: space between your legs and glass under your feet and glass all round." Greene was in "the leading plane of four."

They flew out over the North Sea, then turned back. "The engines were shut off and each plane in turn dived steeply down, cutting through the great summer castles of cloud" and flew "on to the target in Berkshire—a maximum height of about 200 feet at 200 m.p.h., too low for gunfire; nor could any fighter in the upper air observe us as we bumped just above the hills and woods the same colour as ourselves." Greene "felt a momentary horror at the exposure of a whole quiet landscape to machine-gun fire–this was an area for evacuation, of small villages and farms . . . . It was completely open to the four aircraft which swept undetected from behind the trees and between the hills. There was room for a hundred English Guernicas."

Here was the forerunner to a bombing raid Greene went on over a decade later while the French were preparing to face the first important Viet Minh counter-attack on Phat Diem. In a letter to his son, Francis, from Hanoi on 16 November 1951, he wrote:

> I went on two missions. The first was to bomb & machine gun round a little town which the Communists had captured. My aircraft went alone. Tiny little cockpit, just room for the pilot (who was also gunner & bomber) the navigator & me—an hour's flight each way & then three quarters of an hour over the objective. We did fourteen dives. It was most uncomfortable, coming rapidly & steeply down from 9 thousand to 3 thousand feet. You were pressed forward in your seat & then as you zoomed up again your stomach was pressed in. I began to get used to it after about four dives. Coming back we went down to about 200 feet, and shot up a sampan on the Red River.

Details are sketchy. When some detail is added a month later, on Christmas Day 1951 in a letter to his mistress, Catherine Walston, the conflict is clarified and creative:

> "I got where no newspaperman was allowed, into surrounded Phat Diem—the rebels all round within 6 hundred yards, flames, far too many corpses for my taste, & constant mortar fire . . . . The bodies, especially those of a poor woman & her small boy, who had got in the way of war, drove me to confession."

This was presumably the second mission mentioned in Greene's letter to his son.

We now have the beginning of a seminal scene in *The Quiet American* written partly in private letters over several decades; from Greene's sick-bed to Vivienne in October 1926 there is the raw selfishness, excitement and guilt at watching the death of the small boy in hospital, and from two bombing raids, the first in an article, the practice one in 1939 with its imagined "hundred English Guernicas," the second in a letter to his son about the raid at Phat Diem at the end of 1951, where "a sampan was shot-up." Then there is the letter to

Catherine Walston with its "far too many corpses," and the bodies of "a poor woman and her small boy who got in the way of war" and drove Greene to Confession.

On 12 July 1952 "Indo-China: France's Crown of Thorns" was published in *Paris Match*. Along with an historical discussion about Vietnam, it turned Greene's private observations at Phat Diem into a publishable report:

> "It is hard to assess the losses of the Viet Minh: here and there the canal was filled with a thick gruel, heads floating above the accumulation of bodies below." Among his "most striking memories" is that of the "bodies of a woman and her small boy caught in a crossfire between the parachutists and the enemy. This mother and child suddenly lost their anonymity when I realized that their faith and mine were the same.

Here part of the combined private image is made public, and it is a little less personal than when it ended in the Confessional. It is also more horrific. As detail is added, it is done in the way Greene suggested in his 1941 review of American newspaperman, Ralph Ingersoll's account of the Blitz with imaginative rather than emotional sympathy. The "too many corpses" are now "the gruel of bodies in the canal." The "woman and her small boy who had got in the way of war" are now "caught in a crossfire between the parachutists and the enemy." The privacy of the confessional has become at once universal in Catholicism, and the mother and child are no longer anonymous, rescued from the image of gruel in the canal. This image will change again.

In "Before the Attack" on 16 April 1954 in *The Spectator,* Greene says he is waiting "for a plane on the shuttle service to Dien Bien Phu" from Hanoi's military airport:

> I always have a sense of guilt when I am a civilian tourist in the regions of death: after all one does not visit a disaster except to give aid—one feels a voyeur of violence, as I felt during the attack two years ago on Phat Diem. There violence had already arrived.... It was very present in the canal so laden with bodies that they overlapped and a punt of parachutists stuck on a reef of them: and it came suddenly home on patrol when two shots killed a mother and child who found themselves between the opposing forces. What panic had they felt? I felt a little of it myself when for a few moments I lost my companions and found myself stumbling between the Viet Minh and the Foreign Legion. I told myself then that I hated war, and yet here I was back—an old voyeur at his tricks again.

Here in 1954, the private and public accounts from 1926, 1939, 1941, 1951, and 1952 begin to merge. In 1939 Greene saw at a distance the possibility of "a hundred English Guernicas." On two Vietnamese missions in 1951 he watched his pilot "shoot up a sampan" and saw the faces of the dead mother and her son, an image he could not forget. In 1926 he was self-conscious about watching when the boy died, a similar self-consciousness he praised in Ralph Ingersoll in 1941. In 1951 that emotion made him flee to the Confessional. By 1952 he joined the mother in Catholicism and she and her child "suddenly lost their anonymity." By 1954, his self-conscious guilt has become the sin of voyeurism, and he "a civilian tourist in the regions of death ... a voyeur of violence ... at his tricks again," hating war.

When our voyeur then published "A Memory of Indo-China" in September 1955, he recalled a vertical bombing raid he went on in December 1952 as "a way of killing time." Boredom had set in. There had been too many bodies. In 1939 in the practice bombing he admitted with bravado "I wasn't the only one sick—the second pilot was sick, too, and the navigator passed me an encouraging note—'Not feeling too good myself'." But in Vietnam "before the second dive" the older Greene "felt fear—fear of humiliation, fear of vomiting over the navigator's back, fear that middle-aged lungs would not stand the pressure. After the tenth dive I was aware only of irritation—the affair had gone on too long, it was time to go home." Then, as the bomber turned, and in the relief of finding himself still alive even the fear of being shot down left him, the plane dived again, "flattening out over the neglected rice fields, aimed like a bullet at one small sampan on the yellow stream. The gun gave a single burst of tracer, and the sampan blew apart in a shower of sparks; we didn't even wait to see our victims struggling to survive, but climbed and made for home. I thought again, as I had thought when I saw a dead child in a ditch at Phat Diem, 'I hate war.' There had been something so shocking in our fortuitous choice of a prey—we had just happened to be passing, one burst only was required, there was no one to return our fire, we were gone again, adding our little quota to the world's dead." The scene is identical in *The Quiet American*, which was published the same year.

That in a "A Memory of Indo-China" Greene says he recalls the vertical raid of December 1952 while the sampan blowing apart in a shower of sparks is in his letter to Francis dated 16 November 1951, and the dead mother and her child are mentioned to Catherine Walston on Christmas day of that year, only underlines the way he gathered his image toward fiction.

The "absolute selfishness" and aesthetic excitement of the writer's gaze is from its beginning in 1926, entangled with the guilt of watching someone else's pain, as if to watch and listen were to betray the suffering rather than a measure of sympathy for their plight. In 1939 on the practice bombing raid the possible pain and fear are imagined as "a hundred English Guernicas." In Vietnam the private man finds a public way to deal with himself as a voyeur, first in a visit to the confessional, then in the realization of a shared religion when the mother and her son lose their anonymity and their pain takes on a wider meaning, perhaps lessening the sting of individual guilt. Soon, as the voyeuristic detail of Greene's reporting finally comes to rest in fictional metaphor, the sampan and the dead child are in Fowler's mind when he decides he has to take sides to remain human and chooses the Viet Minh.

As Greene wrote in "Bombing Raid" in 1939, he always preferred "the ruled to the ruler." But Fowler's choice in 1955 is far more pointed and carries with it his conflicted involvement in Pyle's death, and perhaps Greene's own in taking a direct political stand in a novel. The oversound of discomfort remains, but the recurrent guilt of voyeurism has subsided in action. If we move on to *Travels With My Aunt* in 1969, the novelist's selfish stare is excused as life giving.

Early on Greene insisted that it was a writer's responsibility to tell the truth, and he was so irritated when critics called his view of the world *Greeneland* that he accused them of wearing blinkers. He procured his material the hard way and he prided himself on its accuracy. Yet here as he gathered his facts from personal impressions through public professional renderings into fiction, we find changes, dramatic additions, even a dating error. They are small and we might well say, so what: *The Quiet American* and *Travels With My Aunt* are far better for them. But that is to miss the point.

Re-editing *Reflections,* I saw how the hard discipline of writing forced Greene to find his own truth. He was led to it by his uneasy conscience and his sense of personal failure more than by his need to recycle material to pay his bills, something he did throughout his life. As he reconfigured his facts into fiction, reality into art, he too was changed, his words seeming cleverer than their writer. His reporting pulled him toward that powerful scene in *The Quiet American* where he finally decided that "the affair had gone on far too long, it was time to go home"—time to let go. But what he began to see in 1926 was not finished with him until 1969 in *Travels With My Aunt*, the novel that marks his move from England to France at the beginning of 1966 and the only one he said he ever had fun writing. Then, when Aunt Augusta's lessons about reading and recording life finally got through to Henry, Greene was able to acknowledge that "the splinter of ice in the heart of every writer" is life giving. Here was forgiveness for Aunt Augusta, liberation for Henry, and new creative freedom for Greene, what Seamus Heaney might have called an achieved grace.

**Professor Judith Adamson** has written many books, including *Graham Greene and Cinema, The Dangerous Edge*, a political biography of Graham Greene, *Charlotte Haldane*, a biography of JBS Haldane's first wife, and *Max Reinhardt: A Life In Publishing*. She edited and introduced *Love Letters*, the thirty year correspondence between Leonard Woolf and Trekkie Ritchie Parsons, and selected and introduced the essays in Graham Greene's much acclaimed last book, *Reflections*, which she recently re-edited for the new Vintage edition. She lives in Montreal where she is a Research Scholar in Residence at Dawson College.

# Shades Of Greene In Catholic Literary Modernism

## Mark Bosco, S.J.

The 2009 Graham Greene International Festival

*"Christianity does not make art easy. It deprives it of many facile means, it bars its course at many places, but in order to raise its level."*
—Jacques Maritain, *Art and Scholasticism*

An implicit historical assumption in the narrative of western culture is that the modern age witnessed the death of God and the waning influence of Christianity. Modernist writers of the late nineteenth and twentieth centuries, among those most aware of their own "modernity," did much eulogizing of religious faith, relegating it to an outmoded cultural nostalgia or a reactionary maneuver that tethered art to traditional categories of cultural power such as the church or the state. The challenge to religious faith is one of many ways Modernism defined itself by what it attempts to cast off. In 1918, Edwin Muir titled an essay, "What is Modern?" His answer was intimately bound up with the demise of religion. "We see outside our field of conflict a region of Christian calm, but never, never, never can we return there, for our instincts as well as our intellect are averse to it," he writes. "We refuse to escape by reactionary backdoors—Christianity and the like ... religion has dried up."[1] For Muir and his contemporaries, the challenge of modernity was making meaning without resorting to worn-out religious traditions. And yet the success of this Modernist project is complicated by the persistence of Catholic modes of cultural expression informed by and responding to the theoretical and artistic underpinnings of modernist formulae. Indeed, twentieth century Catholicism, as a globalized, philosophical, and artistic tradition, often mapped out alternative visions and fictions of reality in dialogue with the rise of modernist aesthetics. Whether understood as an artistic revival that reached across national boundaries to pose fundamental questions about art and culture, or whether understood solely as the emergence of a supposedly new genre of "Catholic" novel that peaked at the end of the mid-twentieth century, one finds a cultural confluence between three unlikely terms: Catholicism, literature, and modernism.

Putting these terms into conversation seems, at first glance, a difficult task. If part of the literary avant-garde's agenda had been to dismiss religion's ability to enlighten what is considered modern, then Roman Catholicism certainly attempted to dismiss the avant-garde as misguided, as well. The papacy, suspicious of those attempting to study Catholic belief with the rationalist tools of modern science and historical-critical methodologies, deployed the word *modernism* as a catchall for the errors of the age. The infamous "Modernist Crisis" appeared within the official texts

---

1 Edwin Muir, *We Moderns: Enigmas and Guesses* (London: George Allen & Unwin Ltd., 1918) 91-92. Muir published this, his first work, under the pseudonym Edward Moore.

of the Catholic Church between 1907 and 1910, after the Papacy had already lost control of the Papal States in Italy (1870) but before the traumatic events of the Great War. Pius X's papal condemnation of the sins of modernism focused around historical criticism in biblical scholarship and contemporary rationalist philosophy (Pascendi Dominici Gregis).Within the same year Pius condemned a list of sixty-five propositions as modernist heresies (*Lamentabili Sane Exitu*). Finally, two years later, he mandated an oath against modernism that all Catholic clergy and seminary professors had to forswear (*Motu Proprio Sacrorum Antistitum*).[2] To be identified as a Catholic intellectual through the first decades of the century was, by its very nature, an anti-modern pose. Such an appraisal would not seem to bode well in discussing a growing Catholic artistic community that understood itself in conversation with the theoretical claims of literary modernism.

Cultural critics also contest the term *modernism*. What Baudelaire could refer to in 1863 as "that indefinable something we may be allowed to call "modernity"[3] has, since then become a complicated, self-conscious debate that involves a diverse canon of artists, literary and otherwise. Once understood as the rupture of epistemological concerns from metaphysical categories, modernism quickly broadened to refer to a set of aesthetic movements united in the practice of destabilizing accepted formal, social, and cultural conventions.

Modernist aesthetics assumed that the anxious dislocations and traumas of modernity could find its coherence only in the artist's creative act, through one's encounter with the artwork itself. T. S. Eliot's *The Waste Land* became, for many artists, a defining work, poetically reaching for an experience beyond dualisms, a search for "a pinpoint in time" or, at the very least, a gathering of the "fragments shored up against [our] ruin." In the assessment of one critic, the conceptualization of "modernism continues to reveal its oppositional and subversive powers through various shapes of its new figurations."[4] And yet as Modernist studies continue to be re-contextualized in various cultural environments, there is little discussion of its Catholic figurations.[5] There is no little irony that the success of the Modernist "project" is complicated by the persistence of religious tropes and topics throughout Modernist literature. Artists keenly focused on the dialectics of modernist aesthetics include Georges Bernanos, Francois Mauriac, T.S. Eliot, W. H. Auden, Evelyn Waugh, Graham Greene, Walker Percy, and Flannery O'Connor. For them, Christian faith was not only source material, but also a necessary response to the modern world. Thus we find ourselves at a moment in literary studies when this Modernist assertion as anti-religious or anti-Catholic is very much in doubt as an important claim or even a true picture of modernism. Indeed, for many twentieth century artists and intellectuals, being Catholic was a possible way to be modern.[6]

---

2 The oath against Modernism (1910) was in effect until 1967, near the end of the Catholic Church's Second Vatican Council.
3 Charles Baudelaire, "The Painter of Modern Life," in *Selected Writings on Art and Literature* (Viking,1972) 395.
4 Astradur Eysteinsson, *Modernism* (Amsterdam: John Benjamins Publishing, 2007).
5 The survey of recent international symposia and new essays in the field verify its marginalization. In the two-volume work, *Modernism*, edited by Eysteinsson and published in 2007, over 50 essays extend the conversation about historical and aesthetic developments in literary modernism, yet no title deals with religious conversion or Catholic

My aim in this essay, then, is to trace the development of a particularly Catholic configuration of modernism, from its roots in nineteenth century France through its evolution in England, and ending with a sustained meditation on the British writer and Catholic convert, Graham Greene. I will suggest that in Greene's most important fiction one grasps that the Catholic literary revival is actually a kind of Catholic literary modernism. To cover this all in one paper is probably too ambitious a goal, but I hope that I can at least express some of the context and the theological contours of the Catholic revival, primarily focusing on France and England, so important to Greene's own development as an artist.

In order to understand the genesis of literary modernism and its Catholic configurations, we must first return to the French and the English enlightenment and the concomitant revolutions that marked what is called "the Modern"—the modern consciousness, the modern state, and modern philosophy. These categories developed from initial stirrings in eighteenth century French culture, fostering a belief, often enshrined in the term "philosophical positivism," that science and natural evolution would progressively remake the world into a better place. Fast forward a century to Charles Darwin's *The Origin of Species (1859)*, and there was an emerging consensus among Western philosophers, scientists, and intellectuals that the human person was biologically and socially determined, and that reality was merely the empirical phenomena seen, the scientific observations recorded and interpreted.

The legacy of philosophical positivism in western culture was the subsequent elevation of anthropology, psychology, and sociology as the *de facto* discourses that best explained human life and offered the best solutions to improve it. One of the consequences of this belief was the relegation of religion to the past, as something that would be abandoned over time for the more certain truths of modern science. Religion, if it were discussed at all, would more and more be understood as the realm of the ignorant at worst, or the work of the imagination at best. It would be only a matter of time, so the logic went, that reason would subordinate the flights of religious fancy to scientific constructions of human life and development. This legacy continued to bifurcate faith and science, religion and modern society, mutually exclusive terms, if not categorically antagonistic to one another.

One can envision the intellectual salons of France and England during the last years of the nineteenth century: Charles Darwin

---

impulses so prevalent during the twentieth century period. Very little, for instance, expounds upon Eliot's and Auden's religious turn in poetry and there is no mention of Catholic novelists.

6 Four recent studies of the last decade offer a truer picture of Modernism as each grapple with various modernist authors, thinkers, and cultural critics in their quest to reimagine the relationship between Christianity and culture. Stephen Schloesser's *Jazz Age Catholicism: Postwar Paris 1919-1933* (Toronto, 2005), *Pericles Lewis's Religious Experience and the Modernist Novel* (Cambridge, 2010), Elizabeth Anderson's *H.D. and the Modernist Religious Imagination* (Bloomsbury, 2013), and Erik Tonning's *Modernism and Christianity* (Palgrave Macmillan, 2014), all offer diverse notions of the perceived crisis of Western civilization, yet each draws on the idea that a revival of elements of (Catholic) Christian tradition had provided either a solution to or some negotiation of that crisis. These critics insightfully argue that contrary to common perception, religion played a large part in the aesthetics of our secular age, an argument that the philosopher Charles Taylor would readily accept. Taylor's revision of the relationship between religion and secularization theories has opened a door for scholars to see the centrality of Catholic aesthetics at work in a variety of modernist impulses.

has just proposed that all of life—not just human life—is a violent competition between species. Karl Marx has theorized that all of human life is a violent struggle between social classes. Nietzsche has just proclaimed that the weakest links—especially those burdened by religion—would die out while Übermensch would survive and build a brave new world. Freud was just beginning to develop his theory of the mind whereby the unconscious sway of the id, ego, and superego were said to control and determine our actions and our sanity. And yet the cultural effect of this triumph of science and secularization brought a feeling of disenchantment for many, especially in a highly industrialized and impersonal world. As the philosopher Charles Taylor suggests, there existed a strange ambiguous tension in cultural discourse in the late nineteenth and early twentieth centuries: on the one hand, the positivist belief in inevitable progress; on the other hand, a dark deterministic world devoid of the possibility of human freedom, let alone any providential intervention.

This disconnect first found its literary roots in the stark realism of French naturalists like Honoré de Balzac and Emile Zola. They portrayed in almost photographic detail the contemporary afflictions affecting society. Their outlook was informed by two basic principles of positivism: biological heritage and social setting. The human person is merely the sum total of genetic inheritance and social environment. The sordid and revolting aspects of life were now literary subjects, usually centered on the social upheavals wrought by the rampant industrialization of the period. Whether in the seedy, drab life of a Paris boarding house in Balzac's *Le Père Goriot* (1835) or the miserable portrayal of Zola's coal miners in *Germinal* (1885), these novels eschewed any romantic escape into sentimentality. Rather, the aim of this aesthetic attempted to expose both human nature and society as they really were. Its artistic goal was to lift the veil of ignorance through acute observation, forcing readers to understand the brutal reality behind the comforting facades of modern life.[7]

Part of Catholicism's reappearance on the cultural and intellectual stage began as an aesthetic reaction against this "Reign of Science" that inundated the intellectual and political discourses of culture. Indeed, there is a flurry of famous French artists and intellectuals converted or re-converted to the Catholic faith during this period, and their texts are filled with conversions as well. In this literary turn to Catholicism, they found a way to narrate what the critic Ellis Hanson calls "the odd disruption, the hysterical symptom, the mystical effusion, the medieval spectacle . . . in an age of Victorian Puritanism, enlightenment rationalism, and bourgeois materialism."[8] By returning to Catholic belief and themes as the material for their work, these artists created a specific vision of French Catholicism, one that was prophetic in denouncing both the rationalism of the state as well as the bourgeois Christianity that made a too easy concourse with industrial society. Many of these artists gained the attention of a wider French audience because Catholicism was never served up with triumphant, epistemological certainty or as morally uplifting drama; rather,

---

7 See Schloesser's *Jazz Age Catholicism* (pages 18-26), for a fuller exposition of Balzac, Zola, and others of the French Realist-Naturalist School of the late nineteenth century.

8 Ellis Hanson, *Decadence and Catholicism* (Harvard University Press, 1997) 26.

Catholicism was inscribed in the midst of fallen, poor humanity, a place of constant struggle where the mysterious irruptions of grace might shine forth or manifest in profound ways in the lives of characters.

Nowhere was this revival more in evidence than in French literature. Beginning with such figures as Joris-Karl Huysmans, León Bloy, and Charles Péguy in the late nineteenth century, and continuing on in Paul Claudel, Georges Bernanos, and François Mauriac into the mid-twentieth, these artists made Catholic literature and drama into an accomplished literary form that defended the spiritual reality of human life. With an emphasis on aesthetic considerations over rational modes of discourse, their literary works served to address and critique the reigning manners of bourgeois, materialist French society. Catholicism offered both a critique of the modern state, and also a powerful philosophical and artistic alternative. As Hanson again suggests, an alternative Catholic vision of the world was more creative, an artistic matrix that allowed the rational and irrational phenomena of life to coincide. The aesthetic and historical heritage of Catholicism—its theology, its cathedrals, its communion of saints, its rituals and sacraments, its music and art—spoke more powerfully of the full range of human experience. Hanson provocatively remarks, "Catholicism is itself an elaborate paradox . . . The Church is at once modern and yet medieval, ascetic and yet sumptuous, spiritual and yet sensual, chaste and yet erotic, homophobic and yet homoerotic, suspicious of aestheticism and yet an elaborate work of art."[9] Hanson proposes that it is these lived paradoxes that made Catholicism such a powerful alternative to the rationalized, bourgeois state: to be Catholic—to have a Catholic vision of life—was to make of one's life an artistic adventure, to understand one's life as a work of art. Catholic faith became a cultural container and conceptual signifier for the paradoxes within the "modern" individual. Ironically, Catholicism becomes for these artists not so much a reaction against the modern but a new way to consciously negotiate the discourses of modernity.

As noted, Modernism, in its earliest iterations in the literary arts, also negotiated a paradox: for all the desire to rupture the epistemological from the metaphysical categories of aesthetics and meaning, Modernism still yearned for something unitive behind or beyond the dualisms of scientific positivism. If their aesthetics assumed that the anxious dislocations of post-World War I trauma could only find its coherence in the artist's creative act, or through the encounter with the artwork itself, then the sacramental system of Catholic faith suggested an analogous journey. By this I mean that if theologically a sacrament is an ontological encounter with something outside the mode of rationalization, then the early Modernists—whether T.S. Eliot, Ezra Pound, or William Carlos Williams (with his famous dictate "No idea but in things")—is very much a reconfiguration of Catholic thought on sacramentality. It is the orthodoxy of Thomas Aquinas, especially writ large in the neo-Thomism of Jacques Maritain. The artwork, like a sacrament, is an encounter with mystery, with a form of knowledge that is not utilitarian, nor conceptual. Modernist aesthetics and Catholicism, as an aesthetic or

---

9 Hanson 7.

sacramental vision, echoed and paralleled one another. One might call this Thomistic objectivism—that the object or the form in front of a person is a dramatic unfolding of some felt knowledge. This is certainly the case with Maritain's dialogue with avant-garde artists, and it is definitely true of the New Criticism that became such a force in literary theory in the United States of the 1940s and 50s. Catholic artists learned from the French naturalism of Balzac and Zola that bourgeois faith was often held hostage to religious sentimentality, what we might describe as Catholic kitsch today. Hagiographic and pious artistic productions proliferated within institutional Catholicism as a way to counteract what was perceived as the deadening effects of modern life. Poetry, fiction, drama, and painting imagined a transcendent world at work in the world despite reality. But there was also an intellectual and artistic counter-narrative of faith where Catholic writers, imbued with the philosophical and aesthetic underpinnings of modernism, create art that eschews any form of religious feeling as sentimental or melodramatic. There might be a melodramatic tinge to the stories of Mauriac or Greene, but the Catholic turn or religious insight in their works is never sentimental but hard won and often an arduous one. As Flannery O'Connor noted, "A faith that just accepts is a child's faith and all right for children, but eventually you have to grow religiously as every other way, though some never do. What people don't realize is how much religion costs. They think faith is a big electric blanket, when of course it is the cross. It is much harder to believe than not to believe."[10]

In a perceptive essay, the novelist and critic David Lodge suggests four key features of a literary aesthetic as variously employed by Catholic modernist authors of the early twentieth century, especially in the manner that French novelists and poets of the first decades of the twentieth century employed it.[11] Lodge succinctly describes them as the idea of the sinner at the heart of Christianity, the doctrine of "mystical substitution," the implied criticism of materialism, and the tireless pursuit of the erring soul by God, the "Hound of Heaven" motif in Francis Thompson's famous metaphor.[12] I want to offer a fifth ingredient to Lodge's summary, one especially germane to Graham Greene: the heightened tension of the narrative and plot in the conflict between the corrupt flesh and the transcendent spirit, usually devised as sexual tension between male and female protagonists ascending to a spiritual suffering, that finds its reference in Christ's crucifixion. I will engage this element in more detail later when we look at Greene's *The End of the Affair*.

Lodge takes Charles Péguy's famous phrase, the "sinner at the heart of Christianity" as the premiere attribute of a modernist, Catholic literary strategy. Far from the moralism and sentimental pieties of what might attract a Catholic bourgeoisie, these novelists dramatized the story of great sinners—thieves, prostitutes, drunks, derelicts, and apostates. Mauriac's novel

---

10 Flannery O'Connor, *The Habit of Being: Letters of Flannery O'Connor*, edited by Sally Fitzgerald (New York: Farrar, Straus & Giroux) 254.
11 Some scholars note that 1913 was the beginning of a consciously French modernism, with the publication of Proust's *Living with Swann*, Stravinsky's *The Rite of Spring*, and a sensational exhibition by Marcel Duchamp. It was also the year that saw the publication of Catholic writers: León Bloy's *On Huysman's Tomb*, Charles Péguy's collection of poems, *The Money Suite*, and François Mauriac's first novel, *Young Man in Chains*.
12 David Lodge, "Introduction," *The Viper's Tangle* by François Mauriac (New York: Carroll & Graff, 1987)

*Thérèse* (1927), for instance, valorizes his title character, a woman married to a boorish husband. Discovered to be slowly poisoning her husband with arsenic, she is quickly locked up by the two families in order to save face. After much suffering, Thérèse is told to give up her daughter, and is banished to Paris. Though she stands as a criminal and outcast, Mauriac's sympathy—and the reader's—is with Thérèse, making the novel's condemnation rest firmly on her family. Thérèse is thus one of Mauriac's tragic studies of a woman who risks all to get out of her encaged life, becoming in the end a sort of saint. Mauriac subverts orthodox notions of saintliness in order to offer a kind of Catholic vision that fulfills Péguy's axiom that the sinner—not the righteous believer—is the heart of Christianity, the reason why Christ came to save. This is where the real drama is to be found.

The second property of a Catholic modernist strategy is the notion of "mystical substitution," an idea perfected by the French writer Georges Bernanos. Bernanos denounced the distortion of Christianity into respectable and genteel mediocrity, protesting in his works the collusion of the French Catholic hierarchy with the rich and powerful. Works such as *Under Satan's Sun* and *Diary of a Country Priest* illustrate what Bernanos thought Christian life was like literally when lived "under Satan's sun." His protagonists are often saint-heroes whose virtues lie not in super-heroic, conventional saintliness but in their human frailty. Bernanos' concept of mystical substitution is dramatized in the way his heroes willingly participate in Christ's agony on the cross by giving their life up for another. In *The Diary of a Country Priest*, the priest cries out impulsively, "I'll answer for your soul with mine."[13] In theological language, this articulates the doctrine of *kenosis*, an act of self-sacrifice made out of love for another as rehearsed in Paul's hymnic proclamation that Jesus "emptied himself and became a slave" (Phil. 2.7). This trope is a constant theme of the Catholic literary modernism, perfected in Bernanos's works, and very much a key dramatic movement in the novels of Graham Greene.

The third property of a Catholic literary aesthetic shared with secular modernist strategies of art concern a suspicion of crass materialism and the bourgeois and buffered classes it engendered. This trope was often embodied in the drama of a fourth and crucial element, an understanding of a God that "hounds" us "with unhurrying chase and unperturbed pace," in the words of Thompson's celebrated poem.[14] The "Hound of Heaven" vividly illustrates the soul fleeing from a God it both fears and rejects, desperately hiding itself, only to feel at the end a final despairing turn toward this divine presence. What seems like crisis and anxiety in a character's ability to master oneself dramatically becomes another form of kenosis, an un-mastering of the self's importance, not so much a defeat as a new awareness and acceptance of a deeper reality at work. There is this paradoxical sense that even in our freedom to disavow God, God continues to play checkmate with our souls. If the French Catholic modernists helped to give this theme pride of place in the modern novel, it was Graham Greene who perfected it.

---

13 Georges Bernanos, *The Diary of a Country Priest*, trans., Pamela Morris (Cambridge, MA: Da Capo Press, 2002) 255.
14 Francis Thompson, "The Hound of Heaven," verse 10-11. The poem was first published in 1893 and included in the *Oxford Book of English Mystical Verse* in 1917.

A story of pursuit and chase is, of course, central to Greene's literary imagination and he takes the modernist techniques of the thriller and puts them at the service of a metaphysical, cosmic chase.

The expression of Modernist aesthetics in French Catholic artists and intellectuals began during the first thirty years of the twentieth century but quickly crossed the channel into the British Isles in various ways.[15] English Catholicism, a minority tradition in predominantly Protestant England, only gained some legitimate status in the 1840s. Following from this legal victory and aided by John Henry Newman, a convert from Anglicanism's own religious revival, the Oxford Movement, a small but effective Catholic revival flourished in England for over a century.

From the beginning it was dominated by English converts who shared a vision of the world as fallen, or in Newman's words, "implicated in some terrible aboriginal calamity." English Catholicism, and especially those who converted to the faith in the early twentieth century, involved a decidedly intellectual constituency: writers, poets, artisans, theologians, and clergy who had found the Anglican dispensation either intellectually untenable or too compromised by political collusion with the state. This era's diversity of Catholic converts and their works—the Jesuit poet Gerard Manley Hopkins, the writer G.K. Chesterton, the novelist Madox Ford, the poets Siegfried Sassoon and Edith Sitwell, and the priest-scholar Ronald Knox, to name just a few—allowed Catholicism a distinct voice in the intellectual life of England at the time.[16] Yet even here converts treaded difficult terrain within both the Catholic Church and within Protestant elite society. Because these converts were educated or well-known individuals, they were suspected by fellow Catholics of having liberal or modernist tendencies; at the same time, they had to defend to their Protestant peers the view that religious and intellectual freedom was an essential element of their new-found faith.

A difference between the status of French Catholicism and that of Protestant England concerned who owned the language of faith. One can find a latent religious discourse threaded through such writers as Samuel Taylor Coleridge, William Wordsworth, George Eliot, and Matthew Arnold, but their work describes the trajectory of faith in literature in terms of a *Deus Absconditus*, of religion evermore eclipsed by Enlightenment rationalism, science, and philosophical positivism. What is left of the "religious sense" in late nineteenth century British literature is expressed in either the moral melodramas of a Charles Dickens novel or in the philosophical displacement of religious feeling in many of the English poets. The impression that religion had lost its power within British culture only gained force in the Victorian elegies that mourned the loss of meaning in bourgeois culture and the implicit loss of religious belief. Eliot's *The Waste Land* (1922) expressed the disillusionment,

---

15 Modernism as a conscious trope in Anglo-American literature arrived with the Imagist movement, founded by Ezra Pound in 1912, but it was T.S. Eliot's *The Waste Land* and James Joyce's *Ulysses*, both published in 1922, which shaped the broader discourse of British literary Modernism.

16 There were also well known British Catholics who were not converts, among them two caught up in the Catholic "Modernist Crisis": George Tyrell (1861-1909), expelled from the Jesuits in 1906, and the lay theologian and apologist, Baron Friedrich von Hügel (1852-1925).

confusion, and seeming chaos that afflicted the generation of artists still reeling from the First World War. Many intellectuals in England during the 1930s and 40s turned to orthodox religious belief in the Anglican Church as well, most notably T. S. Eliot, C. S. Lewis, Dorothy Sayers, and W. H. Auden. Just as in France but from a different route, organized religion had regained some cultural prestige, a fashionable alternative for many British intellectuals. Like France in the early decades of the twentieth century, Catholic Christianity in Britain found a place at the cultural table of intellectual debate.[17] With the novels of Evelyn Waugh and Graham Greene, the Catholic revival found a popular preeminence in England in the 1930s through the 50s. Waugh's conversion was anchored in his belief that the essential truths of Catholicism had been dissipated by an English society uprooted from its Catholic birthright.

His early satires exposed modern society as a vacuous spectacle adrift from its roots. Beginning with the novel *Brideshead Revisited* (1944), Waugh attempted to use Catholicism not only to frame the issues of modernity, but also to offer Catholicism's vision and doctrine as an antidote to the present crisis in Western, and specifically English, civilization. Waugh's later books, true to the author's own religious conversion to Catholicism, portrayed characters searching for the certainty and the triumph of a creedal faith that had been obscured or eclipsed by the mores and values of modern European society.

Graham Greene, also a convert, shares with Waugh much of the same Catholic concerns and issues in his writing, but, in many ways, comes closer than Waugh to dramatizing modernist themes as embodied by his French contemporaries. The classic ingredients elucidated by David Lodge concerning François Mauriac's Catholic vision—the sinner at the heart of Christianity, mystical substitution, a critique of materialism, and God as the Hound of Heaven—can be found in many of Greene's most celebrated works. These novels—*Brighton Rock* (1938), *The Power and the Glory* (1940), *The Heart of the Matter* (1947), and *The End of the Affair* (1951)—illustrate Greene's own absorption in the French modernist strategies of the Catholic Revival. Greene takes Péguy's famous text "The sinner is at the heart of Christianity" as the epigraph of *The Heart of the Matter*, but it could be the epigraph and the theological lens for all of his novels from this period: the spiritual life of the sinner has the privileged status of experiencing "the appalling strangeness of the mercy of God."[18] Greene's novels of the thirties, forties, and fifties were constantly discussed in terms of the dialectical nature of counter—Reformation Catholicism, texts that stood against both Protestant religious discourse and the materialism and secular ideologies of the modern age.

---

17 For a fuller investigation of British conversion in the twentieth century, see Patrick Allit's *Catholic Converts: British and American Intellectuals Turn to Rome* (Cornell, 2000). For an excellent discussion of the Catholic intellectual's response to World War I, see *Roman Catholic Modernists Confront the Great War*, edited by C.J.T. Talar and Lawrence F. Barmann (Palgrave Macmillan, 2015). For an incisive chapter on the conversion of Ford Madox Ford and how it altered his stance on the aesthetics of literary modernism, see Timothy J. Sutton's *Catholic Modernists, English Nationalists* (University of Delaware Press, 2010).

18 Graham Greene, *Brighton Rock* (Penguin 1938, 2004). 268. At the end of the novel, the character Rose confesses to a priest that if her dead husband, the gangster Pinkie, must be damned in hell, then she wants to be with him because she is still in love with him. The priest replies, "There was a man, a Frenchman...who had the same idea as you," explicitly referring to Charles Péguy.

Let me conclude by giving a rather extended example of Greene's shade of Catholic literary modernism from one of his most celebrated novels, *The End of the Affair* (1951). In the earlier novel, *Brighton Rock*, Greene makes reference to the "appalling strangeness of the mercy of God." It seems that in *The End of the Affair* this strange mercy of God becomes Greene's very subject, for Greene attempted to embody this strangeness in the adulterous affair between two people who stand ostensibly outside of Catholicism. I choose this novel over Greene's *The Power and the Glory*, which is justifiably his greatest novel, because I wanted to expose that fifth property of Catholic modernist aesthetics—the way in which sex and sexuality becomes a "way to God."[19] In *The End of the Affair*, Greene heightens the conflict between the flesh and the spirit through the sexual tension between his male and female protagonists, so that they ascend to a spiritual suffering and a spiritual exaltation that finds its reference in Christ's crucifixion.[20]

Set in London during World War II and immediately afterwards, the story is told by a novelist, Maurice Bendrix, who had begun a passionate love affair with Sarah, the wife of a senior civil servant named Henry. Four years into the affair they are together in his apartment during an air raid. Bendrix goes downstairs and is buried under the front door in a bomb explosion. Sarah rushes down, believing him to be dead. When Bendrix recovers consciousness and goes back upstairs to their bedroom, he finds Sarah on her knees. Unbeknownst to him, she is vowing to "anything that existed" that if Bendrix is restored to life, she will give him up as her lover and return to her husband, Henry. She sticks to her vow, but Bendrix assumes that she has ended their affair only to begin another. Eighteen months later and still in a jealous rage from being dropped by Sarah, Bendrix hires a private detective, reporting on her movements and procuring her private journal from her house. Reading the journal, Bendrix finds out about Sarah's vow, and is relieved to know that she is still in love with him. From the journal we learn that, though first hating and resentful of the God she now believes in, she slowly comes to a deeply felt peace. In a late journal entry she begs God to take her peace and give it instead to her ex-lover, a kind of mystical substitution. Bendrix, on the other hand, is convinced that he can compete against an illusory God and tries to confront her. Sarah avoids him, runs away in the rain, and dies from pneumonia a week later. Bendrix and Sarah's husband, Henry, both in mourning, find out that Sarah was under religious instruction with a Father Crompton, yet Bendrix bitterly advises Henry not to give Sarah a Christian burial. At her cremation, he discovers from Sarah's mother that she was secretly baptized a Catholic at age two. After this revelation, the coincidences keep piling up. In the end, Bendrix moves in with Henry at his invitation, yet still hateful and jealous of Sarah's God, in whom he too has reluctantly come to believe. Forced to confront Sarah's convictions in her diary, and these semi-miraculous coincidences, Bendrix is reluctantly and defiantly led to the same place as Sarah. The provocative point here is this: Sarah's adulterous encounter with

---

19 Greene shares this deployment of sexual decadence as a crucible of faith with François Mauriac.
20 This exploration into Greene's novel is a summation of my own work. See Mark Bosco, *Graham Greene's Catholic Imagination* (Oxford, 2005) 58-69.

Bendrix becomes the occasion for her religious encounter with God, and Sarah becomes the touchstone, the encounter, for Bendrix's own belief in God.

One can see in this short plot summary the Catholic tropes of Greene's modernist novel[21]: the adulterous Sarah at the heart of Christianity; a "mystical substitution" in her willingness to give up her love affair for Bendrix's life; the upended rationalist ideologies of the cynical secularist, Bendrix; and of course, the amorous God who hounds Sarah and, at the end of the novel, hounds the unwilling Bendrix. Because Sarah has neither belief nor any rudimentary religious instruction, she is convinced of her belief in God only through the miraculous restoration of her lover. It is a vow made in an extreme moment, dialectical in its intensity to commit her to an "all or nothing" decision, which over time becomes an undeniable conviction of her belief. Only later does she develop any sense of faith, fostered precisely in the realization of her sexual longing for Bendrix as a spiritual form of suffering. We might put it this way: Sarah begins her journey without the benefit of any material signs of God, except one: the body of her lover. She is led by her abandonment of this body to put her faith in signs of divine presence in another body, the suffering body on the crucifix.

This is the most provocative aspect of the novel: the human body as the fundamental sign of God's presence, whether it be bodies in pain, bodies disfigured, or bodies in erotic intimacy. Greene proposes to place the doctrine of the Incarnation at the center of this realistic novel, thereby pushing the ramifications of the doctrine to extreme moments of sexual ecstasy and of intense suffering because of the loss of the beloved's body. If God has become human flesh, then every finite body is a possible conduit of God's grace. It is the strongest claim of Catholic sacramentality in any of Greene's oeuvre, making "the appalling strangeness" of God's presence stand out in the profound realism of both Bendrix's critical, rationalist narration of events and Sarah's sometimes hysterical meditations in her diary. Sarah's hysteria swings from savage hatred of a God she only slightly believes in, to momentary glimpses into a spiritual peace.

Bendrix, too, always recalls the physicality of his and Sarah's love-making in vivid, concrete, visceral terms, so intense that he begins to use religious, mystical vocabulary: "Eternity is said not to be an extension of time but an absence of time, and sometimes it seemed to me that her abandonment touched that strange mathematical point of endlessness, a point with no width, occupying no space."[22] Sexual love becomes the still point in time, a kind of death experience that is extraordinary and ineffable, a moment of "absolute trust and absolute pleasure, the moment when it was impossible to quarrel because it was impossible to think"(71). Sex with Sarah is so ecstatic that Bendrix is forced to consider it in terms of prayer, meditation, and contemplation as the nearest comparable experiences.

Sarah is one of the few women characters in Greene's vast repertoire who is actually described as beautiful. Indeed, she is very comfortable in her beauty, aware of the power of her body as source of her

---

21 Interestingly, Greene critics argue that *The End of the Affair* has many modernist affinities, especially in the play of diachronic and synchronic time and in the shift of narrative consciousness.
22 Graham Greene, *The End of the Affair* (Penguin, 1951,1975) 51. All further pages referenced parenthetically in the text.

charisma. Distraught about her vow to break up with Bendrix, she wonders, "Why shouldn't I escape from this desert if only for half an hour? I haven't promised anything about strangers, only about Maurice. I can't be alone for the rest of my life with Henry, nobody admiring me, nobody excited by me" (98). Yet it is Sarah's meditations in which God is identified with the finite world of bodies that is central to the theological vision Greene constructs. God first becomes real for Sarah as another suffering, naked body sharing every human attribute. The centrality of the body as divine signifier comes to its apex in her long diary entry of 2 October 1945, written after having paused in a Catholic church to get out of the rain:

> [The church] was full of plaster statues and bad art, realistic art. I hated the statues, the crucifix, all the emphasis on the human body. I was trying to escape from the human body and all it needed. I thought I could believe in some kind of a God that bore no relation to ourselves, something vague, amorphous, cosmic, to which I had promised something and which had given me something in return... like a powerful vapor moving among the chairs and walls.
> [I saw] the hideous plaster statues with the complacent faces, and I remembered that they believed in the resurrection of the body, the body I wanted destroyed forever. I had done so much injury to this body... [I thought] of my own body, of Maurice's. I thought of certain lines life had put on his face as personal as a line of his writing: I thought of a new scar on his shoulder that wouldn't have been there if once he hadn't tried to protect another man's body from a falling wall. And so I thought, do I want that body to be vapor (mine yes, but his?), and I knew I wanted that scar to exist through all eternity. But could my vapor love that scar? Then I began to want my body that I hated, but only because it could love that scar. We can love with our minds, but can we long only with our minds?
> And of course on the altar there was a body too—such a familiar body, more familiar than Maurice's, that it had never struck me before as a body with all the parts of a body, even the parts the loincloth concealed... So today I looked at that material body on that material cross, and I wondered, how could the world have nailed a vapor there? A vapor of course felt no pain and no pleasure... I looked up at that over-familiar body, stretched in imaginary pain, the head drooping like a man asleep. I thought, sometimes I've hated Maurice, but would I have hated him if I hadn't loved him too? Oh God, if I could really hate you, what would that mean?... I walked out of the church in a flaming rage, and in defiance of Henry and all the reasonable and the detached I did what I had seen people do in Spanish churches: I dipped my finger in the so-called holy water and made a kind of cross on my forehead. (109-112)

Sarah's reflections move from wanting to flee the body, to looking at the crucified body, to a consideration of Maurice's body, and then to a final insight into the importance of the human body to God. An impersonal, vaporous, disembodied spirit seems less believable to Sarah in this world of flesh. Sarah submits to a person—the person on the cross—even if this person is never addressed directly, only observed. The theological aesthetic is most pronounced here, for in discovering what is at stake in believing in this incarnated God, she becomes a more willing participant in the form of Christ, of identifying herself with the suffering Christ. The diary entry ends with her defiant baptismal gesture, crossing herself with holy water as she leaves the church. It is the transformative moment, the spiritual key to unlocking a mystical, even erotic identification with God.

Sarah's diary continues to swing from a willing surrender to an intense desire for escape with Bendrix. That the experience of God and of Bendrix have become conflated in her mind is illustrated in the way she addresses God as "You," a term always used in addressing Bendrix: "I remembered the time when I had stuck my nails into my palms, and I didn't know it but You moved in the pain. I said, 'Let him be alive,' not believing in You, and my disbelief made no difference to You. You took it into Your love and accepted it like an offering... I wasn't afraid of the desert any longer because You were there" (113). Yet a month later she writes, "I'm not at peace any more. I just want him like I used to in the old days... I'm tired and I don't want any more pain. I want Maurice. I want ordinary corrupt human love." In Augustinian fashion she ends the entry, "Dear God you know I want your pain, but I don't want it now. Take it away for a while and give it me another time" (89). In her final letter to Bendrix, informing him that she will not break her vow and go away with him, she writes, "I've caught belief like a disease. I've fallen into belief like I fell in love. I've never loved before as I love you, and I've never believed in anything before as I believe now. I'm sure. I've never been sure before about anything" (147). Even religious belief, Greene suggests, subversively carries with it bodily signification, a virus inscribed in Sarah's ailing body. But Greene poses another bodily image of religious belief that subverts Sarah's metaphor: her mother tells Bendrix after the cremation ceremony that Sarah was actually a Catholic. She confides that she had her daughter secretly baptized at the age of two, claiming, "I always had a wish that it would take. Like a vaccination" (164). Sarah's body becomes the primary site for the totalizing love of an incarnate God. Belief is both like a disease that consumes her in a mystical annihilation and abandonment of self, as well as a vaccine that has silently inoculated her from taking any simple and easy route in her struggle with her vow to God.

The revelation of Sarah's secret baptism is an important factor in illustrating Greene's Catholic imagination. Greene once again wants to emphasize the mystery of sacramental grace in ontological terms, a visible marker of God's mediation in the life of a human person. Sarah's baptism stresses the vertical relationship with the divine, a work of God by the Church that marks indelibly the soul of the baptized. The news of the baptism betrays Greene's enchantment with Catholic scholastic discourse on *ex opere operato* notions of grace so prevalent in this time period of Catholic culture. But it does so in order to magnify the struggle in the text for any clarity about where truth lies—whether in mere coincidences or in a personal destiny. Bendrix has tried to write a novel of this love affair based on his claim to interpret what is happening to him and Sarah.

The fact of the baptism places in doubt his claims, becoming Bendrix's final "crack" in his perception of events. He is forced to wonder if he too is becoming hysterical. The narrative of his thoughts is strikingly similar to Sarah's own changing attitudes in her diary: "I'm a man of hate. But I don't feel much hatred; I had called other people hysterical, but my own words were overcharged. I could detect their insincerity. What I chiefly felt was less hate than fear" (190). From the moment that the baptism is revealed, Bendrix reluctantly finds himself addressing a God he hates, afraid that he will "leap" as Sarah has leapt into religious belief. The form of Sarah's leap is theologically framed more in terms of kenosis than in existential choice: "I might have taken a lifetime spending a little love at a time, eking it out here and there...You were there, teaching us to squander, like You taught the rich man, so that one day we might have nothing left but this love of You" (89). If Sarah is portrayed as "spent" but renewed in God's love through the accumulation of miraculous occurrences that populate the last pages of the novel, the text implies that Bendrix is actually not far behind her. Yet Sarah's baptismal "inoculation" keeps her from any simple and easy accommodation with her vow and growing religious belief; Bendrix is given no such assistance. Feeling spent and tired, he prays: "O God, You've done enough, You've robbed me of enough, I'm too tired and old to learn to love, leave me alone forever" (192). The novel ends with Bendrix in *medias res*, struggling with his belief in God. His hatred and fear is similar to Sarah's moments of hatred and fear, an early expression of love in a spiritual desert. God is still hounding Bendrix, the reluctant believer.

One final point that echoes modernist aesthetics: it is the artist's work that coheres in a world of chaos and dislocation. Bendrix, the comfortable atheist, who thinks religious faith is irrelevant to modern life, begins the novel by stating that, at best, God is a mathematical entity: "I find it hard to conceive of any God who is not as simple as a perfect equation, as clear as air" (11). Bendrix emphasizes that his way of love is "ordinary human love," understood as an uncomplicated consequence of biology: "Hatred seems to operate the same glands as love: it even produces the same actions" (27). He notes that Sarah's love for him is different, more difficult to reduce to such formulations, lacking the jealousy that is always surfacing in his longing. Emotions are all part of an equation for Bendrix, something quantifiable and open to precise formulation. Love, hatred, and jealousy are mathematical fractions of biological drives forever trying to cancel each other out. Sarah continually takes him into a world where the equation founders. It is a new territory in which there is no escape. He thinks that his profession as a writer is one that conveys the truth of life, and his inability to control the ending of his own story makes him question the very ability to make any totalizing claims on reality. And yet he notes that just as an author succeeds in bringing to life only certain of his characters, so too might God succeed only with the saints:

> Always I find when I begin to write there is one character who obstinately will not come alive. There is nothing psychologically false about him, but he sticks, he has to be pushed around, words have to be found for him...he never does the unexpected thing, he never surprises me, he never takes charge. Every other character helps, he only hinders. And yet one cannot do without him. I can imagine a God feeling in just that way about some of us. The saints, one would suppose,

in a sense create themselves. They come alive. They are capable of the surprising act or word. They stand outside the plot, unconditioned by it. But we have to be pushed around... We are inextricably bound to the plot, and wearily God forces us, here and there, according to his intention, characters without poetry, without free will, whose only importance is that somewhere, at some time, we help to furnish the scene in which a living character moves and speaks, providing perhaps the saints with the opportunities for their free will. (185-86)

Being a saint, in Bendrix's estimation, makes one free, and thus more alive, because saints have a different perspective and relationship to a society conditioned to drag one into a complacent and agnostic irrelevancy. Greene is subtly distinguishing in this text the Catholic *difference* in understanding contemporary secular and materialist culture: faith in God grants a poetry to one's life. The reader realizes that Bendrix is comparing himself to Sarah, she who "takes charge," who has that poetry in her to become more fully human. Sarah is drawn in an ascent to the beautiful form of Christ on the Cross still hidden from Bendrix's spiritual perception. She leaps out of her bourgeois state of affairs reflected in both her easy-going agnosticism as well as in an explicitly institutionalized Catholic observance. In the process she is made a thing of poetic beauty taking on that form which becomes for Bendrix another sign of God's poetic presence, however difficult a sign that might be for him.

*The End of the Affair*, then, is, in many ways, Greene's most persistently theological novel. Closer to the modernist strategies of French Catholic authors, Greene attempts to convey the complexities of the appalling strangeness of God's grace. A writer immersed in the political and religious events of the twentieth century, he came of age during the height of literary modernism. In this regard he stands in the company of other modernists—Eliot, Sitwell, Waugh, Auden—to name just a few artists who found in Catholic and Anglo-Catholic faith a literary way to negotiate modernity. The Greene shade of Catholic literary modernism is, in the end, a palette very much woven into the pattern of faith and belief today.

**Mark Bosco, S.J.**, is associate professor of English and Theology at Loyola University Chicago, and the director of their Joan and Bill Hank Center for the Catholic Intellectual Heritage. His main research focuses on the intersection of religion and art, especially on the 20th century Catholic literary revival in Britain and North America. He is the author of *Graham Greene's Catholic Imagination* (OUP, 2005), and editor of *Academia as Satire: Critical Studies in an Emerging Genre* (Edward Mellin, 2007). *Revelation and Convergence: Flannery O'Connor and the Catholic Intellectual Tradition* (CUA Press) is forthcoming in 2017. His current research includes a full-length documentary on the life of Flannery O'Connor, now in postproduction, with PBS/American Masters.

# Figures In Greene's Carpet: *The Power and The Glory* to *Monsignor Quixote*

## Robert Murray Davis

The 2007 Graham Greene International Festival

In the patently autobiographical novel *The Ordeal of Gilbert Pinfold*, Evelyn Waugh has Mr. Pinfold maintain that "most men harbour the germs of one or two books; all else is professional trickery of which the most daemonic of the masters—Dickens and Balzac even—were flagrantly guilty;" indeed, he envies "painters who are allowed to return to the same theme time and time again, clarifying and enriching until they have done all they can with it."[1] Graham Greene did not cite Waugh, but he did concede that he might be "a two or three book man."[2]

The figure in Waugh's carpet—to use the phrase of Henry James, whom both men admired—is obvious even to the casual reader. It is essentially circular in that the hero may learn but is not fundamentally changed.

Greene acknowledged that there might be patterns in his carpet, but he wanted "to remain unaware of them. Otherwise I think my imagination would dry up." He did not reread his novels because "I know I would come across all too many repetitions due quite simply to forgetting what I had written before. I've not the slightest wish to have my nose rubbed onto 'the pattern in the carpet'."[3]

Since Greene can no longer be bothered by critical meddling, which in any case he regarded as legitimate, I'll discuss the pattern I have found, one drawn from Francis Thompson's "The Hound of Heaven." I'm thinking not of "the labyrinthian ways," which furnished the American-imposed title of *The Power and the Glory* that Greene disliked. It is not inapt, but more apropos are these lines, from which I have tried unsuccessfully to remove the theological implications:

Now of that long pursuit
Comes on at hand the bruit;
That Voice is round me like a bursting
sea: "And is thy earth so marred,
Shattered in shard on shard?"[4]

Many if not most of his novels and entertainments—if Greene's old and intermittently discarded distinction is worth preserving—deal with the theme of pursuit through a marred world, from *The Man Within* through *A Gun for Sale*, *Brighton Rock*, *The Power and the Glory* and its twin *The Confidential Agent* down through *Monsignor Quixote*. Sometimes the pursuit is geographical, across political borders; sometimes it is psychological, as in *The End of the Affair*. In any case, the movement,

---

1 Waugh, Evelyn. *The Ordeal of Gilbert Pinfold*. London: Chapman and Hall, 1957, 2.
2 Allain, Marie-Françoise. *The Other Man: Conversations with Graham Greene*. Trans. Guido Waldman. New York: Simon and Schuster, 1981, 24.
3 Ibid, 23.
4 Thompson, Francis, and Jean Young. *The Hound of Heaven*. Harrisburg, PA: Morehouse, 1992., 155-159

whether it is eschatological or melodramatic, is linear, toward a definite resolution or conscious irresolution.

Looking at the novels in this way can allow us to deal with the problem that Peter Christensen finds in most criticism of Greene's fiction. It has, he argues, tended to regard novels published after 1973 as "more or less an appendage rather than an integral part of his development."[5] I cannot promise to integrate all of Greene's later novels with his earlier ones, but looking at his 1940 *The Power and the Glory* and the 1982 *Monsignor Quixote* may point the way to a solution. Both are variations of the pursuit/quest pattern. *The Power and the Glory* traces the flight of an unnamed priest, the only one left in the area, through the seedy towns and villages and desolate jungles of southern Mexico as he attempts to function as a dispenser of the sacraments and of God's word, all while avoiding capture and execution by atheistic authorities who regard his actions as treason. A "whisky priest" who has fathered a daughter whom he desperately loves, he has no one to hear his confession even if he could repent the action that produced the child; moreover, and in strict theological terms he commits another mortal sin every time he takes communion at Mass. Twice he almost escapes from the dangerous territory, but both times he is called to minister to someone who is supposedly dying. The second time, he is captured and, just before his execution, feels "like someone who has missed happiness by seconds at an appointed place. He knew now that at the end there was only one thing that counted—to be a saint."[6]

It could be said that the whisky priest moves from experience, if not to innocence, then to sanctity. In contrast, Greene's monsignor seems to move from innocence, or a holy simplicity, to experience. But on the surface, *Monsignor Quixote* seems to have little in common with the claustrophobic intensity of *The Power and the Glory*. The contrast is largely due to a very different background—the fictional *Don Quixote* and the actual pleasant and leisurely journeys around Spain that Greene took with Father Leopoldo Durán. Created a monsignor on a traveling bishop's whim, Fr. Quixote is enjoined "to go forth like your ancestor Don Quixote on the high roads of the world" and tilt at windmills since that is the way "that Don Quixote found the truth on his deathbed."[7] A character being evicted from his comfortable life sounds like a Waugh novel, and for a time the travels of the Monsignor and his friend the Communist ex-mayor called Sancho, seem to be a series of farcical incidents interspersed by debates about the merits of Communist and Catholic doctrine. But at the end of the novel Monsignor Quixote dons his battle regalia—a purple pechera rather than a barber's basin—and like his fictional ancestor attempts to rescue the Blessed Virgin from the simoniac extortions of village priests. Pursued and injured, he dies after saying a version of the Mass that his pharisaical bishop has forbidden him to perform.

Despite differences in inspiration and tone, the two novels have obvious similarities in pattern and theme, both physical

---

5 Christensen, Peter. "The Art of Self-Preservation: Monsignor Quixote's Resistance to Don Quixote," *Essays in Graham Greene: An Annual Review*, 3 (1992), 25-42, 41.

6 *The Power and the Glory: Text, Background, and Criticism* (hereafter *P&G*), ed. R.W.B. Lewis and Peter J. Conn. New York: Viking, 1972., 284

7 *Monsignor Quixote* (hereafter *MQ*). New York: Simon and Schuster, 1982, 25. .

and psychological. One can look at the parallels in fairly basic terms by describing what they are—a fairly simple though not unrewarding task—and by attempting to account for the differences between the two and by looking at what had happened to Greene, the Catholic Church, and the world in the more than four decades that elapsed between the writing of the novels.

Most simply, and most obviously, the Monsignor expresses humorous concern about becoming "a whisky priest," a direct allusion to the earlier novel, although unlike the unnamed fugitive in *The Power and the Glory,* he has no trouble procuring alcohol, including wine, none of which he uses to say Mass. There are a number of less blatant parallels, incidental and structural. The Spanish monsignor goes to a blue film, deceptively titled "A Maiden's Prayer," and finds it funny rather than shocking. The Mexican priest, spending the night in a crowded prison cell, overhears the sounds of sexual pleasure, at first with horror, then with the realization that "*That* is beautiful in that corner—to them."[8] He is forced to endure the stench from a slop-bucket and asked by an intolerably pious woman to hear her confession. He tells her to "Say an act of contrition . . . . and trust God . . . to make allowances."[9] The Monsignor, after fearing that a mysterious man in a bar, perhaps a secret policeman, is going to execute him, is forced to hear his confession in the lavatory—"a lavatory, a church. What's the difference?"[10] The man is an undertaker who, like all of his colleagues, removes handles from caskets and reuses them. The Monsignor says, "Do you think God cares so much about a thing like that? . . . don't feel so important. Say that you are sorry for your pride and go home."[11]

Both priests encounter bank robbers. The Mexican's is real—a murderer—and when the priest returns across the border to administer last rites, he is captured and jailed to await execution. Monsignor Quixote's robber, whom he helps to escape and who, like the galley slaves freed by Don Quixote, steals some of his clothing, turns out merely to have robbed a convenience store. But his bishop, fearing scandal that would affect the Church's reputation, has Quixote imprisoned in his room on the grounds that he is, like his literary ancestor, mentally deranged.

Both priests are aware of the distinctions between priests who are self-satisfied and those who are self-sacrificing, and both condemn, the Mexican in himself and the Spaniard in others, pious extortion for religious services that seem to promise salvation. Both encounter conventionally good people who, to adopt Greene's distinction in *Brighton Rock,* operate in the economy of right and wrong rather than one of good and evil. Both, after their deaths, are replaced, literally or symbolically, by a priest who, in the case of *The Power and the Glory,* carries on the mission of maintaining, against nearly impossible odds, the presence of God in a godless place and, in *Monsignor Quixote,* a monk who came through doubt and Descartes to a Trappist monastery where he upholds the spirit of the law against the letter and the belief in mystery rather than physical proof—perhaps a milder form of what, in *The Power*

---

8 *P&G*, 176.
9 Ibid, 175.
10 *MQ*, 119
11 Ibid, 118.

*and the Glory*, Greene calls "the dark and magical heart of the faith."[12]

On deeper and more complex levels, the most obvious parallel between the two novels can be seen in characters who represent clashing ideologies, the priest and the lieutenant—Greene's "two protagonists," whom he invented for what he called "the only novel I have written to a thesis."[13] And in a 1957 interview with Philip Toynbee[14], he said, in response to Toynbee's comment that *The Power and the Glory* dealt with "the conflict between church and state in Mexico," that "I see that only as a background of the book. It is really an attempt to understand a permanent religious situation: the function of the priesthood. I was much more interested in the theological point of view than in the political one."[15]

In *The Power and the Glory*, the priest believes that religion offers the hope of peace and plenitude in a harsh and often loveless world, that "pain is part of joy."[16] His nemesis, the Lieutenant of police, has been scarred by his early experience of the Church's disregard for the poor and wants to sweep away all superstitious hope in the hereafter and to hunt down and kill the last priest in the state. Ironically, the two men have much in common. Midway through the novel, the Lieutenant releases the priest, whom he does not recognize, and gives him five pesos. The priest realizes that he has been given "the price of a Mass," and calls the Lieutenant "a good man."[17] Later, temporarily flush with fees for baptisms and knowing that he is going to betrayal and certain death, the priest gives most of his money to a socialist schoolmaster to buy food and clothing for destitute peons.

As Greene had done in *Brighton Rock*, he implies a contrast between characters with a sense of right and wrong and those with a sense of good and evil. The Lieutenant has the look of a priest or "a theologian going back over the errors of the past to destroy them again"[18] or "a mystic" who "had experienced . . . vacancy—a complete certainty in the existence of a dying, cooling world, of human beings who had evolved from animals for no purpose at all."[19] He is ascetic, with no desire for drink, women, and money, feeling "no sympathy at all with the weakness of the flesh."[20] In the slovenly decrepitude which engulfs all of the other characters, he alone is clean, with a highly polished holster. When surrounded by children admiring his automatic pistol, he knows that he is fighting "to eliminate from their childhood everything which had made him miserable, all that was poor, superstitious, and corrupt . . . . He was quite prepared to make a massacre for their sakes—first the Church and then the foreigner and then the politician—even his own chief would one day have to go. He wanted to begin the world again with them, in a desert."[21] In an odd way he resembles

---

12 P&G, 208.
13 Greene, Graham. *Ways of Escape: An Autobiography*. New York: Simon & Schuster, 1980, 87-88.
14 Philip Toynbee interviews Graham Greene on The Job of the Writer." *The Observer*, 15 September, 1957.
15 *P&G*, 498.
16 *P&G*, 94.
17 Ibid, 189.
18 Ibid, 32.
19 Ibid, 33.
20 Ibid, 34.
21 Ibid, 77.

Bendrix in *The End of the Affair,* who, Sarah says, "thinks he hates, and loves, loves all the time—even his enemies,"[22] and as the priest tells him, God's love "might even look like hate."[23] The Lieutenant won't go that far, but he is charitable, even sympathetic, toward the destitute man whom, as already stated, he does not recognize as a priest. And the night before the priest's execution, he practices one of the corporal works of mercy by giving drink to the thirsty, in this case bootleg brandy—and tries to practice a spiritual work of mercy in comforting the sorrowful by seeking a confessor.

As Greene has admitted, the Lieutenant is constructed as a foil to the priest who defined a vocation as a way to become "rich and proud,"[24] who spoke empty words to pious societies and wished to rise in the hierarchy, who, as "the only priest left in the state . . . thought himself the devil of a fellow carrying God around at the risk of his life; one day there would be a reward . . . ." [Ellipsis is Greene's.][25] But this pride led him to disregard his duties to fast, pray, and say Mass and instead to succumb to drink and fornication.

The priest thinks that "if there's ever been a single man in this state damned, then I'm damned too," adding, "I just want justice."[26] Earlier he thinks that his first duty is to save his own soul, but for one thing: he cannot repent his sin of fornication because he cannot disavow its result, his daughter, whom he loves, as he comes to see, as he should love the whole world. Lacking a confessor "to draw his mind slowly down the drab passages which led to horror, grief, and repentance,"[27] he cannot move his self-condemnation for his acknowledged sins "from formula to the fact."[28]

In later years, Greene said that he had never believed in Hell,[29] but it is obvious that in his Catholic novels his characters needed to in order to reach the paradoxical endings most obvious in *The Power and the Glory* and *The Heart of the Matter,* endings in which the chance of salvation is forced on the reader, victim of a card trick like the whisky priest's "Fly Away Jack." In *Brighton Rock,* the priest says that Pinkie has a chance to receive God's mercy, but Pinkie makes it a much tougher uphill battle for his large-C creator if not for the lower-case one. In *The Power and the Glory*, the chance of salvation is first suggested early in the novel as "The simple ideas of heaven and hell moved in his brain: life without books, without contact with educated men, had peeled away from his memory everything but the simplest outline of the mystery."[30]

That mystery includes his powers as a priest. As he tells the Lieutenant, it would make no difference if all priests were like him, for he and others "can put God into a man's mouth" and "can give him God's pardon."[31] Moreover, he goes to almost

---

22 Greene, Graham. *The End of the Affair*. Penguin, 1975, 124.
23 Ibid, 269.
24 Ibid, 92. 25 Ibid, 129.
26 Ibid, 269.
27 Ibid, 173.
28 Ibid, 281.
29 Greene, Graham. *Articles of Faith: The Collected Tablet Journalism of Graham Greene*. Ed. Ian Thompson. Oxford: Oxford University Press, 2006, 128.
30 Ibid, 89.
31 Ibid, 263.

certain death to give that pardon to the dying American bank robber—his double as wanted man. And, though Greene does not use the line from the Gospel of John, his favorite, the relevance is perhaps too obvious for him to quote "Greater love hath no man than this, that a man lay down his life for his friends."[32]

Greene contrasts the priest's torturous path toward death and implied sanctity with the treacly piety of the story of Father Juan, perfect from boyhood through the moment of his execution, shouting "Vive El Cristo Rey." Although the real priest can mumble only something that sounds like "Excuse" (him? his executioners, in imitation of Christ?), in death he becomes part of the succession of martyrs and converts the boy who listened to the story, impatient for the shooting to begin, from admiration for the Lieutenant to a dream of the funeral at which "the dead priest winked at him"[33] to welcoming the new priest and potential next martyr.

The Lieutenant is left with the boy's spittle on his holster, a sense that his life has lost purpose, and a dream of which he can remember nothing "except laughter, laughter all the time, and a long passage in which he could find no door."[34] Unlike the General who executes the last Pope in Greene's much later story, "The Last Word," the Lieutenant does not wonder if what the dead man believed was true, but clearly the last word in *The Power and the Glory* belongs to the priest.

*The Power and the Glory* is about faith in God as a key motivation, about the spiritual power of Catholicism against materialist forces, and about the struggle for sanctity against various thorns in the flesh. *Monsignor Quixote*, published 42 years later, presents doubt as more nourishing than certainty; the collusion between ecclesiastical and secular power; and what the American critic Patrick Henry calls "the progressive convergence of the self and the other."[35] But here the other is not God but another human being—who is, like the Lieutenant, an atheistic materialist, in fact a Communist, and the self is a simple parish priest with no sexual temptations who finds much good in Karl Marx.

While in *The Power and the Glory*, as John Desmond puts it, in the best discussion of the theology of *Monsignor Quixote* I have seen, "the opposition between materialist and redemptive visions is unmeliorated,"[36] the Monsignor "affirms the spirituality of matter."[37] And Mark Bosco, S.J., who thinks it a "great novel," sees it as "more a new development—stylistically and thematically—than a mere coda to Greene's celebrated Catholic cycle."[38]

As these critics have shown, *Monsignor Quixote* is one of Greene's theologically most complex novels, rivaling *The End of the Affair*. However, I share Greene's taste for simplicity over complexity and will focus on his treatment of the spirit versus the letter. As I said earlier, Greene often referred to books in various genres to

---

32 John 15:13 33 *Articles of Faith*, 300.

34 Ibid, 280.

35 Henry, Patrick. "Cervantes, Unamuno, and Graham Greene's *Monsignor Quixote*," *Comparative Literature Studies*, 23:1 (Spring 1986), 12-23, 13.

36 Ibid, 62-63.

37 Desmond, John. "The Heart of (the) Matter: The Mystery of the Real in *Monsignor Quixote*," *Religion and Literature*, 22:1 (Spring 1990), 59-78 , 70.

38 Bosco, Mark. *Graham Greene's Catholic Imagination*. Oxford University Press, 2005, 138, 139.

show the difference between received opinion and the texture of lived experience. In *Monsignor Quixote*, the most rigid example of the letter is Fr. Heribert Jone's *Moral Theology*. Unlike some books cited in other Greene novels, this one is real, described on the Family Life Center International website as "a handbook that condenses moral theology to its conclusions" in "a crystal clear treatment of every conceivable aspect of morality . . . . Jone shows what is a sin and what is not; what is a venial sin and what is a mortal sin . . . . This book's thoroughness and completeness will boggle the mind."[39]

Jone's book certainly boggled the mind of Monsignor Quixote, who likens it to "a book of military regulations,"[40] remarks that most secular priests are "too busy to be moral theologians"[41] and later adds, "moral theology is not the Church."[42] Greene opposes to Jone the Monsignor's "books of chivalry . . . Saint John of the Cross, Saint Teresa, Saint Francis de Sales,"[43] which are to him "all the faith I have and all the hope."[44] St. Francis wrote 800 pages about God's love and never mentioned mortal sin.

The Monsignor's nemesis Fr. Herrera—as clean and precise as the Lieutenant in *The Power and the Glory*—is Jone's chief disciple in the novel. Herrera concedes dismissively that "one accepts the gospels, naturally,"[45] and he prefers Matthew, who mentions Hell fifteen times.

Calling Matthew "the Gospel of fear,"[46] the Monsignor, like Greene, prefers John, who does not mention Hell at all, and although the opening of John's Gospel—"In the beginning was the Word, and the Word was with God, and the Word was God"—had along with Latin been banished from the Mass, the Monsignor still recites it privately.

As the Monsignor travels with his friend Sancho—who like the Lieutenant is mistaken for a priest, and, as the Monsignor says, "perhaps a true Communist is a sort of priest"[47]—he reads *The Communist Manifesto* and realizes that "There are many holy words written which are not in the Bible or the Fathers"[48] and that Marx "was a really good man at heart."[49]

As the novel progresses, both men realize that while their respective books of chivalry can inspire them, the words have often been grotesquely twisted, with the Kremlin and the Roman Curia representing the corruption of the best intentions. The Monsignor dreams of Christ descending triumphantly from the Cross, obliterating all doubt and establishing a world in which "everyone is certain that the same belief is true"[50] and prays that he—and Sancho—will be saved from that kind of belief. In the waking world, the friends spend the night in a brothel, go to a mildly blue film, collude in the escape of a robber, and evade the Guardia. Their adventures and debates of

---

[39] familylifecenter.net.
[40] *Articles of Faith*, 82.
[41] Ibid, 75.
[42] Ibid, 81.
[43] Ibid, 39.
[44] Ibid, 77.
[45] Ibid, 40.
[46] Ibid, 67.
[47] Ibid, 93.
[48] Ibid, 109.
[49] Ibid, 107.
[50] Ibid, 70.

Part I of the novel end with the Monsignor saying, with a laugh, "You are my moral theologian, Sancho."[51]

Part II of the novel, much shorter, deals with the Monsignor's imprisonment by his bishop, who would rather think him deranged than criminal, and his deliverance by Sancho. At the climax of the novel is his most quixotic act, denouncing the profanation of the Virgin's procession by simoniac priests, where he is injured by a swinging censer (perhaps Greene's pun on "censor"). While fleeing the secular authorities—unlike the Mexican the Monsignor is accompanied by his materialist colleague—his beloved car Rocinante crashes, and he falls into delirium. After promising Sancho not a governorship but a kingdom, he goes through a form of the Mass, at the end of which he collapses after putting a phantom Host on Sancho's tongue. Like his double the Lieutenant, Sancho feels uneasy, but, more like Maurice in *The End of the Affair* than the Lieutenant, he fears not that his task is at an end, but whether "the love which he had begun to feel for Father Quixote" can continue—"And to what end?"[52]

At least as instructive as the similarities between *The Power and the Glory* and *Monsignor Quixote* are not just the differences but the complicated and sometimes intellectually torturous reasons for the differences. Behind *The Power and the Glory* lay Greene's awareness of parallels between the persecution of the Church in Mexico in the 1920s and 1930s, especially the execution of Father Pro, and the Elizabethan persecution of Edmund Campion and his fellow priests. He had wanted to go to Mexico to write about the persecution of the Catholic Church as early as 1936, but the need to support his family made it necessary for him to finish writing *Brighton Rock* and to accept the job of literary editor of *Night and Day*, the distinguished, short-lived magazine that died at the end of 1937, freeing him from "a busy but boring life."[53]

But he was anxious to get out of England. Norman Sherry reported that Greene told his agent, "I don't know how I shall get the vitality to think of another novel unless I can get out of bloody Europe" and thought that Greene desired to escape from "the incessant work, the loss of *Night and Day*, and from living the life of a 'gentleman' author in a 'gentleman's establishment'."[54]

Greene's distaste for England is clear in the opening pages of his travel book *The Lawless Roads*, where he contrasts present suburban England, with its suicides and sordidness, with the people who "had lived here once and died with their feet crossed to show they had returned from a crusade." The present has corrupted the past: a photographer's shop has a "diamonded Elizabethan pane—a genuine pane, but you couldn't believe it because of the Tudor Cafe across the street." Anticipating the trip to Mexico, he thinks, "why Mexico? Did I really expect to find there what I hadn't found here? 'Why, this is hell,' Mephistopheles told Faustus, 'nor am I out of it'."[55]

In Mexico, reading Trollope's *Barchester Towers*, Greene concedes that "The world is all of a piece, of course; it is engaged

---

51 Ibid, 144.
52 Ibid, 221.
53 Sherry, Norman. *The Life of Graham Greene: Volume I: 1904-1939*. Penguin, 1990, 656.
54 Ibid, 659, 660.
55 Greene, Graham. *Another Mexico* (hereafter *AM*). New York: Viking Compass, 1964. Originally published in England as *The Lawless Roads*, 1939, 6.

everywhere in the same subterranean struggle, lying like a tiny neutral state, with whom no one ever observes his treaties, between the two eternities of pain and—God knows the opposite of pain, not we." He does see a difference between "quiet and active sectors" of the battle line. But, he adds, "So many years have passed in England since the war began between faith and anarchy; we live in an ugly indifference."[56]

Except very briefly—in the small region between the debilitating altitude of Mexico City and the claustrophobic tropics, for example—Greene is never comfortable. Fleetingly aware of "something simple and strange and uncomplicated, a way of life we have hopelessly lost but can never quite forget,"[57] he hates the slovenly, corrupt police and the swaggering pistoleros who hang about the politicians. He hates with equal vigor the world represented by an American woman's magazine—"it wasn't evil, it wasn't anything at all, it was just the drugstore and the Coca-Cola, the hamburger, the graceless, sinless, empty chromium world."[58]

Greene also hated most of the Mexicans, except the back-country Indians, and almost everything about Mexico. But if in Mexico there "were idolatry and oppression, starvation and casual violence . . . you lived under the shadow of religion—of God or the Devil."[59] Back in London, he is no more comfortable with England than when he left. He sees new posters for Air Raid Precautions. Looking at the ugliness of the city, he asks, "How could a world like this end in anything but war?"[60] And at Mass, so different from the ones he attended in Mexico, he thinks, "We do not mortify ourselves. Perhaps we are in need of violence."[61]

Then a plane flies overhead and everything changes for a moment as people wait to see what will happen and "The telephones were cut off, the anti-aircraft guns were set up on the common outside, and the trenches were dug. And then nothing happened at all—the great chance of death was delayed."[62]

In reviewing *The Lawless Roads*, Evelyn Waugh decided that Greene was "an Augustinian Christian, a believer of the dark age of Mediterranean decadence when the barbarians were pressing along the frontiers and the City of God seemed yearly more remote and unattainable . . . . Contemplation of the horrible ways in which men exercise their right of choice leads him into something very near a hatred of free-will."[63] Waugh might have cited, though he did not, Greene's bilious admission that the buzzards, pervasive in both the travel book and in *The Power and the Glory*, on one occasion "looked domesticated, as if they were going to lay an egg. And I suppose even a bird of prey does sometimes lay an egg."[64] That seems only part of the natural order, but elsewhere

---

56 *AM*, 27.
57 Ibid, 207.
58 Ibid, 225-6.
59 Ibid, 225.
60 Ibid, 277.
61 Ibid, 278.
62 Ibid, 278.
63 Waugh, Evelyn. *The Essays, Articles and Reviews of Evelyn Waugh*. Ed. Donat Gallagher. London: Methuen, 1983, 249.
64 *AM*, 146.

Greene admits that "Nature appalls me when unemployed or unemployable."⁶⁵

The trip to Mexico and political events in Europe did have more positive effects on Greene and, more important for his readers, on his writing. Until 1938, he said, "My professional life and my religion were contained in quite separate compartments, and I had no ambition to bring them together." That changed because "of the socialist persecution of religion in Mexico, and . . . General Franco's attack on Republican Spain," both of which "inextricably involved religion in contemporary life," though, one might think, in opposite ways. As a result, Greene came to feel, "Catholicism was no longer primarily symbolic, a ceremony at an altar" but "closer now to death in the afternoon."⁶⁶

In this vein, Greene quotes a surviving Mexican priest as saying of Pro and the other martyrs, "The Church needed blood . . . . It always needs blood."⁶⁷ At least as important here—and for years to come—is Greene's sense that "Catholicism...had to rediscover the technique of revolution"⁶⁸ because "the only body in the world today which consistently—and sometimes successfully—opposes the totalitarian State is the Catholic Church."⁶⁹

*The Lawless Roads* can be profitably read as a sourcebook for characters, incidents, and mood in *The Power and the Glory*, as Greene made quite clear. Perhaps most important not only for these two books but for *Monsignor Quixote* and perhaps for many others, if I live long enough and no one beats me to the idea, is Greene's use of intertextual references, if the term can be stretched to include generic and imaginary as well as real texts. *The Lawless Roads* frequently alludes to Trollope's novels and to other literary and journalistic texts. In *The Power and the Glory*, the sentimental saint's life counterpoints the whisky priest's struggles and ends with the martyr's execution just after the priest is shot. *Monsignor Quixote* has a whole library of references, which I shall examine later, not only to Cervantes' novel but to theology and casuistry from the Gospel of John to *The Communist Manifesto*. Greene's use of these counter-texts is obviously very complex, but at present I can only simplify and say that he uses them to represent conventional thought against which his characters can react—or, to put it even more simply, the dead letter against the living and often suffering spirit.

To move from the theoretical to the biographical and historical, the differences between the two novels can be partly explained by forty years of very complicated life, and though Greene did not do a total about-face, his emphasis did shift. Even in 1937, he commented that some novels he was reviewing for the *Tablet* were "concerned with social justice, and they all avoid the merely political approach. The trouble is: what approach can you have but the political or the religious?"⁷⁰ Into the 1950s, he emphasized the religious approach in his fiction and nonfiction. He had come back from Mexico with a stronger emotional connection to the Catholic faith, which before then had been more intellectual. Then, paradoxically—how else with Greene?—his

---

65 Ibid, 64.
66 *Ways of Escape*, 78-9.
67 *AM*, 260.
68 Ibid, 20-1.
69 Ibid, 80.
70 *Articles of Faith*, 105.

affair with Catherine Walston led to a deeper faith. In 1952, the year after their relationship was reflected in *The End of the Affair*, he wrote to her, "I would still stay in the fringes of the church if you left me—perhaps not even in the fringes, for almost all my *Catholic* writing has been done since I knew you and I have certainly been to the sacraments far more often in our five years than in the previous eight."[71]

Although the definitive break with Walston does not seem to have come until 1958, Greene had moved by 1955 from the religious to the political approach in *The Quiet American* and, with the arguable exception of *A Burnt-Out Case* and the obvious exception of *Monsignor Quixote*, for the rest of his career. This may be in part due to the restlessness which took him to Africa, Vietnam, and South America and in part to his increasing interest in and admiration for Marxist-nationalist-leftist leaders like Ho Chi Min, Fidel Castro, and Omar Torrijos.

By this time, Greene had begun to hope for a rapprochement between Catholics and Communists. The roots of this hope may be seen in 1941, when he maintained that "Conservatism and Catholicism should be as impossible bed-fellows as Catholicism and National Socialism."[72] By the 1960s, partly in light of the Second Vatican Council, he had begun to see hope for a truly revolutionary Church in the liberation theology of some Catholic activists in South America, and almost twenty years before he wrote *Monsignor Quixote* he saw in Cuba hope that "Marxism here seems to be shedding much of its nineteenth-century philosophy" and opening "a first breach in Marxist philosophy (not in Marxist economics)" and quoted Fidel Castro's view that "a revolutionary can have a religious belief. The Revolution does not force men, it does not intrude into their personal beliefs. It does not exclude anyone."[73] And in 1987, in a speech given in the Kremlin, he asserted that "There is no division in our thoughts between Catholics—Roman Catholics—and Communists."[74] As I said in my review of *Reflections*, this would have come as a surprise to many of my Hungarian friends.

These views may have overlapped with what seems to have been a waning of his faith or at least his practice of the rituals of the faith. In *A Sort of Life* he talked about Confession: " . . . we may become hardened to the formulas . . . and skeptical about ourselves: we may only half-intend to keep the promises we make, until continual failure or the circumstances of our private life finally make it impossible to make any promises at all and many of us abandon Confession and Communion to join the Foreign Legion of the Church and fight for a city of which we are no longer full citizens."[75] This passage echoes the confession of the title character in "A Visit to Morin," first published in 1957. The elderly author, prominently known as a Catholic but no longer practicing, tells his visitor that "Perhaps I wrote away my belief" in the course of "twenty years and fifteen books"—Greene's years as a practicing novelist and the right number of books, if one discounts the suppressed *The Name of Action* and *Rumour at Nightfall*. Having excommunicated himself because he could

---

71 Sherry, Norman. *The Life of Graham Greene: Volume II: 1939-1955*. New York: Viking, 1995, 502. 72 Greene, Graham. *Collected Essays*. Penguin, 1970, 262.

73 *Reflections*, 218, 219

74 Ibid, 316.

75 Greene, Graham. *A Sort of Life*. New York: Simon and Schuster, 1971, 169.

not repent his love of a mistress, Morin cannot return to the Church because "I had cut myself off for twenty years from grace and my belief withered as the priests said it would.... I know the reason why I don't believe and the reason is—the Church is true and what she taught me is true." He refuses to return to the sacraments because "my lack of belief is an argument for the Church. But if I returned and they failed me, then I would really be a man without faith...."[76]

Perhaps there was also some influence from what the younger Catholic novelist David Lodge called the disappearance of Hell in the 1960s. Before that, Lodge says in *How Far Can You Go?* "the whole system of religious authority and obedience in which [his characters] had been brought up, binding the Church together in a pyramid of which the base was the laity and the apex the Pope, depended on the fear of Hell as its ultimate sanction."[77] The key question—one which Greene raises in *Monsignor Quixote* and in his 1989 interview—was birth control because "it compelled thoughtful Catholics to re-examine and redefine their views on fundamental issues: the relationship between authority and conscience, between the religious and lay vocations, between flesh and spirit."[78] As I noted earlier, Greene says in the 1989 interview that "I never *have* believed in Hell;"[79] he is very uncertain about heaven; he finds it harder to believe in God but retains, rather than belief in dogmas, a kind of faith as a Catholic agnostic.

As Greene gained hope from *perestroika*, he became less attached to the Church and began to lose hope in the Church as a potentially revolutionary force after the election of Pope John Paul II. He compared Gorbachev to John XXIII and John Paul II to Ronald Reagan—both of the latter lacked a healthy sense of doubt—in a 1989 interview. And the travels in Spain with Fr. Leopoldo Durán in the years surrounding the writing of *Monsignor Quixote* may have given Greene a fuller sense of the ways in which the Church colluded with the Franco regime, which he never ceased to criticize. He also criticized members of the Catholic hierarchy in America for acting as "the voice of the Cold War."[80] And as Yvonne Cloetta said, "religion belonged to a past he wanted to forget, whereas politics had to do with the present."[81]

But less than ten years after Greene met Cloetta, he sought the acquaintance of Fr. Durán, his traveling companion in Spain, a kind of Boswell, and if not a spiritual advisor, a confessor (though in 1989 Greene said that at eighty-five "I've nothing much to confess")[82] who administered the last sacraments to Greene on his deathbed. This seems an unlikely friendship even judging from Durán's account. Durán staunchly supported Franco as "a discerning man [who] brought recovery to the country" and believed that Greene "never understood Franco's political and spiritual ideology;"[83] thought "the Guardia Civil stand for all that is honourable and orderly

---

76 Greene, Graham. *Collected Stories*. Penguin, 1986. 225, 227.
77 Ibid, 118.
78 Ibid, 120.
79 *Articles of Faith*, 128.
80 *Reflections*. Ed. Judith Adamson. New York: Reinhardt, 1990, 219.
81 Ibid, 95.
82 *Articles*, 126.
83 Durán. Leopoldo. *Graham Greene: An Intimate Portrait by His Closest Friend and Confidant* (trans Euan Cameron. Harper: SanFrancisco, 1994, 78, 126.

in Spain;"[84] regarded Monsignor Quixote's bishop, whom Greene thought "Hell," "a decent man;"[85] disliked many of the enemies of Opus Dei; and thought that he had convinced Greene to give a positive view of the "Mexicans" buying the favors of the Church near the end of the novel.

Given these differences, it seems odd that the men shared jokes—about the Trinity being represented by two and a half, later three, bottles of wine—and more serious views, as when Fr. Durán's "I do not believe in God. I touch him" is given to Monsignor Quixote. Marx's distinction between tragedy and farce is not quite accurate, but *Monsignor Quixote* represents the comic side of Greene that emerged from beneath the "Augustinian Christian" that Waugh saw in the Thirties. Perhaps Greene's lack of belief in Hell—and in the Monsignor's lack of belief—allowed him to relax more than a little. The fact that by the 1970s Greene was comparatively wealthy may also have had something to do with his mood—not to speak of the many bottles of wine that, like the Monsignor and Sancho, he and Fr. Durán shared. The novel that resulted provides little physical context and very little psychological context for the characters, perhaps in order to allow Greene to concentrate on the theological issues raised in the dialogues between the Monsignor and Sancho.

What does remain consistent from 1940 to 1982 is Greene's attraction to mystery, whether theological or a broader hunger for the irrational; his distaste for bourgeois society, whether in its commercial or its stuffy manifestations in religious ceremonies; and, as Yvonne Cloetta put it, Greene's identification with the weak and oppressed against any kind of power, civil or ecclesiastical. As he said in 'The Virtue of Disloyalty,' the writer "stands for the victims, and the victims change."[86] In his books about Mexico, he focused on the Church Suffering and in the travel book sporadically hoped to see the rise of the Church Militant. By the late 1970s, aware that the current Pope was not going to live up to the promises of the Second Vatican Council, allegiance to the Church Militant became less and less possible, and he and the Monsignor turned from the bureaucracy represented by the Curia to a faith—much stronger than mere belief—in the mystery at the heart of Christianity.

Thus, even as his relation to the Church grew more problematic and he changed his label of himself from "a novelist who happens to be a Catholic" to "Catholic agnostic," he never quite abjured his faith. More than forty years before his death, he maintained that his Catholicism "would present me with grave problems as a writer if I were not saved by my disloyalty. If my conscience were as acute as M. Mauriac's . . . I could not write a line" and Greene took comfort in the fact that "the personal morality of an individual is seldom identical with the morality of the group to which he belongs."[87] To adapt George Orwell's line, some moralities are more individual than others. Robert Browning's "Bishop Blougram's Apology," from which Greene

---

84 Ibid, 218.
85 Ibid, 218.
86 Cloetta, Yvonne. *In Search of a Beginning: My Life with Graham Greene*, as told to Marie Françoise Allain, trans. Euan Cameron. Bloomsbury, 2005., 269.
87 *Why Do I Write: An Exchange of Views between Elizabeth Bowen, Graham Greene, & V. S. Pritchett.* London: Percival Marshall, 1948, 31, 32.

drew a favorite line, provides a fitting conclusion for the discussion of *The Power and the Glory* and *Monsignor Quixote*—and a not unsuitable way of summing up Greene's view of himself and certainly our response to him:

> Our interest's on the dangerous edge
> of things.
> The honest thief, the tender murderer,
> The superstitious atheist, demi-rep
> That loves and saves her soul in new
> French books—
> We watch while these
> in equilibrium keep
> The giddy line midway: one step
> aside,
> They're classed and done with.

Greene may have wavered from time to time, but he never quite took the final step over that edge.

**Robert Murray Davis**, professor emeritus, University of Oklahoma, has published extensively on Evelyn Waugh, including *Evelyn Waugh, Writer* and *Brideshead Revisited: The Past Redeemed*, and other 1930s writers; on the literature and culture of the American West; and on post-Communist writing in Central Europe. His creative nonfiction includes three volumes of memoir, two volumes of essays, and a book of advice for middle-aged divorced men. He has also published several books of poems. He has lectured in ten countries besides the USA, and his writing has been translated into eight languages. Since 2002, he has lived on the outskirts of Phoenix, Arizona, and is co-editing *Brideshead Revisited* for the *Complete Works of Evelyn Waugh*, to be published by Oxford University Press.

# Graham Greene's Books for Children

## François Gallix

The 2011 Graham Greene International Festival

*"No one can recover from their childhood."*
*"Nul ne guérit de son enfance."*
—French singer, Jean Ferrat :

The British actress, Emma Thomson, once declared: "There is in Britain a great respect for children's literature: We take it very seriously."

Undoubtedly, the relationship between what adults read and books for children has always been quite different in France and in English-speaking countries. Thus, when T.H. White's agents decided to translate into French *The Sword in the Stone* (1938),[1] the first volume of his modern British adaptation of the Arthurian legends and to publish it in a children's collection (La Bibliothèque Verte) without changing a single word in the text, no French adult wanted to be seen reading it. Curiously, this was one of the books found on President Kennedy's bedside table after his assassination.

It is in fact very revealing that, as for detective or sentimental fiction, many authors feel the need to use a penname when they decide to include a book for children in their catalog of works. This was the case with Greene—who did not authentify his first children's book, *The Little Train*. When it was published in 1946 by Eyre and Spottiswoode, it carried only the name of the illustrator, Dorothy Craigie.[2]

For many generations, English-writing authors have aimed at a double readership, like Charles Dickens, Robert-Louis Stevenson (who was one of Greene's remote cousins), Jonathan Swift, Daniel Defoe, in children-adapted illustrated editions. More recently, J.K. Rowling's *Harry Potter* books were published in most countries in two editions, one for children, one for adults. Bloomsbury produced editions with a different cover picture in Britain and in the United States of America; in France "Gallimard" and "Folio Junior" carried the same text, but with different illustrations and at a cheaper price. The most prominent case was Philip Pullman, who surprised critics when he won the Whitbread prize for adults in 2001 for *The Amber Spyglass*,[3] the third volume of his trilogy intended for children, *His Dark Materials*.

Greene has always been known as an author who aimed at different kinds of readers, writing both what he called *entertainments*, often thrillers, spy or detective stories, and proper "novels" for readers looking for what Roland Barthes called *writerly* texts—narratives implying the reader's participation, and those Virginia Woolf termed, without any negative connotation, as *common readers*. As Neil Sinyard quite rightly put it, "Greene is what, in classical music terms would be called a 'crossover artist' . . . who has the gift of appealing both to the intelligentsia and the masses."[4]

---

1 White, T.H. *The Sword in the Stone*. London: Collins, 1938.
2 *The Little Train*, by Dorothy Craigie, with illustrations by the author. London: Eyre and Spottiswoode, 1946, as by Graham Greene. London : Max Parrish, 1957. Illustrated by Edward Ardizzone. London: The Bodley Head, 1973.
3 Pullman, Philip. *The Amber Spyglass*. London: Scholastic School, 2000.
4 Sinyard, 112.

In her introduction to *The Quiet American*, Zadie Smith ironically considered Greene "a literary double-agent," capable of having himself been influenced by such canonic writers as Conrad and James and by authors of spy novels such as John Buchan, John Le Carré, or of adventure stories like those of Sir Henry Rider Haggard. One could add the Reverend Wilbert Awdry for *Thomas, the Tank Engine*, published the same year as Greene's *The Little Train*, or even Diana Ross with *The Little Red Engine Gets a Name* (1942). These texts have a common theme: a lonely train wrongly deciding to escape to the peaceful daily world so as to obtain the respect of others.

Few authors have so continuously and enthusiastically described the influence that the books they read in their childhood had on their whole lives and on their own writing. Greene even went as far as to claim that the books he read as a child had more influence on his life than the discovery of religion and his conversion to Catholicism. Indeed, he thought that one's personality was definitively determined in the first fifteen years. What Greene wrote in his essay on Charles Dickens in *The Lost Childhood* (1951) might justify his statement: "the creative writer perceives his world once and for all in childhood and adolescence, and his whole career is an effort to illustrate his private world in terms of the great public world we all share."

Greene was a very precocious reader and secretly learned how to read, hidden in his uncle's attic near Cambridge, which surprised his mother. He never forgot that first book: "It was paper-covered with the picture of a boy bound and gagged, dangling at the end of a rope inside a well with the water rising above his waist."[5]

It was in fact one of Dixon Brett's adventures—a popular detective story published in the *Aldine Magazine* in the twenties. Greene later read Conan Doyle when he was ten, and in 1974 wrote an introduction to *The Sign of Four*. He also passionately immersed himself in Sir Rider Haggard's adventurous world of *King Solomon's Mines* (1885)[6] and *She* (1887)[7], which not only influenced his own way of writing, but also turned him into a "globe-trotter," a reporter, and an agent of the secret services:

> If it had not been for that romantic tale of Quartermain, Sir Henry Curtis, Captain Good and, above all the ancient witch Gagool, would I at nineteen have studied the appointments list at the Colonial Office and very nearly picked on the Nigerian Navy for a career.[8]

And yet, reading those adventure novels was not enough and he very often mentioned the importance of his discovery, at the age of fourteen, of a historical, sentimental novel by Marjorie Bowen that is today quite forgotten, *The Viper of Milan* (1906). There he found the phrase he often quoted and commented on: "Human nature is not black and white, but black and grey. I read all that in *The Viper of Milan* and I looked around and I saw it was so."[9] In his 1960 introduction to her book, he paid her an exceptional homage by suggesting

---

5 Greene, Graham. *The Lost Childhood and Other Essays*. London: Eyre and Spottiswood, 1951. Penguin Books, 1962, 11.
6 Haggard, H. *King Solomon's Mines*. London: Cassell, 1885.
7 Haggard, H. *She*. London: Longmans, 1887.
8 Bowen, Marjorie. *The Viper of Milan* (1906), with an Introduction by Graham Greene. London: The Bodley Head, 1960, 13.
9 Ibid., 10.

her book initiated his own literary career: "I think it was Miss Bowen's apparent zest that made me want to write. One could not read her without believing that to write was to live and to enjoy."[10]

He immediately invented new episodes in his copy books, which have unfortunately disappeared and even wrote a pastiche of the novel filled with breath-taking intrigues. There he had also discovered the very Conradian theme which was to influence most of his own fiction, and which he could have also found in Greek tragedies, or in Shakespeare's plays—the moment when fate would inexorably oscillate: "the sense of doom that lies over success—the feeling that the pendulum is about to swing."[11] Similarly, Greene often said that the epigraph from Browning's poem "Apology" (1885) could have summed up most of his own novels :

> Our interest's on the dangerous edge
>   of things.
> The honest thief, the tender murderer,
> The superstitious atheist, demi-rep
> That loves and saves her soul in new
> French books—We watch while there
>   in equilibrium keep
> The giddy line midway.

## A Few Children's Characters in Greene's Fiction

Children always play an important part in the writer's fiction. Thus, in *The Power and the Glory,* it is Luis, the young boy who revealingly opens the door at the very end of the novel to let in the new priest who will assure the continuity of the church after the execution of the whisky priest in Mexico: "'My name is Father . . .' But the boy had already swung the door open and put his lips to his hand before the other could give himself a name.'"[12]

Philip, in the short story, "The Basement Room" (1935), adapted for the screen by Carol Reed as *The Fallen Idol*, impersonates the very Greeneian figure of the innocent child unable to understand the adult world that surrounds him. The young boy involuntarily betrays the man he admires, Baines, the butler.

In the four-page short story, "I Spy," one of Greene's favorites, included in *The Spy Bedside's Book* (1957) and edited with his brother Hugh, Charlie Stowe, aged twelve, hides in his father's tobacco shop to smoke his first cigarette and is then the unwilling witness of his father's leaving the house, framed between two mysterious men wearing raincoats and bowler hats.

"The Destructors" is a premonitory short story taking place in 1950s London about gratuitous vandalism and the extreme violence among certain groups of young people. First published in magazine form in 1954, it was adapted for British television in 1975. By focusing exclusively on a violent group of youngsters, the story somewhat mirrors William Golding's *Lord of the Flies*. In Greene's short story, the youngsters, led by Trevor (T), decide without any reason to destroy completely a 200-year-old house that had survived the Blitz during the absence of its owner, Mr. Thomas, "Old Misery."[13]

---

10 Ibid.,10.
11 Ibid.,15.
12 *The Power and the Glory,* 220.
13 Greene, Graham. 'The Destructors', in *Twenty-One Stories*. The Viking Press, 1949.

## Four Illustrated Books for Children

One may wonder what brought Greene to write four illustrated books for children, also classified as "transport novels": *The Little Train* (1946), *The Little Fire Engine* (1950)[14], *The Little Horse Bus* (1952)[15]; and *The Little Steam Roller* (1953)[16]. In the Spring of 1939, Greene started his long-lasting love affair with Dorothy Glover, a theatre costume designer who, under the penname of Dorothy Craigie, illustrated children's books.

Greene was then at the head of a publishing house, Eyre and Spottiswoode. If he agreed when Dorothy suggested that he write books for children that she would illustrate, it was most probably to avoid what he feared all his life: boredom. The Little Train runs away because he is bored to remain on a country branch line; Toby, the pony in *The Little Fire Engine*, suffers too from this affliction.

The four books were written in London during the German bombings of the Blitz, when Greene and Dorothy Glover were active voluntary members of the Civil Defence. In the books, a vehicle invariably performs a courageous act which inevitably fails. The vehicle is always on the side of law and order, and it often becomes a hunter. The Little Train dreams of a visit to "the world outside, where the great expresses go." In fact, the outer world turns out to be ugly, noisy, and frightening.

The underlying theme in the four books, which are connected as a series, is a nostalgic commemoration of a pre-war rural Britain and the end of an era: motor cars replacing horses, small corner shops giving way to impersonal anonymous stores financed by banks and stern businessmen. Revealingly, in *The Little Train*, the big city, called "Smokeoverall" is presented as Dante's Inferno, a terrible cave of demons where loudspeakers announce connections to 'High Yelling', 'Tombe Junction' and 'Grimborough'—a seedy world reminiscent of Eliot's *The Waste Land*.

The circumstances surrounding the composition of *The Little Train* were recounted by Greene in a signed copy he sent to Catherine Walston with the mention of his collaboration with Dorothy Glover, formerly a stage designer and then a successful writer of boys' books. It was written mainly in a pub called "The Chester Arms" on Sunday mornings during the flying-bomb period of World War II, probably in June 1944. Greene describes how they made a small dummy copy out of a notebook and he made wild pencil suggestions as to how the illustrations should go and of what they should consist; so the book was written and designed simultaneously.

*The Little Train* was originally dedicated to "the guard of the twelve o'clock to Brighton." The manuscript kept at Austin (Texas) consists of 24 tiny pages written in black ink and pencil. The editing and montage by Greene are apparent, for instance, "Double spread of village," pp.5 and 6, "farewell scene." The positioning of the illustrations was clearly indicated by Greene in pencil on the right-hand side of the pages.

---

14 *The Little Fire Engine*, illustrated by Dorothy Craigie. London: Max Parrish, 1950. Illustrated by Edward Ardizzone. London : The Bodley Head, 1973.
15 *The Little Horse Bus—A Tale of StartlingAdventure*, illustrated by Dorothy Craigie. London : Max Parrish, 1952. Illustrated by Edward Ardizzone. London : The Bodley Head, 1974.
16 *The Little Steam Roller—A Story of Adventure, Mystery and Detection*, illustrated by Dorothy Craigie. London : Max Parrish, 1953. Illustrated by Edward Ardizzone London : Doubleday, 1974.

The first edition numbered 20,000 copies of which 12,000 sold quickly. Although that book simply credited "Story and Pictures by Dorothy Craigie," the 1952 blurb on the inside dust-jacket of *The Little Fire Engine* (1950) announced: "IT CAN NOW BE REVEALED that Graham Greene was not only the author of the book which you now have in your hand, but, also its predecessor, *The Little Train*."

In a letter to Max Reinhardt, dated 14th August 1959, Greene had refused an alternative illustrator for a second edition of his third children's book, *The Little Horse Bus* (1952) to be published by Max Parrish: "that would be insult to an old friend who collaborated in the whole affair." However, following Dorothy Glover's death in 1971, the book was re-published and illustrated by Edward Ardizzone. The manuscript of *The Little Horse Bus*, subtitled *A Tale of Startling Adventure,* illustrated by Dorothy Craigie and published in 1952 is contained in a beautiful little "Century notebook." Written in pencil, it specifies the space where the drawings should be included, e.g.: "whole page (31) in color entitled 'Hansom and horsebus'." It was awarded the Boys' Clubs of America *Junior Book Award for 1955.*

*The Little Steamroller*, subtitled *A Story of Adventure, Mystery and Detection,* was first published in 1953. The manuscript is included in the same Century notebook as *The Little Horse Bus*. Both editions of these books were successfully illustrated by two excellent artists using contrasting styles and techniques: in the 1950s by Dorothy Craigie with her typographical effects and her graphic games; and in the 1970s by Edward Ardizzone, already a famous book illustrator whose work was collected by many fans.

The books were translated into several languages, including German, Swedish, Dutch, Italian and French, except for *The Little Steamroller*. The French edition is a thorough adaptation which features a "Frenchification" of the text. This method was quite common at the time, the object being not to disorientate the young reader. Unfortunately, this prevented the young reader from learning about another culture. Thus, in *Le Petit Omnibus*, the original route for the bus, London Bridge to Waterloo Station becomes the very Parisian Madeleine to Bastille. Whitehall and Oxford Circus are changed to Maubert and Place de la Concorde. Scotland Yard is la PJ, Police Judiciaire, situated on the well-known Quai des Orfèvres. In *The Little Train,* the great Jock of Edinburgh, the famous Scottish Express, "*Why ye poor wee train...*," becomes "le grand Mistral" marseillais and has a very amusing Mediterranean accent. Strangely enough, "Guinness is good for you," which appears on a poster, becomes "Buvez du vin!"

Now out of print and valuable collectors' items, there is a strong argument for the four beautifully written books to be be reprinted. Ironically, the theme has now become very fashionable, with the emphasis on the ecological value of a more natural world, away from the noisy, polluted, impersonal industrial cities.

Finally, *The Monster of Capri*[17] and *The Monster's Treasure* are a unique curiosity in the publishing world and a real treasure for the bibliophile. *The Monster of Capri* was originally handwritten by Greene for his two grandchildren on the back of eleven colored postcards, each one featuring a

---

17 *The Monster of Capri,* including *The Monster's Treasure,* ed. by Rolando Pieraccini. Pesaro, Italy : Eurographica, 1985.

different view of Capri. *The Monster's Treasure* is a continuation, this time written on eight postcards.

Reproductions of the postcards were published by Eurographica in 1985 in a signed, limited edition. Included is a handwritten dedication: "*The Monster of Capri*: a story written specially for Andrew and Jonathan by their Grand pic, Graham Greene." This is followed by an Author's note which reads: "These stories, written on postcards, were addressed to my two grandchildren Andrew and Jonathan Bourget many years ago when they were small. Now I am afraid they are too old to much enjoy the book, which all the same is dedicated to them."

In his essay on young Charles Dickens,[18] Greene wrote

The creative writer perceives his world once and for all in childhood and adolescence, and his whole career is an effort to illustrate his private world in terms of the great public world we all share.[19]

Greene also used a thought-provoking image, insisting on the considerable importance of the books found on the family's shelves and read by children. Those books, he concluded, are "a crystal, in which the child dreamed that he saw life moving."[20]

---

18 "The Lost Childhood", 1951.
19 Ibid., 59.
20 Ibid., 12.

**François Gallix** is Emeritus Professor of XXth century British Literature at the Sorbonne. He has presented many contemporary British authors, including Alan Sillitoe, Peter Ackroyd, David Lodge, Julian Barnes, Jonathan Coe, Graham Swift, Hanif Kureishi, Will Self, and he has published several books and articles about them. His research concentrates on the works of Graham Greene. He has recently discovered and published in *The Times* and in *The Strand* a detective novella by Greene. He has edited two volumes on Greene, published by Robert Laffont (2011). His research also includes Nabokov and *Lolita,* and Boris Vian, alias Vernon Sullivan.

# Graham Greene And The Congo, 1959: Personal Memories and Background of *A Burnt-Out Case*

## Michel Lechat

The 2006 Graham Greene International Festival

One morning, some fifty-years-ago in 1959, Graham Greene appeared at Yonda, the leprosy settlement for which I happened to be the doctor. How was it that he came to my place, in the Equateur Province of the then Belgian Congo? It would be nice to say that he emerged one day, stepping down the gangway of the bishop's riverboat as Querry does in the novel *A Burnt-Out Case*. This could have occurred: one "travels without maps" in the heart of the jungle and somehow, sometimes, one may run into dancers on a cricket lawn in a missionary outpost, an evening whisky with the manager of a cotton plantation, or even a leprosy colony. One is in the middle of nowhere, and all of a sudden, at the detour of a tree, passing through some sort of interface one penetrates into another universe. But it was not the case. Greene did not come unannounced. His visit to Yonda had been arranged through a common friend in Brussels. In his letter to this friend, he expressed the wish "for the purposes of a book to spend some weeks in a hospital of the Schweitzer kind in Africa, but run by a religious order."

Of the Schweitzer kind, indeed! I must confess that my first reaction was mixed. Rightly or wrongly, Doctor Schweitzer at that time was not highly regarded by health professionals. He was therefore not the most perfect reference to use. Yonda was very different from the "leprosaria" of yesteryear that Greene had apparently in mind. The place was a large village near the Congo River, with small brick houses along avenues bordered by mango trees and simple technical buildings, housing over one thousand leprosy patients. There was no segregation of the "lepers," this cruel and unnecessary measure meant to prevent the transmission of the disease. Leprosy is not all that contagious, and out of some 100,000 patients at the time in the Congo, no more than ten percent were reputedly infectious. Patients could go freely in and out of the compound. They were accepted with their family, spouses or concubines, and even with their children. There were schools, and children were examined at regular intervals for the possible onset of symptoms, which at an early stage are easy to cure. There were workshops, and families had their plots of land for cultivation, a dozen dugouts, which we called "pirogues," that lay on the banks of the river. Yonda was aiming at becoming the prototype of a modern institution for the care of leprosy. The Sisters called it "*le petit Monaco des Noirs*," the little Monaco of Africans. I felt at that time that this was not a very inspiring context for a novelist.

Hence, I did nothing to prompt him to come. Out of consideration for him, and for the lady friend by whom he was recommended, I did however spend a Sunday preparing a large chart describing a dozen "leprosaria" throughout Africa which, in my opinion, were better suited than Yonda to accommodate him and minister to the birth of a novel.

To speak the truth, I was not that eager to shelter such a visitor in Yonda. In spite of its relative remoteness, the place was on its way to becoming if not yet a tourist attraction, at least a show piece. Of course that was not an issue with Greene. What I was more apprehensive of was that our guest, a famous Catholic writer, might upset the delicate balance between the Mission and me. It is not always that easy to be a mission doctor, the more so when one is at the same time a government employee. How would the father superior react, bicycling non-stop through the avenues chewing at his cheroot? What would the father in charge of construction, who in a previous life had taught Greek in a provincial Belgian town, think? And the brother in charge of carpentry who did not speak a word of anything except Frisian, at times mixed with some presumably horrendous expletives in Malay, which he had brought back from his years in a Japanese concentration camp during World War Two. Not to mention the bishop, described in the *Congo Journal* as 'a wonderfully handsome old man with an 18th-century manner—or perhaps the manner of an Edwardian "boulevardier"?' What if this "pilgrim of the dry season," the sarcastic term used by the colonials to designate passer-by travelers, did not go to Mass? Did he even play bridge? The bishop was reputed for distributing his missionaries among the various stations in the bush according to their readiness to play bridge during his pastoral visits.

In any event, after a couple of weeks arrived a letter expressing his wish to come to our place, and then a second letter:

The book that I have in mind has a leper mission purely as a background and I have no intention, I promise you, of producing a roman à clef.... Nor am I looking for any dramatic material. The more normal and routine-like that I can make the background the more effective it would be for my purpose. (27th October 1958)

and a third letter in December,

... I want to see things as they are.... I want also to reassure you about the subject of the novel. The real subject... is a theological and psychological argument which for reasons I can't go into for fear of destroying this still nebulous idea that should take place against the background of an African hospital settlement.

I went to see the Superior of the Mission in order to make the necessary arrangements for the visit. He did not show reluctance or surprise. He was somewhat accustomed to the visitors I was bringing in, not to say the ones sent occasionally by the colonial administration ('You cannot miss the Belgian Lambaréné!'): a famous American ornithologist, an honorary Belgian consul in Sao Paolo, a Mister Arnold from the State Department, the manager of a travelling circus, a physiotherapist in training, a renowned doctor who had crossed the Atlantic on a raft, a lady socialist senator, a saxophonist, etc. So, it was all go for our English writer. Let us inspect the mosquito net in the bedroom at the Fathers' house, fill the jug with water, and check the soap in the soap dish. We forgot to place a coat hanger; cassocks are apparently not supposed to be hung on a coat hanger, and this caused some embarrassment to Greene.

Greene came, and life went on undisturbed. Nobody asked questions, each of us being engrossed in our own tasks. The fathers went their way, busy driving trucks, mixing cement, repairing generators, all interspersed with teaching, preaching and distributing sweets to the children. The sisters cycled from the convent to the school and from the kitchen to the pharmacy. I went my way. He went his. It must be added that at the time of Greene's visit, the whole mission was teeming with frantic building activities. After years of discussions with the colonial authorities, it had been decided to build a hospital in order to replace the four-room dispensary which, since my arrival five years before, had served as consultation room cum laboratory and maternity ward. The fathers were feverishly drawing blueprints; Edith, my wife, was typing orders. I was ordering equipment (we even have electricity). As a consequence, nobody had much time to devote to our eminent guest.

He showed an utmost capacity for creating regular habits. In the morning he would walk down the meadow to the banks of the River, the Congo, sit in an old "pirogue" and read until the heat became unbearable. At various times of the day, habits overlapped. He generally had lunch at the fathers', during which the foursome of missionaries exchanged innocent jokes in Flemish, bursting into laughter that left him nonplussed. At the end of the day he would come to our house for a rest on the veranda and dinner with my wife and children. Now and then he joined me in the dispensary and sat on a chair between the door and the open window, observing the patients and asking questions. Needless to say, he was impeccable in his approach to them. (Twenty years later, he casually mentioned in one of his letters to me the "fear I have felt the first few hours with you in the leper colony". I had not noticed.)

What a pity that nobody took a photograph of Greene staring at a patient, for example Imbonga Bernard, the man without fingers who had been taught to knit as well as any sister. Or the woman with the palsied eyelids who could not close her eyes or even blink. "The doctor had bought her dark glasses but she would not wear them because they were not a medicine—she had trust only in drugs" (Congo Journal, Febr.10th). Greene added that patients with mutilated feet who were given orthopedic shoes put them on only on Sundays.

That was the way of life at Yonda for all of us, and he was part of the group. He was like everybody else, doing his job, which in his case was struggling to deliver a novel. We had, however, to protect him from people's curiosity. There are Parkinsons everywhere who have a gift for nosing around. At the post office, this British gentleman, Mr. Graham (as he chose to introduce himself), being seen in the company of the doctor of the leprosarium, soon became Mr. Greene. The most obvious nuisance came from the people who were longing to have his opinion on some manuscripts they kept in a drawer. The number of individuals in a colonial town in want of a publisher for their novels is amazing. They usually showed up after five o'clock, "just to have a beer." We had the scenario all prepared and well-rehearsed. As soon as a car was spotted turning off the road and into the long alley of palm trees, Graham rushed back to the house, jumped through the window of our bedroom, and out into the forest.

The settlement at Yonda was beginning to encroach on the equatorial forest whose edges unfolded like huge green cliffs: "The great trees with their roots like the ribs of ships. From the plane they had stood from the green jungle carpet browning at the top like cauliflowers. Their trunks curve a little this way and that giving the appearance of reptilian life" *(A Burnt-Out Case,* Part 2, Chapter 1). A beautiful description. "These woody spaces would remain unexplored ... for longer than the planets." The craters of the moon were better known than the forests at the door." I am convinced it was while stepping over the rim of our bedroom's window to run away from the unwanted afternoon bores that Greene imagined the flight of Deo Gratias, Querry's boy, into the forest at night, on "a rough track which ... led towards what geographers might have called the center of Africa" *(A Burnt-Out Case,* Part One, Chapter 2) What was there? Clearings in the forest with abandoned villages? Dormant ponds? Hidden paths meandering between the swamps? The smelling exhalations of an unchartered country? For years, at the rear of the house, we had, Edith and I, contemplated this inextricable tangle of greenery extending for hundreds miles on our doorsteps without ever having been able to make way into it.

Greene was, of course, a formidable observer. He seemed inattentive, though always on the lookout, gleaning small bits of trifling information and storing them for further processing.

"I am wondering, does he play bridge?" asks the Bishop of Mrs.Rycker.

"That atheist ..." said Rycker of the Doctor: "Do you remember when last year I tried to organize a Leper's Day .... Four hundred dresses had accumulated ... and he refused to distribute them, just because there were not enough to go round", (This was a true story only were there blankets or tins of sardines? I forget.)

"Father, why are you so against Mr. Querry?" asks Father Thomas of the Superior.

"What other man in his position–he's world famous, Father, even if Father Paul may never have heard of him— would bury himself here ... ?"

In a few words transpires the whole resentment of Father Thomas, who is dead wood, towards Father Paul, who is building the hospital, and also some of his discomfort with the missionary work. Who knows? Even when there is no significant event, Greene would create life out of futility.

Greene never looked at people as though they were butterflies or cockroaches. As he stresses in the prologue to *A Burnt-Out Case* it would be a waste of time to try to spot or decode the central characters in the novel. The characters are "formed from the flotsam of thirty years as a novelist." Marie-Françoise Allain, the French journalist, refers to Greene's sagacity as though he has a gift as a medium. I would rather say that in general he officiates, so to speak, as an *accoucheur*. He was seeing right through what people could have been or might become, at different times, in different situations, in different universes. We all have virtual personalities which can come out according to the circumstances of life.

The Superior in the novel is a striking illustration thereof. A most inconspicuous character, he is an innocent piece of the *décor* who does not see the difference between a bidet and a footbath. Nonetheless he is led to make *en passant* a number of sharp remarks that nobody in Yonda would have expected from him. Yet, several years later, the country being in a state of complete upheaval, he actually became archbishop, revealing himself to be much closer to the assertive and robust character displayed in the novel than to the laconic priest he was during his years in the leprosarium.

Greene was nevertheless, in some respect, deceptive. Visitors to Yonda were at times very thought provoking. They could often point out things whose interest for me had eroded after years of routine, which had become casual, and were escaping my attention. Graham, while a most pleasant companion when visiting a retired veterinarian in his cocoa plantation, strolling among the giant bamboo trees in a dilapidated botanical garden, or looking at strange scaffoldings along the road reminiscent of ancient tribal rituals, was also, should I say, concealed, keeping his observations to himself, not sharing them easily, as though they had to mature. Therefore I must confess that he did not bring me that much during his stay in terms of helping me to renew my vision of Yonda. But after all, why should he have done so? I had to wait for the book.

It was between us a sort of tacit pact of mutual reserve: he would have called it a "duty of reticence." This attitude was not one-sided. I never of course took advantage of his presence, at times for hours in the car going to some distant station, to put him questions about religion. He never asked me about my beliefs, half-beliefs and non-beliefs. Otherwise, life would have become impossible. The nearest we came to discussing religion was on a Sunday driving to Coq' to attend Mass at the native parish, the church in the African township. He told me "Michel, I hope it is not for me that you are going to Mass." I returned the question. Otherwise, we never engaged in the subject. It was my way of protecting him. Harassed by so many people eager to put to him their religious anxieties—and there was quite a bunch of them around—I believe that he appreciated my restraint. It might be the reason he dedicated the novel to me, and explains why we kept our friendship alive until the end of his life.

Let me quote here a letter he sent me before the novel was published (23 March 1960):

I am struggling towards the end of my novel which is now called *A Burnt Out Case* and I am wondering if I don't as I am inclined to do put it in the fire whether you would allow me to dedicate it to you as a poor return for all your kindness.

I always abstained from reporting to him situations or anecdotes that could have provided the framework of a novel *'à la Greene'*. There were, of course, a number of them. The colonial environment, including the missionary world, is a breeding ground for all kinds of conflicts and entangled situations. How self-gratifying it would be to skillfully suggest a script to a famous author! Thus, during his visit, I avoided whispering in his ear anything which could interfere with his search for an appropriate story. I think it was subconscious on my part, a kind of reflex: a fear of usurping his creative power, sterilizing his freedom to explore and discover.

In this respect, I had a strange experience. When I arrived at the leprosarium as a young doctor, I had a fierce conflict with some the missionary sisters regarding the care of the patients, a quarrel between the ancients and the moderns which, owing to the tropical climate and the stuffy colonial society, reached earthshaking proportions. It was indeed the consummate scenario for Greene. With all the ingredients. At the time of his visit, I did not tell him a word about it. Twenty-five years later, however, while we were having lunch together at Felix's in Antibes, I raised the subject. He interrupted me, saying that when he was in Yonda, he had heard some rumor about this *affaire*, and that he had always been grateful to me for not having told him about it at the time, because it would have destroyed—I do not remember the exact word he used—but it sounded like: "spoiled the whole thing . . . . no book would have come out".

In the *Journal* Greene describes his morning walk through the meadow down to his "pirogue":

Egrets like patches of arctic snow stand among the small coffee-coloured cattle. The huge Congo flowing with the massive speed of a rush hour out over the great New York bridges. This had not changed since Conrad's day.

The reference to Joseph Conrad surprised me. Yonda, indeed, was the heart of darkness. As ship's officer, Conrad had maneuvered his wood-burning stern-wheeler, the *Roi des Belges*, on the Congo River, passing by Yonda, which of course did not exist then. (Klein, a commercial agent and his travelling companion, who as Kurtz was to become the hero of *Heart of Darkness*, is buried downstream.) We were at the time, my wife and I, avid readers of Conrad. Although I refrained from talking literature with Greene, I mentioned Conrad once and I immediately got the feeling that I had made a *faux-pas*. I was quite interested to learn, years later, that the book he was reading when lying in his pirogue in the morning dawn was indeed by Conrad, perhaps as a sort of exorcism.

The publication of *A Burnt-Out Case* raised a petty controversy. A few respected leprologists criticized him for having chosen leprosy as the background of his novel. One of them wrote: "Querry's God is not the God of the Christian . . . This novel will bring pain and distress, and for this reason it would have been better if it had never been written." Graham had been very affected by this letter. This is of course part of a huge *malentendu*. Provided the subject is treated with respect, which is the case, a novelist has the right to choose any topic he feels appropriate. As I wrote to this most eminent colleague: "Leprosy is part of life, like war, corruption, lost expectations, hatred and love. These are no precincts reserved to the retired generals, moralists, psycho-analysts or sex counsellors, no more than leprosy is the exclusive domain of the leprosy specialist." I shall of course refrain from embarking here into a semantic debate on the use of the word "leper," that for decades some people have been trying to eradicate from the English vocabulary. One of Greene's critics reckoned that he used the evil *L-word* no less than fifty-one times in the novel. That undoubtedly is a mortal sin.

I mentioned how tolerant were the missionaries at Yonda regarding moral issues. From the very second day after his arrival, having had dinner the previous evening at the Fathers', Greene raises the point in the Congo Journal (February 4th):

The social problem: the husbands are less inclined to follow their wives than the wives the husbands. The husband will set up in his village with another woman, and when the wife finds a lover to look after her in the colony, the husband descends demanding justice and the return of his 'dot'. The Protestant missions allow this to happen, but the Catholic fathers give the husband short shrift. People here are left alone and there are no moral inquisitions.

This attitude transpires throughout the novel. It is the story (a true story) of the catechist with no fingers nor toes left who brought to church for baptism a baby that he had fathered to a woman crippled from polio: "... there were no questions and no admonitions. The fathers were too busy to bother themselves with what the Church considered sin—moral theology was the subject they were less concerned with" (*A Burnt-Out Case*, Part 4, Chapter 1).

The fathers were unconcerned with private lives. Except of course, at least in the book, Father Thomas, who is indignant about the Sisters keeping as teacher in the school Marie, a young woman "having a baby every year by a different man ... allowing her to teach with her cradle in the class. She is pregnant again. What kind of an example is that?" The Superior replies "We are here to help, not to condemn."

The more I think about it, the more I imagine Greene's surprise when he arrived in Yonda, an institution which perhaps did not meet his expectations. Here was a situation where it was not sin, but rather the disease that took precedence. The disease was becoming the sin, and TLC, to use the jargon, was replacing moral theology. He must have been faced with a dilemma. Is it possible that to some extent it hampered his drive to write *A Burnt-Out Case*? Could it explain why, after his visit, he repeatedly complained to me that he was quite unsure a novel would ever surge out of his stay. In *Ways of Escape*, he says that "never a novel proved more recalcitrant [...]." In the *Congo Journal*, he confesses:

> The priests are more concerned with engineering; electricity, navigation and the like, than with the life of man or God.—(Querry) has come seeking another form of love and is faced with electric turbines and problems of building, and he fails to understand the priests as much as they fail to understand him (*In Search of a Character, Congo Journal,* Febr.12th).

These priests were everyday missionaries for everyday life, quietly doing their jobs, not torn apart between one or another perdition and some ultimate redemption. Greene indeed was apt to adjust to whatever routine there might be, or however unusual the circumstances (and perhaps preferably when those were unusual), he adjusted. Since there were no inspiring events, he was able to instill life into the most commonplace occurrences.

Was Greene satisfied with the four weeks he spent at Yonda? Did he find in the "léproserie" and in the fathers and patients (and the doctor) what he was expecting? I cannot help believing that a great part of the depression, which according to many sources affected Greene during the writing of *A Burnt Out Case*, was not so much due to his unhappy cohabitation with Querry, but to the fact that he had not met the appropriate context in which to breed his novel. He was faced with the thorny dilemma of having to make the best of an inauspicious situation. But at the end, he succeeded. And the result was a superb book.

And then, from the Congo, Greene flew to Douala, in the Cameroons. He wrote us a warm note of thanks, adding:

> I forgot to tell you that I went to one other léproserie ... a mixture of the sentimental and the squalid.... Altogether it made one to realize all the more strongly what you have accomplished at Yonda.

A couple of weeks later, he sent me an intriguing letter:

I have just received an account in a local Cameroon paper of a meeting with me in Douala and feel extremely annoyed because I am reported as saying that I preferred the little léproserie of Dibamba to those in the Belgian Congo—better built, industrialized and less human! I am quoted as saying that I would have liked to have passed a fortnight at Dibamba. Needless to say I said none of these things.

I did not doubt for an instant that Greene would not denigrate Yonda, especially in front of a journalist. But I wanted to know more about this place in Dibamba. I obtained a copy of the article. It must have been quite an interesting interview indeed, defined forthright by the clerical journalist as " un peu de tout, à la française" (a little of everything, in the French way). Greene was presented as "ce géant aux yeux clairs" (this giant with pale eyes), "qui prend la vie comme un collégien en vacances" (seizing life like a college boy on holiday). It was a sort of lyrical elegy to Greene, comparing him to King Arthur in search of the Grail, a high class Don Giovanni, the bizarre trio of Epicure, Rabelais and Saint John the Baptist, with the robust health of catholic writers like Claudel, and Bernanos, and Mauriac, and also to Chesterton, Mao-Tse-Tung, Maurice Barrès and even Victor Hugo. In this orgy of comparisons and endorsements, the Dibamba/Yonda contest stands out as an insignificant and almost ludicrous footnote.

Graham must have been terribly embarrassed. I was not. I wrote to reassure him:

> Please do not worry about the Douala's article.... It could well be that the "léproseries" in the Congo are less compassionate than those in the Cameroon.... Africans are not children. We are not here to use them for our self-fulfilment, We are here to help the patients into developing their responsibility as human beings... We are not looking for gratitude. We want them to get cured, whenever possible, and then to forget us afterwards. I believe that it is the only way to show interest in individuals.... It would be good that your Jesuit journalist thought about that.

These comments were well translated by Greene in the mouth of Doctor Colin: "A patient can always detect whether he is loved or whether it is only his leprosy which is loved. I don't want leprosy loved. I want it eliminated".

With years passing, I cannot, however, help asking myself whether there is not a bit of truth, a little bit of truth in that Douala interview. Later, as a sort of cryptic reply to my plea, Greene wrote a heartfelt review of a book on Lambarene (*Days with Albert Schweitzer*, by Frederick Franck) in which he stresses the human sides of this leper colony, by contrast with the "scientific" ones: "The sentimental hospital offers something to the human mind in pain or despair which the scientific may not be able to do, and the scientific sometimes fails by reason of its own dogmas."

Greene, of course, uses the term *scientific* for want of a better word. Nowadays, one would talk of management. Yonda was definitely an example of good management. But management has its dangers. Would it be possible that Greene had foreseen the present-day drift of management towards a faceless world of cost-effectiveness, where cure is a return for health investment, people are human resources, partners are stakeholders, and patients will soon become clients, disguised behind statistics and decimal figures. Doctor Schweitzer was, perhaps, not that wrong after all.

No comments were made after *A Burnt-Out Case* was published, just as no questions were asked while Greene was in Yonda. The fathers and the sisters went on treating the patients. The book, I suppose, joined the few romans policiers and the stock of missionary journals on the chocolate-colored dresser in the fathers' common-room. They probably did not read it. They had no time.

What happened to Yonda afterwards, how, thanks to the sisters who joined me in 1953, it survived in the middle of the chaos, is another story. It could have been the subject of another Greene novel.

**Professor Michel Lechat** was a renowned Belgian epidemiologist who worked at the Catholic University of Louvain and later at the Tropical Institute at Antwerp. He published more than 300 scientific papers, including more than 200 on leprosy. In 1953 he went to Iyonda in the then Belgian Congo to run the leprosarium. In 1959 he agreed to play host to Graham Greene, who stayed with him and his family for several weeks while the writer was researching for his novel *A Burnt-Out Case*. Subsequently Professor Lechat became a lifelong friend of Greene. He died in 2014.

We are grateful to his widow Edith Dasnoy for granting us permission to use his original lecture notes.

# The Furthest Escape Of All: Darkness And Refuge In The Belgian Congo[1].

## Michael Meeuwis

The 2014 Graham Greene International Festival

## Introduction

Graham Greene's *A Burnt-Out Case* (1960)[2] is set in the Belgian Congo, the colony in Central Africa over which Belgium ruled from 1908, the year in which it took it over from the private hands of King Leopold II, to 1960, when the Congo gained its independence. In the first months of 1959, Greene spent five weeks in the Congo in preparation for this novel. My intention here is to contextualize Greene's Congo trip in more detail than what is available in the literature so far (i.a., Hulstaert 1994[3]; Lechat 1991, 2007[4]; Sherry 2004; Meeuwis 2013).

I will do so among others on the basis of information found in the personal archives of Dr. Michel Lechat (1927–2014), the Belgian leprologist who was Greene's main contact during his stay, whose discourse and insights he transposed to Dr. Colin's in *A Burnt-Out Case*, and to whom he also dedicated the book. Shortly before Lechat's death in February 2014, his wife Edith Dasnoy handed me the Greene-related part of his archives. This included photocopies he had made of the documents he had donated to the Harry Ransom Center of the University of Texas at Austin in 2007, such as letters between Greene and himself, but also a number of documents he had newly discovered after 2007, as well as his private and unpublished memoirs, which Edith Dasnoy found on his computer and in several printouts only in 2013–2014. A second major source for me is the original manuscript of the diary Greene kept while traveling in the Congo, in possession of the Harry Ransom Center. The diary was published in 1961 as *In Search of a Character: The Congo Journal* (Greene 1961)[5], but this published version diverges in significant ways from the diary manuscript, revealing many deleted bits of sensitive information as well as wholly different perceptions Greene had of events and people he had

---

1 A first version of this paper was presented in 2014 at the Graham Greene International Festival in Berkhamsted, UK, under the title "Merriment or Make-Believe? Reflections on the *Congo Journal*, Missionaries, and a Home Video Showing Graham Greene in the Belgian Congo." I am grateful to the members of the audience for their feedback. My special gratitude goes to Honoré Vinck for his suggestions, and to Mike Hill and Jon Wise for their invaluable help with identifying the right archives and, not a minor challenge, with decrypting Greene's handwriting.
2 Greene, G. (1977 [1960]). *A Burnt-Out Case*. London, Penguin.
3 Hulstaert, G. (1994). Graham Greene et les Missionnaires Catholiques au Congo Belge. Annales Æquatoria 15: 493-503.
4 Lechat, M. (1991). "Remembering Graham Greene". *The Bulletin: The Newsweekly of The Capital of Europe* 18 April 1991: 14-16.
Lechat, M. (2007). Diary: Graham Greene at the Leproserie. *London Review of Books* 29(15): 34-35. Meeuwis, M. (2013).
5 Greene, G. (1961). *In Search of a Character: Two African Journals*. London, The Bodley Head.

met in the Congo. In addition to Greene himself, another important 'censor' of the diary manuscript was Dr. Lechat, who, asked by Greene to correct the galley proofs, beseeched the writer to omit or change quite a number of unfavorable descriptions of persons still living and working in the Congo before the diary went to print. I intend to list and critically interpret the discrepancies between the consecutive versions of the diary in a future study. Thirdly, I also draw information from additional literature and from other, minor archives, all of which will be identified in due course. Lastly, I rely on the many conversations I continue to have with Edith Dasnoy, who has become a dear friend, as well as with several members of the Belgian branch of the congregation of the Missionaries of the Sacred Heart, the priests among whom Greene spent almost all of his time in the Congo.

My account is organized chronologically, following Greene's itinerary. In section 1, I first try to come to grips with Greene's choice of the Congo when looking for a suitable background for his new novel. For that, I will be referring to the help he requested in 1958 from the Belgian Baroness Hansi Lambert, to whose *beau-monde* circle Greene belonged, as well as to Lechat's invocations of Joseph Conrad's *Heart of Darkness* in his first letters to Greene. I will also discuss the remarkably apolitical intentions with which Greene went to the Congo. In section 2, I explain how all these preparations and intentions culminated in Greene's spending the last week of January in Brussels, with a mistress he nicknames "Tony" in the diary manuscript, waiting for his departure by airplane on 30 January 1959. Greene spent his first two days in the Congolese capital Leopoldville (31 January–1 February), after which he traveled on to the city of Coquilhatville, some 600 kilometers to the north, in the heart of the equatorial rainforest. His final destination was Iyonda, situated only 15 kilometers south of the center of Coquilhatville. Iyonda was a small village and station of the Missionaries of the Sacred Heart, which included the leprosy[6] colony and hospital managed by Dr. Lechat.

Greene spent two periods in Iyonda, namely from 2 through 11 February and again from 26 February through 5 March 1959. As I discuss in section 3, during the first term he was torn between on the one hand an escapist comfort offered by the Iyonda priests' unconcern with his celebrity, and on the other the disappointment of not finding among them the deep religious reflexivity he had hoped. I also consider the exasperating attention Greene received from those colonials who did take an interest in the personality that he was. In section 4, I relate how, from 12 through 25 February, he traveled the Ruki-Momboyo river, a tributary branching off from the main Congo river at Coquilhatville, in order to visit two other mission stations and leprosariums. This two-weeks' river journey, which Greene made by steamer, is of importance for several reasons. First, during the

---

6 I avoid the term "leper," which, as Brandsma and Deepak explain (2012: 326), is nowadays deemed offensive towards leprosy patients. Other terms for "leprosy hospital and colony," indicating the settlement where leprosy patients are treated and isolated from the rest of the population, are "leprosarium" and, borrowed from the French, "leprosery." Brandsma, J. W. and S. Deepak (2012). "Surgical and Social Rehabilitation". In: *Leprosy: A practical guide*. ed. E. Nunzi and C. Massone. Milan, Springer: 321-327.

idle hours on the steamer, Greene took to rereading *Heart of Darkness*, the long novella Joseph Conrad had written on the basis of his own steamer journey on the Congo river in 1890. This rereading allowed Greene to come to a thorough reinterpretation of the novella's merits. Secondly, much of the narrative in *A Burnt-Out Case* revolves around a leprosarium situated on the banks of a river that likewise is not the main Congo but one of its smaller tributaries. Greene's journey on the Ruki-Momboyo and the individuals and localities he saw on its banks thus served him as an important source of inspiration for the book. Finally in section 5, I deal with Greene's second term in Iyonda (26 February–5 March 1959), during which a remarkable home video was shot of him, for which I provide background information and an interpretation, as well as with his last days back in Leopoldville (5–6 March), his brief visit to Brazzaville in French Equatorial Africa (7–8 March), and to Douala in Cameroon (8–12 March), where he visited a fourth leprosarium.

## 1. Finding a destination for an apolitical trip

Already while writing and finalizing *Our Man in Havana* (1958), Greene was conceptualizing his next novel, envisaging to set it in a leprosy hospital and colony somewhere in the tropics: "a new novel [was] already beginning to form in my head by way of a situation–a stranger who turns up in a remote leper settlement for no apparent reason".[7] The traveling author that he was, Greene planned to spend some weeks in such a remote leprosarium, in order to personally collect all contextual and technical information needed to compose a background, and maybe also some dramatic material. For this purpose, in September 1958, he contacts his Belgian friend Baroness Johanna "Hansi" von Reininghaus-Lambert (1899–1960), widow and heir of the famous Brussels banker Baron Henri Lambert (1887–1933)[8]. Hansi Lambert was a lady of the Belgian high society, collecting art, among which paintings by no lesser names than Miró, Chagall, and Picasso, and always keen on inviting, in old salon-style, famous artists, writers, composers, and politicians for lunch or dinner. As her son Philippe Lambert (1930–2011) remembers, Greene was one of the celebrities in Hansi's entourage:

"My mother [. . .] was the product of a world where appearance and demeanor mattered, and had a great savoir-faire combined with anirresistible charm. [. . .] Hansi was lucky to have financial means to support her strong need for friends and influence. She dreaded being alone and took every opportunity to expand her social circle and surround herself with interesting people. Whether it was in her homes in Fudji, Avenue, Marnix or Gstaad, [. . .] she gathered around her writers and poets like Nicholas Nabokov, Graham Greene, the Spenders".[9]

In his letter of 15 September 1958 to Hansi, Greene specifies that he wants to spend some weeks "in a hospital of the

---

7 Greene, G. 1981 [1980]. *Ways of Escape*. Harmondsworth, Penguin, 269.
8 Lambert, Philipe. 2013. *Long Ago (and Far Away)*. Brussels, Editions Racine.
9 Ibid., 138-139.

Schweizer kind in West or Central Africa (because already I have certain knowledge of the background)."[10] With "knowledge of the background" we can suppose he refers to his earlier West-African experiences, i.e. his 1935 trip to Liberia, leading to *Journey Without Maps* (1936),[11] and his life as an MI6 officer in Sierra Leone in the early 1940s, the basis for *The Heart of the Matter* (1948). He continues his letter explaining that he has already located a possible leprosarium, namely in Bamako, Mali, but adds that it is situated in the Sahara, "which I don't know," and that it is not run by priests but by nuns "and I wouldn't feel at ease with them!" Greene knew that Baroness Hansi's late husband as well as her two sons had connections in the Belgian Congo, where they traveled widely and were engaged in large-scale business investments. With that knowledge, he concludes his letter by suggesting to Hansi: "It occurred to me that there might be some place in the Belgian Congo. If you could help me I would be very grateful."

A week later, on 27 September 1958, Hansi Lambert forwards Greene's letter to Dr. Michel Lechat, who had been working in Iyonda since 1953. Lechat and Hansi knew each other through Hansi's son Léon, with whom Lechat had been very good friends since their student years in the 1940s. Lechat was a regularly invited guest at Hansi's society dinners; in fact, there is a note in Lechat's personal archives, in his hand, saying that on 6 November 1950 Greene and he were both present at one of the Baroness's dinners, but they hardly exchanged words on that occasion. On 27 September, as mentioned, Hansi forwards Greene's letter of 15 September to Lechat, adding a note in which she requests him to contact Greene directly and comments that "Greene is a very agreeable and very problematic man. It would be amusing if the Belgian Congo would offer him a background for a novel."[12].

A correspondence between Graham Greene and Michel Lechat quickly ensues. Lechat already writes a first letter to Greene on 3 October 1958. He provides him with a long list of Catholic leproseries in Africa, with details on organization, infrastructure, and the like. He adds that the "most interesting ones"[13] are to be found in Nigeria, Spanish Guinea, Cameroon, and in the town of Tshumbo, the Belgian Congo, but strikingly he does not mention his own leprosery of Iyonda. At first Lechat was not very enthusiastic about hosting a celebrity staying over for research, fearing that this would demand too much of his time and attention (Edith Dasnoy, pers. comm.). But he certainly also wanted to anticipate any unrealizable illusions Greene was entertaining. In his letter Lechat makes subtle efforts to downplay Iyonda as a suitable destination, stressing that the medical infrastructure is not finished, that the hospital and research center are still under construction, that everything human and

---

10 Letter Greene to H. Lambert, 15/9/1958 (photocopy in Lechat archives, author's possession).
11 Greene, G. 2010 [1936]. *Journey Without Maps*. London, Random House.
12 Letter H. Lambert to Lechat, 27/9/1958 (photocopy in Lechat archives, author's possession). My translation from the French.
13 Letter Lechat to Greene, 3/10/1958 (photocopy in Lechat archives, author's possession). My translation from the French.

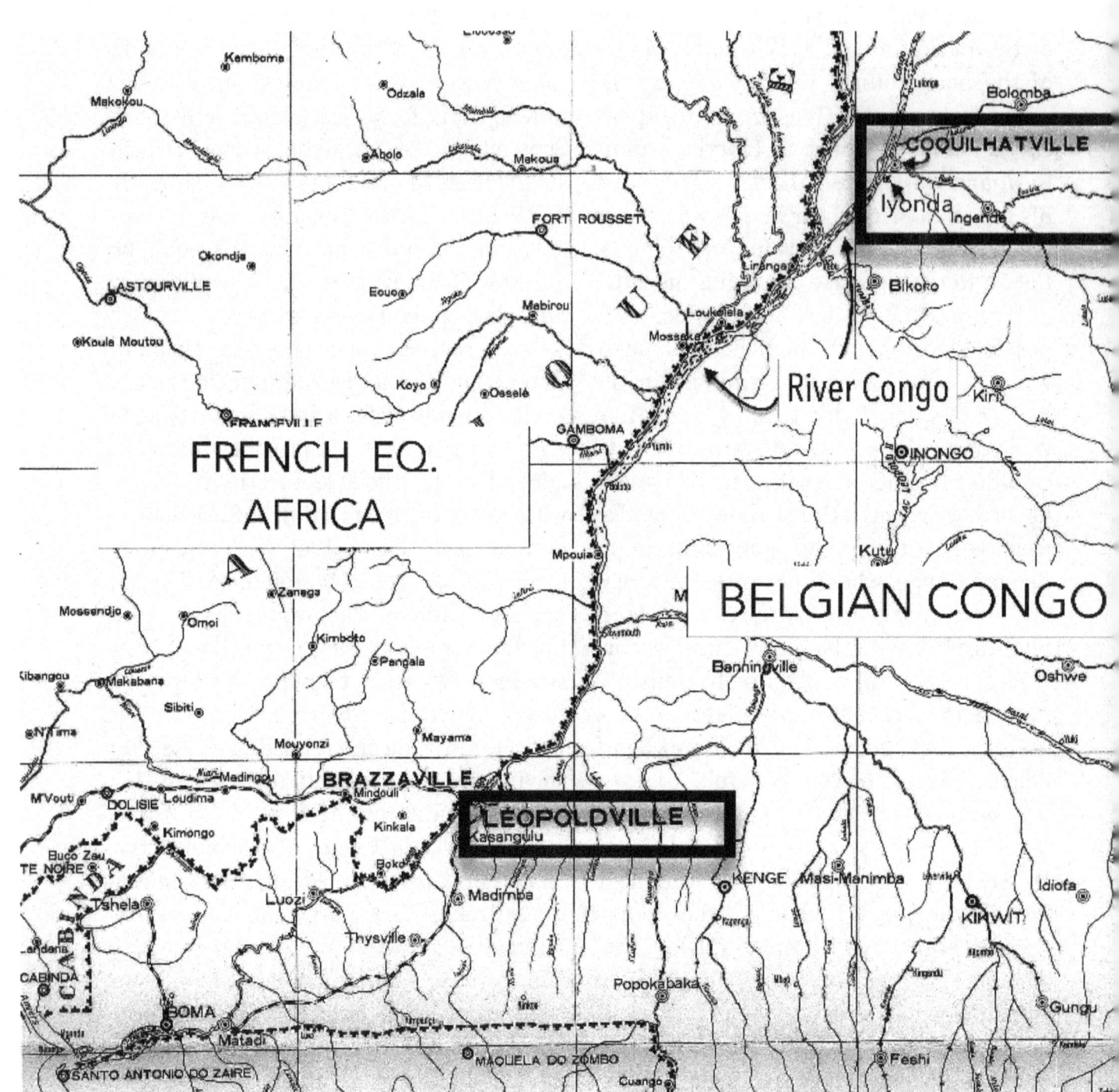

Map 1, indicating the major cities and towns visited by Greene.

Information added by author to a base-map from the Belgian Royal Academy for Overseas Sciences, publicly available on http://kaowarsom.be/en/online_maps. Congo belge.

Ministère du Congo Belge et du Ruanda-Urundi (1940-1941). *Annuaire Officiel-Officieel Jaarboek.* Brussels, Lesigne.

cultural has been sacrificed for the sake of efficacy, and that therefore there is nothing picturesquely African left about it, all in order to preempt Greene's hopes to find a leprosarium "of the Schweizer kind." Lechat also mentions that there are two other leprosariums in the region, namely at the mission stations of Imbonga and Wafanya-Lombolombo, but underscores that they are "situated in a zone hardly penetrated" and can therefore only be reached with difficulty, by steamer. In order to emphasize the loneliness and sordidness of the three locales together, he characterizes them as situated "in full Heart of Darkness," a qualification with which he hopes to dissuade Greene from choosing this region.

But all this information, not in the least the references to Joseph Conrad's *Heart of Darkness*, have exactly the opposite effect on Greene. In four consecutive letters, Greene shows his excitement about the prospect of visiting the Belgian Congo for the first time in his life, where he "was at one time nearly stationed during the war."[14] In a letter of 2 January 1959, Lechat makes another reference to Conrad and again typifies as a gloomy heart of darkness the difficult environment in which he and the missionaries have to work: "five kilometers from my place there is the seat of a commercial company that holds in its archives a dossier of Joseph Conrad, and I think he described the heart of darkness admirably."[15] Greene replies: "I am very intrigued by what you say about the dossier of Joseph Conrad and would very much like to see it."[16]

In his four letters, Greene also stresses that he hopes not to be a trouble, that Lechat should not worry about his comfort, and that with his visit he is neither "looking for any dramatic material" nor plans on "producing a roman à clef,"[17] but only needs to compose a background in order to arrive at what will fundamentally be a "theological and psychological argument."[18]

*A Burnt-Out Case* has indeed proven to be such a "theological and psychological argument," and, Greene's Congo experience as a whole, one of his most solipsistic undertakings. As many commentators have explained (van Dalm 2002[19]; Foden 2004[20]; Sherry 2004[21]; Aitken 2005; Brearley 2011[22]), around 1958 Greene found himself eaten away by his culminating success, which he himself qualified as "a mutilation of the natural man"[23] He was overwhelmed by a great sense of inner emptiness, and felt depressed by frustrations in his personal life, not in the least the extinguishing relationship with Catherine Walston. He was in dire need of getting away from

---

14 Letter Greene to Lechat, 7/10/1958 (photocopy in Lechat archives, author's possession).
15 Letter Lechat to Greene, 2/1/1959 (John J. Burns Library, Boston College, Massachusetts.
16 Letter Greene to Lechat, 16/1/1959 (photocopy in Lechat archives, author's possession).
17 Letter Greene to Lechat, 27/10/1958 (photocopy in Lechat archives, author's possession).
18 Letter Greene to Lechat, 15/12/1958 (photocopy in Lechat archives, author's possession).
19 van Dalm, R. E. (2002). *A Burnt-Out Case: An Autobiographical Suicide* (Occasional Paper number seven). Berkhamsted, The Graham Greene Birthplace Trust.
20 Foden, G. 2004. Introduction to *A Burnt-Out Case* by Graham Greene, 2004 Vintage edition. London, Vintage.
21 Sherry, N. 2004. *The Life of Graham Greene*, Volume 3: 1955-1991. New York, Viking.
22 Brearley, M. 2011. "Graham Greene and *A Burnt-Out Case*: A Psychoanalytic Reading." In: *Dangerous Edges of Graham Greene: Journeys with Saints and Sinners*. ed. D. Gilvary and D. J. N. Middleton. New York, Continuum: 166-180.
23 Burstall, C. 1992. "Graham Greene takes the Orient Express." In: *Conversations with Graham Greene*. ed. H. J. Donaghy. Jackson, University Press of Mississippi: 46-62, 52.

the attention and societal shallowness, and of finding a refuge where he could come to terms with his inner struggles. The Congo offered exactly that, a place of escape. Before his departure, he wrote to Catherine Walston: "the Congo will be a good escape".[24] And 20 years later, with all the benefit of hindsight, he again qualified his trip to the Congo as "the furthest escape of all (and I don't mean geographically)".[25]

The corollary of Greene's inward-looking state of mind in these years was that his Congo trip turned out to be a remarkably apolitical enterprise, that is for the political traveler and author that he was known to be. In the first week of January 1959 there had been violent demonstrations for independence in the Congolese capital Leopoldville, accompanied by riots and acts of aggression against Westerners. When the news that Greene, known to like to travel to troubled places and to set his novels in countries in political turmoil, was to visit the Congo at the end of that month, many Europeans in Leopoldville believed he came exactly for these reasons. This explains the armies of journalists that besieged him from the first hours of his arrival in the capital, as well as during his last days in Brazzaville. In the published *Congo Journal* he added a footnote making it clear how much the journalists were mistaken: "There had been bad riots in Leopoldville two weeks before and nothing could persuade the journalists that my journey planned months ago was not occasioned by them".[26] In the entire diary, references to the incidents or to key political actors and upcoming ideologies are not absent but strikingly few in number, and they are all comments from hearsay. Nowhere does he show any genuine interest in encountering a Congolese political leader or organization in person. Greene travels in his own bulb, primarily occupied with the demons and abyss of his own soul.

*A Burnt-Out Case,* with its almost a-historical and a-contextual atmosphere, is in fact a perfect reflection of Greene's mindset during the trip. Anti-colonial riots or politics in general are hardly used as a functional theme in the drama, and if they are,[27] they are backgrounded as very remote from the protagonists' environment and daily concerns: "[the Fathers] were not interested in the tensions and changing cabinets of Europe, they were barely interested in the riots a few hundred miles away on the other side of the river".[28] Querry, moreover, also stresses that he "didn't believe in politics".[29] The Congo in which the novel is set is not a historical or geopolitical place; it is, as Greene poignantly summarized in his introduction, merely "a region of the mind"[30]—a troubled mind.

---

24 Sherry 2004, 159.
25 Greene, Graham. *Ways of Escape*. 1981, 147.
26 Greene, Graham. *Congo Journal*. 1961, 14.
27 Greene, Graham. *A Burnt-out Case* 1977 [1960], 12,43.
28 Ibid., 14.
29 Ibid., 114.
30 Ibid.,5.

## 2. In Brussels with "Tony" and in Leopoldville (26 January–1 February 1959)

With regard to the days before Greene's departure for the Congo, biographer Norman Sherry, judging from the telegraph correspondence between Greene and Catherine Walston, suggests that Greene spent one night in Brussels.[31] Yet, a letter Greene wrote to his friend and confidant John Sutro,[32] on letterhead of the Palace Hotel in Brussels and dated "Friday" (Friday 30 January 1959), contradicts this. Greene explains to Sutro that "I couldn't ring you on Monday because I (we) overslept. [...] A wild scramble, then four hours waiting at London airport, a drive to Gatwick, arrived in Brussels six hours later, without luggage." This leads me to conclude that Greene was in Brussels not just one night, but five days, namely from Monday 26 through Friday 30 January.

We also learn that Greene was not there alone: the "we" he added between parentheses and as an insert refers to the fact that he spent those five days in Belgium with a woman whom he brings up more than once in his handwritten diary, but all of whose mentions he eliminated for the 1961 publication. Even in the manuscript, he first wrote her name in full but then crossed out each instance and put the nickname "Tony" above it. He describes her as a 29-year-old married woman, and reveals that she has traveled with him from England to Brussels, i.e. on that Monday 26 January. He had an affair with her, equally described in more than one place in the diary manuscript, while still involved with Catherine Walston (which explains why in his telegram to the latter he pretended to have spent only a night in Brussels). In my follow-up study of the diary versions, I will attempt to probe more deeply into Tony's identity and the extent of the affair. Suffice it here to add that in his letter to Sutro, Greene writes that he sees Tony off at Brussels train station on Friday 30 and that he qualifies his past five days with her, which included an excursion to Bruges, as "all very pleasant."[33]

In the diary entry of Saturday 7 February 1959, Greene writes "A week ago at this hour I was still in Brussels,"[34] which would suggest that his plane left Brussels on Saturday 31 January. But Greene is confused here. In his prior letter to Lechat of 16 January 1959 he had announced that he would arrive in Leopoldville on Saturday 31 at 9:20 a.m., which means that he boarded a night plane leaving Brussels in the evening of Friday 30. This is also corroborated by the sequence of events narrated in the diary, by a letter of Michel Lechat to the Governor General of 21 January 1959, informing him of Greene's arrival date and time, and by Greene's own remark "Now for Leopoldville" in his letter of Friday 30 to Sutro.

---

31 Sherry 2004, 164.
32 Letter Greene to Sutro, 30/1/1959; Sutro archives, Bodleian Library, Oxford UK. Kindly indicated to me by Jonathan Wise.
33 Letter from Greene to Sutro, 30/1/1959.
34 This and all other quotations that are not identified otherwise, are from the manuscript of Greene's Congo diary. Courtesy of the Harry Ransom Center, the University of Texas at Austin.

The first impression Greene has of Leopoldville upon arrival on 31 Saturday is that it is "a brand new city with miniature skyscrapers." During the rest of this Saturday, he has lunch, does press interviews with the many journalists wrongly construing his visit as motivated by an interest in the political situation, and later has dinner with a businessman. The morning of the next day, Sunday 1 February, the same man gives him a tour of the city, after which he has lunch with an information officer, followed by another "intrusion of the press."

## 3. First term in Iyonda (2–11 February 1959)

### 3.1. Acquiring a routine

On Monday 2 February, Greene finally leaves Leopoldville on a domestic flight to Coquilhatville, the capital of the northern Equateur province and in those days abbreviated to "Coq" in Belgian colonial parlance, which would become "Luc" in *A Burnt-Out Case*. Greene is collected at Coquilhatville's little airstrip by Dr. Lechat, who immediately drives him to Iyonda (then often spelled "Yonda" or "Ionda"). In addition to the leprosy hospital and colony, Iyonda consisted of a house for the missionary Fathers, another house belonging to the missionary Sisters who assisted the doctor nursing the leprosy patients, a few technical buildings, and the house where the Lechat couple lived with their children. Greene occupied a room in the missionary Fathers' house. Most of the days he also had his dinners with them and his lunches with the Lechat family in their house, but this was sometimes reversed or lunch or dinner were had at the same place.

Throughout this first period in Iyonda, Greene's daily routine was to do his reading of the pile of novels he had carried with him, in the morning on the bank of the Congo river, which he reached by crossing the road linking Iyonda to Coquilhatville and passing through a meadow where the Fathers kept their cattle. In his unpublished memoirs, Michel Lechat remembers how "Every morning, he walked down to the Stream, settled into an old pirogue, and started reading until the heat became unbearable."[35] Greene himself in his diary writes that it was "an old tin ship" rather than a pirogue, and that he did this in order to be safe of ants. There is, interestingly, a home video showing Michel Lechat revisiting Iyonda in February 1988 and standing on the very spot where Greene did this daily reading, as he explains to the person holding the camera. We see in fact a rusty old little boat, which could well be the one in question.

### 3.2. Between healthy unconcern and disillusionment

The rest of the day at Iyonda, Greene would spend walking around the mission and the leprosery, conversing with some Fathers, occasionally a leprosy patient, such as Deo Gratias, whose person and real name he would retain for the novel, and observing the doctor's medical activities and asking him technical questions. In Iyonda, no one changed their routines

---

35 Lechat memoirs, author's possession. My translation from the French.

in any way because of Greene's presence. Lechat describes how everyone in Iyonda was friendly towards Greene, but went on with their lives and work as before. The conversations over lunch and dinner, too, were never rendered uncomfortable by Greene's fame or status as a successful author, and were shallow and unconcerned in an easy way. In fact, most of the Fathers at Iyonda, of the unworldly type, were not really aware of, let alone interested in, Greene's position in literature. In a letter Greene wrote to Lechat eight years after the publication of *A Burnt-Out Case*, he asked the doctor whether the priests in Iyonda "are very cross with me" on account of their being depicted in not so flattering terms in the novel, which in a return letter the doctor answered in the negative.[36] Lechat, in his memoirs, later explained this as follows: "[at Iyonda] the novel did not provoke any immediate reaction. I take it that the book was not even read and was simply added to the few detective stories and the pile of missionary magazines lying on the dark brown sideboard in the Fathers' communal room."[37] In this sense, Greene succeeded in finding among the unconcerned Fathers in Iyonda "the furthest escape of all (and I don't mean geographically)"[38] which he so direly needed. In fact, in *A Burnt-Out Case* Greene fully developed this healthy unconcern he enjoyed in Iyonda into a very similar relationship the priests in the novel maintain with Querry:[39] like Greene, Querry is very pleased that almost all the Fathers, in contrast to Rycker, Parkinson, and Father Thomas, never question him about his past as a successful and widely known architect, but hospitably leave him undisturbed.[40] Greene writes: "[Querry] became very aware of his own safety among them [the Fathers]—they would ask no intrusive questions",[41] i.e. exactly the kind of questions Greene himself was peacefully safeguarded against in Iyonda.

This is not to say that Greene, who in these days experienced a serious belief crisis—"the vision of faith as an untroubled sea was lost for ever"[42]—had not hoped to engage in meaningful conversations with the Iyonda Fathers on doubt, maintenance of faith, redemption and the like. He had expected that the deathly and secluded atmosphere of a leprosery, with a disease epitomizing, at least in popular consciousness, loss of human dignity and what could be experienced as God's utter abandonment, would give rise exactly to such conversations. In fact, the reason for Greene's choice to set his new novel against the background of leprosy must have been related to the sense of deepest divine relinquishment this disease represents, as well as to the romantic idea that living among and helping these reprobates and outcasts of society, especially

---

36 Letter from Greene to Lechat, 24/6/1968, and letter from Lechat to Greene, 5/7/1968 (photocopies in Lechat archives, author's possession).
37 Lechat memoirs, author's possession. My translation from the French.
38 Greene, *Ways of Escape*. 1981 [1980], 147.
39 For more lists of obvious resemblances between the experiences and mental states of Greene and Querry, see van Dalm (2002); Lechat (1991, 2007); Sherry (2004); Brearley (2011); Meeuwis (2013).
40 See also: Brearley, M. "Graham Greene and a Burnt-Out Case: A Psychoanalytic Reading." 2011, 173.
41 Greene, *A Burnt-Out Case*. 1977 [1960], 14.
42 Greene, *Ways of Escape*. 1981, 271-272.

if motivated by religious zeal, is one of the strongest forms of self-sacrifice, certain to lead to personal salvation. In this sense, Iyonda was a disillusionment for Greene. From his diary it becomes clear that he was often irritated by the Fathers' lack of religious reflection on what they were doing. He noted how they were easily amused by college types of humor and immature games, how they occupied themselves with all sorts of logistics, such as constructing buildings, running schools, laying in provisions, but hardly made any deeply religious connections between their work in the leprosy environment and the higher goals of truly committed Christianity. Greene noted in his diary that in Iyonda he had "never yet found in a missionary priest either the naivety which I want for certain of them, nor the harshness towards human failing, nor the inquisitiveness." And Lechat summarized it again expressively when he wrote in his memoirs: "those practically minded missionaries were not torn between one or the other perdition and some redemption. Greene must have been very disturbed by this. To tell the truth, I think he must have been terribly disappointed not to find in Iyonda what he had hope to find, a Schweizer type of hospital."

## 3.3. Unhealthy concern

Compared to the rustic Fathers in Iyonda, most of the higher clergy and white colonials living in Coquilhatville and other towns were much more aware of who Greene was and what he represented in literature. In a provincial town where nothing sensational happened and rumors went fast, many of them were excited by his presence and more than eager to meet him, which his initial attempts to travel under the name "Mr. Graham"[43] could not prevent.

In Coquilhatville, Greene received unwelcome attention from the burgomaster, whose golden book he absolutely needed to sign before returning to Leopoldville on 5 March. Another dreaded dignitary was Monseigneur Hilaire Vermeiren (1889–1967),[44] Bishop in the region for the Missionaries of the Sacred Heart. The reader of the published *Congo Journal* is given a positive image of this Bishop, but as I plan to describe in my future study, this is a result of Lechat's most severe cleansing of the journal's galley proofs. Greene was very impressed by Lechat's reprimands, and did not only delete the passages identified by Lechat as unacceptable, but added or replaced many of them with positive ones, some of which involved no less than complete about-faces. In the diary manuscript we learn how in reality Greene was greatly disparaging about the Bishop's sense of pomp and rank and affected 18th century manners, describing him as "a man who could not stand being alone, who read little and liked cards: as a Bishop dignified and immaculate with the big cross round his neck . . . . who had never really done anything at all." Twenty years after the events,

---

43 Lechat, M. "Remembering Graham Greene." 1991, 2007.
44 For biographical information, see Hulstaert (1989) and Van Hoorick (2004).
Hulstaert, G. 1989. Vermeiren (Hilaire). In: *Biographie Belge d'Outre-Mer - Belgische Overzeese Biografie*. ed. Brussels, Académie Royale des Sciences d'Outre-Mer -Koninklijke Academie voor Overzeese Wetenschappen. 7(C): 365-368.
Van Hoorick, W. 2004. Hilaire Vermeiren: De tweede Beverse missiebisschop (1889–1967). *Land van Beveren* 47(1): 11–30.

in a letter to Lechat of 5 September 1980, Greene still made fun of Vermeiren's shallowness, sarcastically asking if his death in 1967 had been caused by his passion for Bridge. The fictitious Bishop in *A Burnt-Out Case*, vainglorious, unspiritual, and fond of Bridge, in fact resembles Greene's real perception of Vermeiren much more closely than the euphemizing depiction in the published *Congo Journal*.[45]

Greene also mentions at least six occasions in which admirers among the colonials went far out of their way to meet him, many of them carrying a copy of one of his books under their arm for him to sign, some even with the desire also to discuss characters or plot turns. Lechat recounts the anecdote of how Greene, upon spotting from afar one such admirer driving in the direction of the leprosery, would dash into the Lechat couple's house, jump out of the rear window of their bedroom, and run away into the forest.[46]

Even more aggravating for Greene were those admirers impatient to approach him for literary advice. The Province Governor and his wife, Alphonse De Valkeneer (1898–1973) and Suzanne De Valkeneer-Briard (1903–1964), are a case in point. He hated the repetitive calls by and invitations from this couple, for which he had to force himself at least five times during his stay in Iyonda. Suzanne De Valkeneer-Briard was an amateur writer who published her collections of colonial short stories at her own expense[47] and whose over-enthusiastic conversations about authoring annoyed Greene greatly, as appears from the diary.[48] She once naively gauged if Greene would be interested in translating her stories into English, and on two occasions unwarily gave him advice on a writer's vision and methods, fanatically showing him the notes she was taking for her next story. One day she sent him a letter, signing it off with *"salutations confraternelles"* (Edith Dasnoy, pers. comm.), which in English would translate as "with collegial greetings." Greene boiled with anger. This woman was not the only one to approach Greene with their own writings. On 11 February, Greene notes "a local mail brings a letter from another local writer and a copy of his book—like Mme V's published at his own expense. Why should this dream of writing haunt so many? The desire for money—I doubt it. The desire for a vocation in a life they haven't really chosen?" He then complements this ponderation with the rhetorical question "The same instinct that drives some people to desire rather than to feel a religious faith?" It is not improbable that this last contemplation emerged from Greene's self-analysis, in a period of his life

---

45 In April 1961 already, which is very soon after the publication of *A Burnt-Out Case*, Hilaire Vermeiren requested one of his confreres in Belgium to send him a copy of the book (letter of Petrus Wijnants to the Superior Jules Wijnants, 15/4/1961; archives of the Missionaries of the Sacred Heart, Borgerhout, Belgium), which shows how curious, maybe anxious, he was about whether and how Greene had used him as a model.
Heraly. Edmond, R. 2006. *Leprosy and Empire: A Medical and Cultural History*. New York, Cambridge University Press.
46 Lechat, M. "Remembering Graham Greene." 1991, 2007.
47 See for instance her collection of colonial short stories, De Valkeneer-Briard, S. 1950. Au bout du sentier: Nouvelles congolaises. Charleroi, Heraly.
48 Again, all the negative descriptions of this couple are changed to blatantly positive ones in the published *Congo Journal*.

in which, as mentioned, he found himself in a deep belief crisis.

Another important intruder on Greene's peace in Iyonda was the schoolmaster R. Van den Brandt (birth and death dates unknown), who taught at a school in an American Protestant mission near Iyonda and who had written a novel in English. Not later than the day after Greene's arrival in Iyonda, i.e. 3 February, Van den Brandt disturbed Greene at the end of his siesta, seeking advice on literary agents: "a rather ratlike man, a Fleming and a teacher in the Protestant school. He had written a novel in English and wanted advice about an agent. Is there any part of the world, in the most remote corner, where an author who is known will not encounter very soon one who wishes to be a writer? Do doctors encounter middle-aged men who still have the ambition of becoming a doctor?" Having given him a few names, Greene hoped to have brushed him off for good. But the next day Greene received a note from him, asking not only for the agents' addresses but also begging for another meeting in order, this time, to discuss spiritual matters. Familiar with some of Greene's books and understanding well how they developed notions of Catholic faith, Van den Brandt wished to talk to Greene about his own recent loss of belief, which "I don't see how I will ever be able to come back to."[49] He wished to link this, in a private discussion, to Greene's literary renderings of Christian premises: "I cannot understand in your book "The Heart of the Matter" how you let your hero commit suicide . . . ."[50] Greene interpreted this request irritatingly as "spiritual blackmail" and reports in his diary to have replied to the man "that I am not competent in matters of faith: he should apply to a priest." As Sherry also indicates[51] Van den Brandt's unhealthy concern with Greene's private faith struggles inspired him when developing part of the character of Rycker in *A Burnt-Out Case*. Rycker, a former seminarian and devoted Catholic, refuses Querry's silence about his belief and insists on forging a meaningful spiritual bond with him.

For the sake of completeness, for other aspects of the Rycker character Greene found inspiration in the retired Belgian veterinarian Albert Jussiant (1898–1971),[52] to whom Lechat and Greene paid a visit on 4 March 1959 in his house on a peninsula in Lake Tumba. As Lechat writes in what he calls his "tardy exegesis" of *A Burnt-Out Case*, a noteworthy new analysis he made of the novel in 1996,[53] it is during this visit to Jussiant and his much younger wife that the latter recognized Greene from a picture in *Time* magazine. This scene is

---

[49] Letter Van den Brandt to Greene, undated, attached to diary manuscript; Harry Ransom Center, the University of Texas at Austin.
[50] Letter Van den Brandt to Greene, undated, attached to diary manuscript; Harry Ransom Center, the University of Texas at Austin.
[51] Sherry 2004, 194.
[52] Biographical information can be found in Ministère du Congo Belge et du Ruanda-Urundi (1940-1941:928). Jussiant published some articles on topical veterinary medicine.
Jussiant, A. 1944. L'organisation de Coopératives en Milieux Indigènes. *Aequatoria* 7: 137-142.
Jussiant, A. 1948. Notes cliniques sur quelques maladies du bétail: La piroplasmose du porc au Congo belge. *Bulletin Agricole du Congo Belge* 39: 631.
[53] Lechat memoirs, author's possession.

amply revived in Part 2 of *A Burnt-Out Case*, where Querry is recognized exactly by Rycker's equally younger wife Marie exactly from a photo on the cover of *Time*.[54]

## 4. On the Ruki-Momboyo river (12–25 February 1959)

### 4.1 *Greene distrusted*

On Monday 9 February 1959, Greene takes steps to be allowed as a passenger on the congregation's river steamer, the *Theresita*, in order to visit other mission stations with leprosariums along the banks of the Ruki-Momboyo. His attempts are difficult: in Coquilhatville, Father André Beke (1912–1970), in charge of the logistics of the entire congregation, tells him that due to technical problems the boat cannot sail for the next weeks or month. But Greene senses that Father André is only trying to thwart his plans. Returning to Iyonda in the evening disappointed, he writes that he finds Father André "egregious and ambiguous" and adds that "I distrust the whole affair. I don't believe in a favourable decision." A question that remains unanswered until today is what exactly may have happened on this occasion, and in particular why Greene qualified Father André as ambiguous. Sherry quotes Greene giving Father André this epithet, but does not elaborate on it.[55] In 1994, Father Gustaaf Hulstaert (1900–1990), belonging to the same missionary congregation, published an article in which he identified with great detail each missionary mentioned in the *Congo Journal*.[56] Like Sherry, Hulstaert is at a loss as to Greene's mistrust of Father André. He surmises that Greene accuses him of collaboration with the German occupier in Belgium during World War II—in Belgium in post-war years, the qualification "ambiguous" was often used with this denotation. But Hulstaert is wrong. In his own handwritten memoirs, Father André notes that he has read Greene's *Congo Journal* in French translation, and has seen Greene's not-so-positive depiction of him. Beke explains, in Flemish, "this was about whether our boat, which was out of order, would sail or not. Because it was out of order, I didn't give him [Greene] a straight answer, I still had to wait and see."[57] Yet Edith Dasnoy showed me a letter she had written from Iyonda to her father in Belgium on 11 February 1959, i.e. only two days after Greene's unsuccessful attempt. It appears that Father André was very skeptical of Greene's presence among the priests in general, suspecting that he would write scornful things about them in his eventual novel. Father André indeed pretended the boat to be inoperative: distrustful, he wanted to protect his fellow missionaries in the other mission stations and leproseries from Greene's great perspicacity in matters of human character and behavior.

In the evening of the same Monday 9 February, the Bishop let Greene know that the boat was in perfect order and gave him the green light to board it two days later:

---

54 see also Sherry 2004: 194.
55 Sherry 2004, 176.
56 Hulstaert, G. (1994). *Graham Greene et les Missionnaires Catholiques au Congo Belge*. Annales Æquatoria 15: 493-503.
57 André Beke's personal notes; archives of the Missionaries of the Sacred Heart, Borgerhout, Belgium. My translation from the Flemish.

"Just as I sat down to dinner L[echat] came in to say he had had a telephone call: all was well. I go on board Wednesday evening." The steamer lay in Coquilhatville on the Congo river, near the Bishop's residence. Although not explicitly stated, it can be deduced from the diary that Greene spent the night of 11 February on the moored steamer and was awakened at 5 a.m. of Thursday 12 February by the boat's starting engines, after which it raised anchor and left, immediately leaving the main Congo river and entering the Ruki-Momboyo.

The itinerary was simple: for the next 14 days, the boat was to head upstream on the Ruki-Momboyo, visit the leprosery of Imbonga on the way, then continue until it reached the mission and leprosery near Wafanya, called "Lombolombo," after which they would return downstream back to Coquilhatville. The turning point, Wafanya, was reached on 19 February. They arrived back inCoquilhatville on 25 February.

During the journey, the *Theresita* housed four passengers: Greene, Father Henri Vanderslaghmolen (1921–2014), whom Greene knew from Iyonda and who was one of the only ones with some knowledge of English, and two other priests, one of them the steamer's captain. The boat would generally keep close to one bank, making regular stops in order to rest, load and unload goods, or pay visits. Some nights were spent on the boat, others in the mission stations on the banks.

## 4.2. "That blasted Pole makes me green with envy": Re-reading Conrad's Heart of Darkness

This two-weeks' journey reminded Greene so much of Joseph Conrad's days as a steamer captain[58] on the Congo river in 1890, that he considered it to be an appropriate context to start rereading *Heart of Darkness*, which he did from the very first day on the boat, 12 February. In this context, Rod Edmond's account that "[Greene] is also repeating part of the river journey that Conrad had made in 1890"[59] is slightly inaccurate: Conrad had traveled the main Congo river, not the Ruki-Momboyo tributary. Incidentally, this confusion is also made, but of course willfully and maliciously, by Parkinson in *A Burnt-Out Case*, who regularly vexes Querry with his boastings of finding himself on soil once trodden by Conrad and the explorer Stanley. Querry insistently but to no avail attempts to correct Parkinson about these mistakes.

---

58 For the sake of historical accuracy, it is appropriate to mention that Conrad went to theCongo with the promise from a Belgian company that he would be made captain of a river steamer (the *Roi des Belges*), that, due to the petty politics and distrust on behalf of some of the company's local agents in the Congo, he was never officially given the promised post but instead always remained second-in-command, and that it was only due to the real captain's serious illness that he was allowed to act as captain for a short period of time (Sherry 1971; Najder 1978; Stengers 1992). Conrad's bitterness and anger about this incident informed much of the atmosphere he constructed for *Heart of Darkness*.
Sherry, N. *Conrad's Western World*. Cambridge, Cambridge University Press.1971.
Najder, Z., Ed. *Congo Diary and Other Uncollected Pieces* by Joseph Conrad. New York, Doubleday. 1978.
Stengers, J. 1992. Sur l'aventure congolaise de Joseph Conrad. In: Papier blanc, encre noire: Cent ans de culture francophone en Afrique centrale (Zaïre, Rwanda et Burundi). 2 vols. ed. M. Quaghebeur and E. Van Balberghe. Brussels, Labor: 15-34.
59 Heraly, Edmond, R. *Leprosy and Empire: A Medical and Cultural History*. New York, Cambridge University Press. 2006, 233.

As mentioned above, Michel Lechat's description of the leproseries of Iyonda, Imbonga, and Wafanya as "situated in full Heart of Darkness" had already been one of the triggers convincing Greene to choose the Congo as the place to visit for preparing his new novel. Sherry (2004: 154), Foden (2004: vii), and Stape (2007),[60] among others, remind us of the fact that Greene in general admired Conrad greatly, to the point of experiencing a sense of inferiority when comparing himself with him. Greene is on record for having referred to Conrad as "that blasted Pole [who] makes me green with envy".[61] Edith Dasnoy recalls how in a conversation with Greene in Iyonda she and her husband once mentioned their great admiration of Conrad's work and style, and how his reaction was unusually evasive and crabby—so crabby that the three never raised the subject again. In Greene's diary, we find several appropriate and spontaneous citations from *Heart of Darkness*. When contemplating Leopoldville during his first days, he briefly cites, without any identification of the self-evident source: "'And this also,' said Marlow suddenly, 'has been one of the dark places of the earth.'" And when admiring the Congo river at Iyonda on 3 February, he notes "This has not changed since Conrad's day. 'An empty stream, a great silence, an impenetrable forest.'" In *A Burnt-Out Case* there is Parkinson's literal mention of Conrad's novella: "I was carried on shore from my pirogue, the frail bark in which I had penetrated what Joseph Conrad called the Heart of Darkness, by a few faithful natives",[62] as well as his mimicking of Conrad's style when typing "The eternal forest broods along the banks unchanged since Stanley and his little band . . ."[63] as the first sentence of his sensationalist column. In addition, I also wish to draw attention to Foden's noteworthy observation that Marlow and Querry both share the same "sense of moral disgust"[64] and that Querry dismisses evolution theory as an "old song of progress",[65] a reference to Conrad's rejection of scientism and, I think, to that other Congolese short story of his, *An Outpost of Progress*. Finally, in his fascinating book on the sociology of leprosy in colonial contexts, Rod Edmond devotes a long section to a critical comparison of *A Burnt-Out Case* with *Heart of Darkness*, going as far as to identify the latter as "the foundation text" for the former.[66]

On 12 February, when he starts rereading *Heart of Darkness*, Greene reports to have read it for the first time in 1932, i.e. at the age of 27 or 28. He confesses in his diary that after that first reading he had abandoned reading Conrad altogether, as it filled him with a strong sense of inferiority: "Reading Conrad–the volume called Youth for the sake of The Heart of Darkness–for the first time since I abandoned him about

---

60 Stape, J. The Several Lives of Joseph Conrad. New York, Bond Street Books.2007.
61 Keulks, G. Graham Greene. In: *The Oxford Encyclopedia of British Literature*. ed. D. S. Kastan. New York, Oxford University Press: 466-471. 2006, 466.
62 Greene, Graham. *A Burnt-Out Case*.1977 [1960], 133.
63 Ibid., 97, see also Sherry 2004: 199.
64 Ibid., ii.
65 Ibid., 124.
66 Heraly,Edmond. *Leprosy and Empire*. 2006, 233.

1932 because his influence on me was too great and too disastrous. The heavy hypnotic style falls around me again, and I am aware of the poverty of my own." At that young age, Greene thus stopped reading Conrad in order to avoid the risk of being too much influenced or overshadowed by him. But, as Greene progresses further in the book, he makes a new assessment of the novel: "Conrad's Heart of Darkness still a fine story, but its faults show now. The language too inflated for the situation. Kurtz never comes really alive[...]. And how often he compares something concrete to something abstract or vague. Is this a trick that I have caught?" What we are witnessing here looks very much like a moment in Greene's life at which he overcomes his earlier, self-degrading veneration of Conrad. The 54-year old, mature Greene, now rereading *Heart of Darkness* "as a sort of exorcism" as Lechat put it,[67] has made demystifying discoveries that enable him to free himself from the burden of Conrad's indelible shadow.

With regard to Greene's thoughts on Kurtz, Greaney[68] takes analyses such as Greene's to task for not understanding that Conrad's underdevelopment of this character may have been deliberate, namely an attempt to stress that Kurtz is nothing more than a myth, the product of a sort of urban legend about whom the other characters in the story have heard and exchange the wildest speculations. Yet, Greene's appreciation is remarkably similar to a confession Conrad himself had made about Kurtz 58 years earlier, namely in a letter to Ford Madox Ford's wife Elsie Hueffer of 3 December 1902: "What I distinctly admit is the fault of having made Kurtz too symbolic or rather symbolic at all. But the story being mainly a vehicle for conveying a batch of personal impressions I gave the rein to my mental laziness and took the line of the least resistance. This is then the whole [apology] for the tardiness of his vitality".[69] Thus, Conrad had admitted a certain literary languor in developing the character of Kurtz, unintentionally resulting in a too symbolic sort of anti-protagonist. Greene was aware of the fact that Conrad had kept a diary while traveling in the Congo in 1890,[70] quoting from it in *Journey Without Maps*.[71] But what Greene was unable to have knowledge of, at least as far as I can discern, are Conrad's letters, of which a collection and edition only appeared in the 1980s,[72] also containing the one to Hueffer of 1902. It is striking, and I believe indicative of Greene's great literary understanding, that his critique of the Kurtz character so accurately matched a plea of guilty Conrad had made in 1902, unknown to Greene.

---

67 Lechat 1991, 16.
68 Greaney, M. 2002. *Conrad, Language, and Narrative*. Cambridge, Cambridge University Press. 72-76.
69 Conrad cited in Karl, F. R. and L. Davies, Eds. (1986). *The Collected Letters of Joseph Conrad, Volume 2: 1898-1902*. Cambridge, Cambridge University Press. 460.
70 Najder 1978.
71 Greene 2010 [1936]: 8.
72 Karl and Davies 1983, 1986, 1988.
Karl, F. R. and L. Davies, Eds. 1983. *The Collected Letters of Joseph Conrad, Volume 1: 1861-1897*. Cambridge, Cambridge University Press.
Karl, F. R. and L. Davies, Eds. (1988). *The Collected Letters of Joseph Conrad, Volume 3: 1903-1907*. Cambridge, Cambridge University Press.

## 4.3. Lovesickness, Lipscomb, and the two other leproseries

The tedium of the river journey, combined with the insupportable humid heat and with as only company the three Fathers whose "euphoria," "continual jests and laughter," and "raillery in incomprehensible Flemish" continue to tire Greene, driving him more inward than ever during his entire stay in the Congo. He increasingly loses himself in melancholy, most of all in reminiscing about his love affairs in Europe. Nowhere else in the diary does Greene mention so many thoughts and dreams of his mistresses as during these 14 days of *ennui* on the steamer: as soon as the second day on the boat, 13 February, he observes "Melancholy shows signs of returning.... Anita [Björk] too much in mind. The relationship with Tony too superficial to act as an anodyne when she is not there, and C.[atherine Walston] too far away." None of these dreams is pleasant: all carry uncomfortable sexuality, jealousy, and anger. In true Leporello-style, he takes inventory of the "fifteen 'honest' women I have been to bed with," concluding that only Catherine Walston and Anita Björk "stay in my blood," and that maybe Tony can be added to the list. He comes to the sad realization that Anita Björk "remains the unattainable dream of peace" and that Catherine Walston is "the only person in my life who has given me everything to its height—even unhappiness." He also ponders the mystery of his very recent affair with the 29-year-old Tony, attempting to understand what may have driven a young and married woman like her into his arms. He realizes how Tony "lifted me out of the hopeless broken-backed state I was in after leaving Anita" but also points to her "juvenility" and lack of sophistication and wisdom. It does not appear unreasonable to hypothesize that, in the same way as Querry in *A Burnt-Out Case* strongly resembles Greene, the character of Marie, Rycker's much younger, unsophisticated wife, who invents an affair with Querry, is in fact inspired by this Tony.

During the trip, the river taking the passengers slowly through the thick equatorial rainforest, he is told that "Incidentally Martin Bormann's son is somewhere here in the bush." This refers to Martin Adolf Bormann Jr. (1930–2013), who was the first-born son of Adolf Hitler's private secretary Martin Bormann, and Hitler's godson.[73] Converted to Catholicism at the age of 17, Bormann Jr. studied theology and was ordained a priest in 1958, in the Austrian-German branch of the same congregation of the Missionaries of the Sacred Heart. Strangely, Bormann went to the Congo for the first time only in May 1961, which means that he could not have been in the region during Greene's 1959 visit. An explanation for this anachronism in Greene's diary is to be found in the fact that Bormann's entrance in the congregation in Europe and his being prepared for work in the missions in the

---

[73] MSC, M. d. S.-C. d. J. 1963. *Album Societatis Missionariorum Sacratissimi Cordis Jesu, A Consilio Generali Societatis ad modum manuscripti pro Sociis editum*. Rome, MSC. 255; see also Bormann 1965, 1996. Bormann, M. 1965. *Zwischen Kreuz und Fetisch: Die Geschichte einer Kongomission*. Bayreuth, Hestia.
Bormann, M. 1996. *Leben gegen Schatten: Gelebte Zeit, geschenkte Zeit*. Begegnungen, Erfahrungen, Folgerungen. Paderborn, Bonifatius.

Belgian Congo had already raised some dust among missionaries and colonials in and around Coquilhatville. Either the priests or Greene himself picked up the news and misinterpreted it, believing Bormann had already arrived.

On 14 February at Flandria, one of the towns along the tributary where the steamer halts, Greene meets the Englishman Chris Lipscomb,[74] whom he will visit again on the down-river return trip on 25 February. Lipscomb was manager of a palm-oil factory at Flandria. The factory of Rycker in *A Burnt-Out Case* is closely modeled on this factory, with its mill where nothing is wasted and with its distinct smell of "stale margarine"[75]. The character of the unsympathetic Rycker, by contrast, is in no way inspired by Lipscomb, whom Greene found very likable. Greene enjoys the company of Lipscomb and his wife very much, if only for the pleasure of "talking English to two intelligent people again." The relief and contrast Greene expresses here are indicative of his general weariness after weeks of linguistic and cultural alienation in the environment of mostly Flemish-speaking priests and colonials.

His visits to the two leprosariums on the Ruki-Momboyo, i.e. the one at Imbonga on 15–16 February and the one near the village and mission of Wafanya on 19–21 February, were not unsuccessful. In Imbonga he is struck by the efficacy with which villages have been built around the leprosery, as well as by their general cleanliness. He notes in his diary: "very well laid out with room for three lines of traffic... with a wide alley of palm trees down the middle." Of Lombolombo he also praises the layout, which provides a "great sense of width and airiness in spite of the heat." Noting the good organization and beneficial patient treatment, he cannot help making a comparison with what he had found in Iyonda: "So much more psychological help given here than at Yonda." Again, Greene's disappointment with the lack of spirituality in Iyonda surfaces.

The voyage back to Coquilhatville begins on Saturday 21 February at noon. Although traveling downstream and thus faster than on the outward journey, it constitutes a real ordeal for Greene. He grows more and more irritated by the heat, sleeps badly because of it and because of the livestock the Fathers have loaded onto the steamer to take back home, and is frustrated by accumulated delays caused by technical problems with the boat. On top, the trip on this small and somewhat secluded tributary did not allow Greene to disappear from the radar of attentive and admiring colonials, who at times went through much trouble to meet him. On the up-river journey already, while seeking shelter for a storm at the mission house in Imbonga, Greene had been taken by surprise by the sudden appearance—copied in the novel to Parkinson's sudden appearance—of a regional officer and a young doctor, carrying a copy of *The Third Man* for him to sign. The two, who lived elsewhere on the river banks, had braved the storm in an open motor boat on the blustery river to meet the famous author. On the way back, other colonials

---

74 see also Sherry 2004, 182.
75 Greene 1977 [1960], 35.

also took advantage of the stops the boat had to make, rushing into their cars or onto their bicycles to greet Greene on board. Trapped and cornered on the small steamer, there was no other possibility but to put his signature on the produced copies of *The Power and the Glory* and *Orient Express*, and wait for the guests to leave.

## 5. Second term in Iyonda (26 February– 5 March 1959), and leaving the Congo (7–12 March 1959)

### 5.1. *Finding a model for Father Thomas*

Back in Iyonda on 26 February, Greene picks up his former routine of reading novels in the morning, except that he does not go to the river bank anymore but does his reading on the loggia of the Fathers' house. On 27 February he writes "The old routine except that I no longer bother to go to the Congo to read." The rest of day he spends with the Iyonda Fathers and especially with the Lechat couple, whose company he more and more appreciates, resulting in a deep and lasting friendship with Michel Lechat, whose wisdom, discretion, and parsimony with words he greatly esteemed. Indicative of this friendship is not only the fact that Greene dedicated *A Burnt-Out Case* to him, but also the duration of their correspondence, which lasted at least until 1988, the fact that the Lechats visited Greene in Antibes in 1980, and especially Lechat's support for Greene in the context of the very negative review of *A Burnt-Out Case* the leprologist Dr. Robert Cochrane published in 1961. Cochrane dismissed the book as sensationalism and as highly disrespectful towards leprosy patients, concluding that "it would have been better if it had never been written".[76] As Lechat wrote in his memoirs, Greene was much affected by this, as well as by the steaming letters he received from Cochrane. Lechat, in a long letter of 1 March 1961 to Cochrane, took up Greene's defense, arguing that a novelist has the right to choose any subject he likes, including leprosy, which is no one's prerogative territory, for "leprosy is part of human life in the same way as war, corruption, scandals, lost hopes, hate and love."[77]

Greene continues his silent observation of the Iyonda Fathers' unsophistication and petty sides, he is again several times invited for "awful duty drinks" in Coquilhatville, and is once more bothered by amateur writers, this time including a poet who wants to show him his volume of verse. He also, on 28 February, meets a certain "Father Joseph", i.e. Joseph 'Jef' Jacobs (1924–2003).[78] Both Lechat in his above-mentioned "tardy exegesis" of *A Burnt-Out Case* and Sherry in his biography[79] maintain that there was no specific model for the anxious, doubting,

---

[76] Cochrane, R. 1961. Review of *A Burnt-Out Case* by Graham Greene. *The Star* 20(4): 10-11.
[77] Letter Lechat to Cochrane, 1/3/1961, quoted by Lechat in his memoirs (Lechat archives, author's possession). My translation from the French.
[78] For biographical information, see Paradijs, M. (2006). *Wij gedenken*. Borgerhout, Misano, 47.
[79] Sherry 2004, 187.

egocentric Father Thomas in the novel, the only priest who annoys Querry with higher spiritual questions and faith doubts and whom Greene himself later typified as representing "an unsettled form of belief".[80] My conviction is that it is Joseph Jacobs who inspired Greene for building the Father Thomas character. Lechat's and Sherry's oversight must be due to Greene's deletion of his description of Father Joseph from the diary for publication. Note also that Hulstaert, who also worked on the published diary, does not list Father Joseph either.[81]

In the diary manuscript, Greene described Father Joseph as suffering from tropical neurasthenia, which Belgian colonials subsumed under the more general label *cafard*, i.e. a depressed state of mind occurring among whites chronically stressed by the humidity and heat in the tropics. Greene adds: "he doesn't work with the others: a discontent. He has been told that he can choose his own work and that he can even return to Belgium . . . . A failed vocation?" Among the other priests of the congregation, too, Father Joseph Jacobs was generally known as a complainer who suffered from character instability and probably also from doubts about the meaningfulness of his vocation.

Greene leaves Iyonda and Coquilhatville on Thursday 5 March 1959: he is driven to the Coquilhatville airstrip by the Lechat couple accompanied by their two small children and Father Henri Vanderslaghmolen. Four other colonials meet them at the airstrip to see him off, among whom was the amateur writer De Valkeneer-Briard. This bonus company is not how Greene had envisaged his send-off: "an awful woman from the Service Social whom I had been avoiding, the Governor's wife whom I had hoped I would never see again."

## 5.2. Greene on film: Merriment or make-believe?

In the morning of Greene's last day at Iyonda, Thursday 5 March, Father Paul Van Molle (1911–1969) realized that neither the Lechats nor the priests had taken any picture or other kind of visual record of Greene. With Greene's departure imminent later that day, Father Paul, an amateur filmer, hastened to make a recording of Greene on his 8mm camera. This five minute 'home video' can be viewed online, as part of my article *Tiny Bouts of Contentment* (Meeuwis 2013),[82] in which I describe the contents of the film in more detail. The original film is in possession of Edith Dasnoy, who had it transposed to DVD-format. Before my own use of the film in the online publication, to my knowledge it left its hiding place only twice. The first time was in the early 1990s, when Donald Sturrock prepared his documentary on Greene for the BBC, *The Graham Greene Trilogy*. Sturrock used only a small selection of fragments of the footage; also, the order in which he presented them did not respect the original course of the film. Secondly, when Norman Sherry was

---

80 Aitken, T. 2005. Ways of Affirmation and Ways of Escape: Graham Greene in Mexico and the Congo (Occasional Paper number 10), 14.
81 Hulstaert 1994.
82 Tiny Bouts of Contentment: Rare Film Footage of Graham Greene in the Belgian Congo, March 1959. *Rozenberg Quarterly* (December).

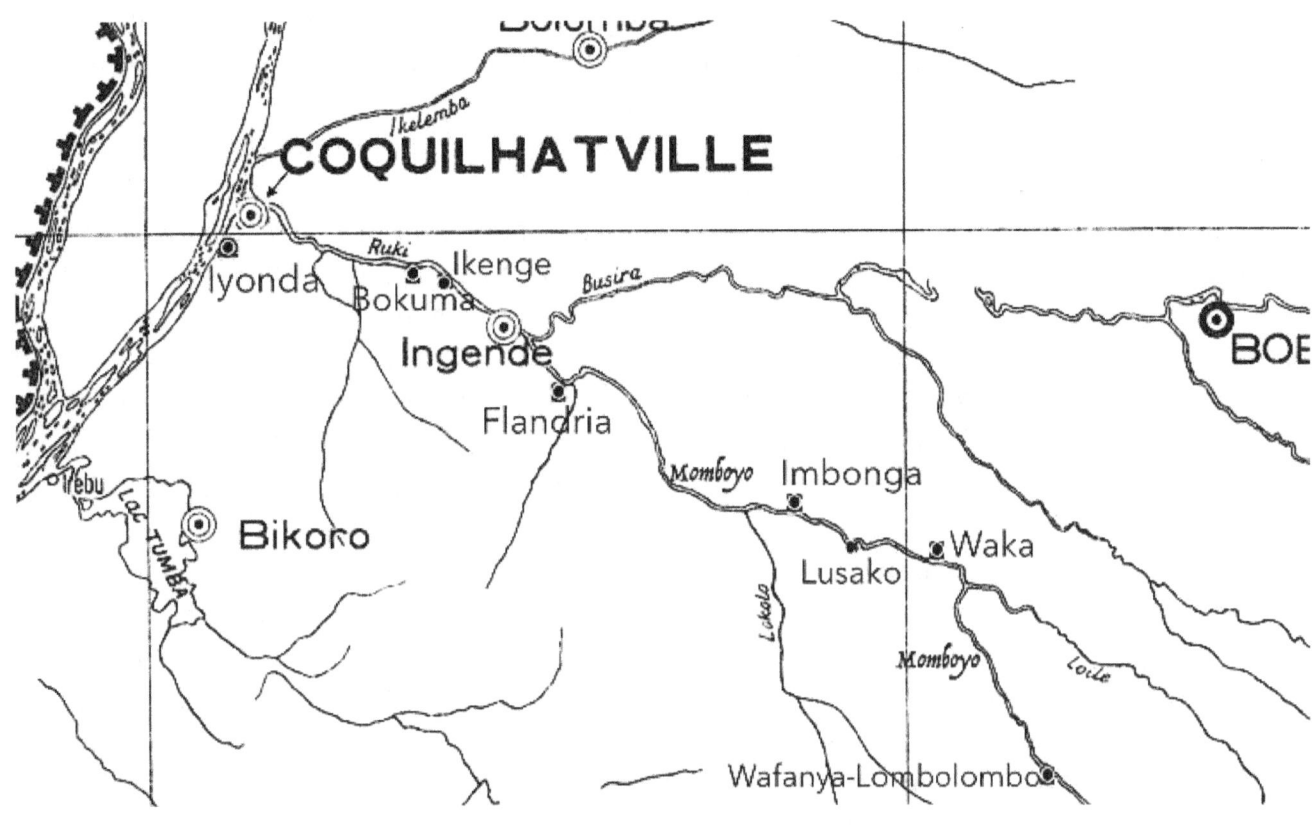

**Map 2** indicating the mission stations where the Theresita halted during Greene's journey on the Ruki-Momboyo tributary of the Congo river, between 12 and 25 February 1959. All place names visible on the map along the banks of the tributary (Bokuma, Ikenge, Ingende, Flandria, etc.) are mentioned by Greene in his diary as places he visited, although he misspells most names.

Information added by author to a base-map from the Belgian Royal Academy for Overseas Sciences, publicly available on http://kaowarsom.be/en/online_maps. Congo belge.

preparing the third volume of his Greene biography, the Lechats lent him a copy of the film. Sherry, however, mentions the film only once, and for that matter in not more than a cursory fashion. He writes: "We have an example on film of Greene entering in the fun, dancing when 'the tall cadaverous joker' Father Henri pulled him from his seat. To screams of pleasure from Dr Lechat's children, Greene, gloomy no more, and Father Henri put on a performance."[83]

The film from start to ending shows a gay, merry Greene. Yet, as already explained, the second half of the 1950s represented one of the darkest periods in his life. In the BBC documentary, relations of Greene's narrate how he was a master in masking away his gloominess, concealing it under the exact opposite. Appearing in off-screen voice, his wife Vivien Greene declares: "I've discovered, and I'm sure I'm right, that people who are great on practical jokes are very unhappy. And I think it was when Graham was most unhappy that he started all these practical jokes . . . . It was I'm quite sure when he was most deeply unhappy that he had this spell of practical joking, which people think of as high spirits but I don't think it is." Her off-screen voice is heard over those parts of the film where Greene is doing a mock waltz with Father Henri Vanderslaghmolen and is looking happily entertained at lunch with the Lechat family. Sturrock's message is clear: Greene's gaiety visible on this footage is make-believe, a shallow pose that when scratched away reveals a deeper, lurking despondency.

In my opinion, this interpretation confuses Greene's stay in the Congo with the later gestation and writing of *A Burnt-Out Case*. Greene on more than one occasion described this writing process as utterly abysmal. In *Ways of Escape* he remembered: "Never had a novel proved more recalcitrant or more depressing. The reader had only to endure the company of the burnt-out character called in the novel Querry for a few hours' reading, but the author had to live with him and in him for eighteen months"[84] and "I had assumed, after *A Burnt-Out Case*, that my writing days were finished."[85] Likewise, to Marie-Françoise Allain he once confided that "my last bout of depression, my worst, I think, coincided with the gestation of *A Burnt-Out Case*."[86]

His stay in the Congo, on the other hand, and regardless of the lack of meaningful religious reflexion in Iyonda, was marked by sparks of genuine merriment. First of all, as mentioned above, Greene felt very much at ease in the company of the Lechat couple, admitting to be able to really relax with them.

Secondly, we have a number of statements by Greene himself, made later in his life, pointing in the same direction. In a letter of 13 April 1959 to Edith Dasnoy, Baroness Hansi Lambert related how Greene, just recently returned, had reported to her about his trip, writing that "Graham Greene has been enchanted by his stay in Yonda and finds you two charming!"[87] Also, in 1988 Greene reacted to the brief, nostalgic trip

---

83 Sherry 2004, 180.
84 Greene. *Ways of Escape*. 1981: 75.
85 Ibid., 87.
86 Allain, M.-F. 1983. *The Other Man: Conversations with Graham Greene*. London, The Bodley Head, 143.
87 Letter Lambert to Dasnoy, 13/4/1959 (original in Lechat archives, author's possession). My translation from the French.

Michel Lechat had made to Iyonda earlier that year. He wrote "I rather envy you your return for a short visit [to] Iyonda. I would like to see the place again and my little hut there and the river going by. But it wouldn't be the same without our lunches together."[88]

Finally, in the commentaries Greene added to Paul Hogarth's book with drawings of "Greeneland," Greene remembered his time in Iyonda, 25 years earlier, as follows: "Most of my memories of the léproserie are happy ones–the kindness of the fathers and friendship of Dr. Lechat to whom the book is dedicated".[89] And he again made the clear distinction between his stay with the Lechats and the Fathers on the one hand, and the gestation of the book on the other: "It was not a depressing experience. What was depressing was writing the novel and having to live for two years with a character like Querry. I thought it would be my last novel."[90]

## 5.3. Leaving the Congo: Brazzaville (7–8 March 1959) and the Douala incident (8–12 March 1959)

Arriving back in Leopoldville on the same 5 March 1959, he is again, as during his first days there, troubled by sensation-seeking journalists whom he has to oblige with interviews, and by another "would-be writer," this time the head of the government's library, who reminds Greene of a fan letter his son had once written to him about *The Little Train*. In the morning of 7 March, Greene traverses the Congo river by boat, leaving Leopoldville and the Belgian Congo behind for good and entering the directly opposite city of Brazzaville, in French Equatorial Africa. Brazzaville immediately appeals to him: "a far prettier and more sympathetic place than Leo—Europe weighs down in Leo on the African soil in the form of skyscrapers: here Europe sinks into the greenery and trees of Africa. Even the shops have more chic than Leo."

He stays in Brazzaville until 8 March, when he boards a plane to Libreville (now the capital of Gabon), the evening of the same day traveling on to Douala, Cameroon. As Sherry suggests that Greene was already back in England by 12 March,[91] he must have spent at most four or five days in Douala. In his brief diary entry of 9 March, Greene only offers information on the cafés and bars he went to in this city. Yet we know that he visited another leprosy hospital and colony, situated near Douala and called after the river Dibamba that flows through the city. In a letter to Lechat written from London on 25 March, he related "I went to one other leproserie outside Douala—a curious mixture of the sentimental and the squalid. The leproserie has been built on a hill top so that there was no proper room between the buildings which were dreary in the extreme. No African infirmiers—only nuns. Altogether it made one realize all the more strongly what you have accomplished at Yonda."[92] Remarkably, this negative

---
88 Letter Greene to Lechat, 4/11/1988 (photocopy in Lechat archives, author's possession).
89 Hogarth, P. 1986. *Graham Greene Country: Visited by Paul Hogarth*. Foreword and Commentary by Graham Greene. London, Pavilion Books, 108-112.
90 Ibid., 108.
91 Sherry, 2004, 209.

depiction of the Dibamba leprosarium and the attendant positive one of Iyonda stand in sharp contrast with what Greene is supposed to have stated in a conversation he had with the French Jesuit Henri de Julliot in a bar in Douala between 9 and 12 March. In his report of this conversation, published in *La Presse du Cameroun* of 17 March 1959, de Julliot wrote that Greene "has preferred our small leprosarium of Dibamba . . . to those of the Belgian Congo, which are too well organized, too industrialized, less humane," and quoted Greene for having said that "Had I known this in advance, it is here that I would have spent those 15 days!."[93] The publication of de Julliot's report in the press embarrassed Greene a good deal. In two consecutive letters to Lechat, he took great pains to deny having said or thought anything of the kind. On 2 April he urged Lechat to believe that "I am reported as saying that I preferred the little leproserie of Dibamba to those in the Belgian Congo—better built, industrialized and less human! I am quoted as saying that I would have liked to have passed a fortnight at Dibamba. Needless to say I said none of these things—in fact I was rather repelled by the atmosphere of Dibamba."[94] On 12 May he even sent Lechat a photo of the Dibamba leprosarium, attaching the note "I enclose a not very good photograph of the leproserie outside Douala, but it may give you an idea of the squalor of the place. It doesn't seem likely that I would have preferred this spot to Yonda does it."[95] Lechat, on 8 April 1959, reassured Greene that he was not at all annoyed, adding that there was, in fact, some truth in his descriptions: at Iyonda, he and his staff strove first and foremost for convenience and dignity for the leprosy patients and refused to seek the picturesque or give way to patronizing sentimentality. In his memoirs, Lechat later related how, if the incident itself did not disturb him in any way, the excessively defensive and denying stance Greene assumed later did manage to provoke some irritation in him: "He defended himself for an incident of such little importance by means of an about-turn that to my taste was a little bit too easy . . . . This left me perplexed, if not irritated. Why these denials? All the more since I am not convinced that he did not send me this article, whose existence otherwise I would have remained unaware of, on purpose in order to let me know, in an indirect way, what he really thought of the leprosarium of Iyonda. This would have been a tiny perversity that would not have surprised me from him."[96] It seems to me that this "tiny perversity" can well be understood when considering how much Greene's Congo trip combined the contradictions of finding a greatly needed place of refuge, being disillusioned by failing religiosity in the face of leprosy, and inescapably having to confront the Conradian darkness of his own heart.

---

92 Letter Greene to Lechat, 25/3/1959 (photocopy in Lechat archives, author's possession).
93 de Julliot, H. (1959). "Rencontre de Graham Greene." *La Presse du Cameroun* 2668(17 mars 1959): 1-3. My translations from the French.
94 Letter Greene to Lechat, 2/4/1959 (photocopy in Lechat archives, author's possession).
95 Letter Greene to Lechat, 12/5/1959 (photocopy in Lechat archives, author's possession).
96 Lechat memoirs, author's possession. My translation from the French.

**Dr. Michael Meeuwis** (born 1968) studied African philology and history at Ghent University and general (socio-)linguistics at the Universities of Amsterdam and Antwerp. He received his Ph.D. from the University of Antwerp in 1997. He is presently Full Professor at the department of African Languages and Cultures of his alma mater, Ghent University. His domains of interest and publication include the missionary and colonial history of the Belgian Congo, the languages and cultures of the western Congo, and the ideological backgrounds of scientific knowledge production in colonial contexts.

# "Memory Cheats": Deception, Recollection, And The Problem Of Reading In *The Captain And The Enemy*

## Frances McCormack,

The 2013 Graham Greene International Festival

T*he Captain and the Enemy* is one of Greene's least well-known and least loved novels. It has received little critical attention, but that is hardly any wonder: it is a frustrating, perplexing, and ultimately unfulfilling read. Greene himself had great difficulty completing it. Leopoldo Durán, in *Graham Greene: Friend and Brother*, notes that

> the revision of *The Captain and the Enemy* almost drove him to despair. He did not like it. He never had liked it. He returned the typescript several times; on various occasions he told me: 'at last it's finished.' And yet, on 9 November 1987, he was still working on this stubborn novel. And to think he had kept it in the drawer of his table for fourteen years.[1]

Despite the challenges of its composition, Richard Greene cautions us against allowing our knowledge of Greene's difficulties with the text to shape our reception of it:

> Greene's dislike for his own books is not to be taken seriously. *The Captain and the Enemy*, though on a smaller scale than the great works of his mid-career, may be an unnoticed masterpiece. It is at the very least a scourging of the rag and bone shop of the heart.[2]

Deeply emotive, dark in its comedy, evasive and narratively untrustworthy, full of lacunae and contradictions, this is, despite (or perhaps because of) its many frustrations for the reader, a provocative and compelling read. Although it is a four-part narrative with a fragmented structure and little continuity between the parts, with a meandering plot and an ultimately unlikeable narrator, it warrants more attention than has been afforded by both Greene scholars and lay aficionados.

The plot defies any kind of structural or narrative unity. It is set in four different time periods: Baxter's distant past, his immediate past, his present, and the time in the immediate aftermath of his death. It takes place in Berkhamsted, London, and Panama. It raises questions that remain unanswered; it follows narrative threads a certain distance before abandoning them; and it leaves the reader without any substantial understanding of characters or their motivations. In his *Preface to Greene*, Cedric Watts notes that

> The structure is loose, and the work as a whole seems rather weakly derivative from previous materials; it gives a sense that a social narrative of a considerably earlier period (concerning the Captain,

---

[1] Leopoldo Durán, *Graham Greene: Friend and Brother*, Broadway: Harper Collins, p. 205.
[2] Richard Greene, ed., *Graham Greene: A Life in Letters*, New York: W.W. Norton, p. 399 n21.

Liza, and Baxter as a boy) is being grafted onto a tale of current politics.[3]

It appears, indeed, that Greene himself had great difficulty with its composition. Jon Wise and Mike Hill, investigating the Greene archives at Georgetown University, have uncovered what they describe as a "messy" process.[4] These archives contain one autographed manuscript and two typescript drafts. The autographed manuscript has dated sections after every few thousand words with the earliest section dated to January 1976. The page numbers are erratic; the narration shifts from first-person to third-person and back again; and on a cover note to the containing folder, Greene has written "Needs arranging." The typescript drafts are equally erratic. The first, dated January 1985, is written entirely in the first person, and is reworked extensively in Greene's hand. The second is undated and incomplete, again with corrections and additions. Wise and Hill conclude, therefore, that the novel was "begun sometime in the mid-1970s, added to quite slowly in the late 1970s and early 1980s, then brought to something like a finished product by 1985, but perhaps recast once more before publication in 1988."[5]

The title of the novel was not any less problematic for Greene: originally, *Getting to Know the Captain*, Greene altered the title to *Knowing the Captain*, before settling on the title taken from George A. Birmingham's novel *Hyacinth* and used as an epigraph to Greene's novel: "Will you be sure to know the good side from the bad, the Captain from the enemy?"[6]

Intriguingly, the autographed manuscript is accompanied by an "Apologia" (revised over two drafts) in which Greene attempts to give an account of the process of composition of the novel. Originally, he intended to publish this with the novel as an explanatory note, but later changed his mind. In the "Apologia," Greene explains that the novel was begun in Antibes in late 1974, two years before he visited Panama. Soon, he abandoned it to resume work on *The Human Factor*, and picked it up again, by strange coincidence, exactly four years later in the exact same spot. He writes:

I prayed last night my usual prayer for those I love or have hurt and without conviction one prayer this time for myself—that I could work again. For the first time in months I woke without melancholy [...]. Whatever happens now it has given me a happy day. If only this book could continue to my end.[7]

The process of composition continues in fits and starts, according to the "Apologia," with the concluding note dated November 22, 1987:

Finished the first complete draft of *The Captain and the Enemy*. I will try not to ask the question which haunts me nearly always at the end of a book: was it worth the trouble?[8]

---

3 Cedric Watts, *A Preface to Greene* (Harlow: Longman-Pearson, 1997), p. 82.
4 Jon Wise and Mike Hill, *The Works of Graham Greene, Volume 2: A Guide to the Graham Greene Archives* (London: Bloomsbury, 2015), p. 208.
5 Ibid.
6 George A. Birmingham, *Hyacinth* (London: Edward Arnold, 1906), chapter 20.
7 "Apologia,", from the autographed manuscript of *The Captain and the Enemy*, Georgetown University Library Archives, cited in Wise and Hill, *The Works of Graham Greene, Volume 2*, p 210.
8 Ibid., p. 210.

The problems Greene faced in writing the novel may help to explain some of its apparently deliberate frustrations of the reader's attempt to decode it. This is a novel that calls into question the role of the author, the nature of autobiography, the reliability of recollection, and the process of searching for meaning in a text mediated by a first-person narrator (and one who, at that, has been raised by a confidence trickster). It interrogates the value of fiction and asks us to reflect on our own role in the reception of the text. Its readers are often left floundering, trying to construct or determine meaning, attempting to navigate the text's various obstacles and obfuscations, endeavoring to understand the essence of a text that is often obscure, disjointed, and as resistant to attempts to read it as it was resistant to its own composition.

Baxter, as a narrator, is notoriously unreliable: setting down his text as an autobiography, there is a self-consciousness to his composition that is absent from conversational first-person narration; it is crafted rather than spontaneous, and at many points Baxter reflects on what he is writing and how he is writing it. Throughout the text, he calls attention to the capriciousness of memory. The word *remember* is used 66 times in total throughout the novel, and *memory* fifteen. *Remember,* when it occurs, sometimes marks Baxter's surprise at his memory for minor details of his past (for example, "I can still remember the wetness of the gravel under my gym shoes,"[9] "I still remember a few of the entries,"[10] "I can remember the exact phrase she used to this day"[11]). At other times it is employed in imperatives uttered by the Captain to Baxter (or others) to remember details ("You'll remember, won't you, that I've left my suitcase behind the bar,"[12] "Remember that it's never too late to learn from a man like myself,"[13] "Now remember what I told you,"[14] "Finding's keeping—remember that"[15]). Elsewhere, however, Baxter uses the word *remember* to abdicate responsibility from telling the truth:

> I don't pretend that I can remember correctly the details of this conversation. There are certain words which I do remember, but I invent far more of them, in order to fill in the gaps between their words, because I want so much to hear in my ears again the tone of their two voices. Above all I want to understand the only two people in whom I could recognize what I suppose can be described as a kind of love, a kind which to this day I have certainly never felt myself.[16]

The repeated emphasis on memory suggests that the reader place this faculty at the center of their interpretation of the book, and yet Baxter's flawed memories and his substitution of invention for memory cause that same reader to become distrustful of the faculty as it manifests itself throughout the novel. Memories ought to arouse the reader's suspicion; Greene reiterates, throughout this text and others, that they are unreliable, uncertain, precarious.

Greene is quoted by Robert Olen Butler as having said that "all good novelists have

---

9 Greene, *The Captain and the Enemy*, p. 9.
10 Ibid., p. 32.
11 Ibid., p. 43.
12 Ibid., p. 16.
13 Ibid., p. 16.
14 Ibid., p. 26.
15 Ibid., p. 31.
16 Graham Greene, *The Captain and the Enemy* (Penguin, 1989), p. 17.

bad memories. What you remember comes out as journalism; what you forget goes into the compost of the imagination."[17]

The realm of autobiography, it seems, should lie somewhere between the two extremes of the setting down of vivid memories and the reconstruction of those that are more faint. James Olney, writing on the autobiographer's task in the twentieth century in particular, remarks that

> an agonized search for the self, through the mutually reflexive acts of memory and narrative, accompanied by the haunting fear that it is impossible from the beginning but also impossible to give over, is the very emblem of our time.[18]

In *The Captain and the Enemy*, Baxter sets out to narrate his life, to make sense of his past, but his experiences are filtered through the amorphousness of memory. He is conscious of the problematic nature of autobiography, and so allows himself the liberty of fictionalizing details of the past in order to make sense of the present. He asks himself "Is it only with today's eyes that I seemed to see at that moment a certain shiftiness in his? Memory cheats.[19]"

Greene himself displays a consciousness of the fragility and unreliability of memory in *A Sort of Life*. He thinks back to his earliest memory of sitting in a pram at the top of a hill with a dead dog at his feet, and works backwards to try to reconstruct the facts: the dog was a pug owned by his older sister; it was run over, perhaps by a horse-carriage, and killed; and his nurse thought that the best way to bring the cadaver home was by placing it at his feet in the pram. He notes that "The memory may well be a true one [...]" and relates his mother's recounting of this narrative and his early utterance of "poor dog" as evidence, leaving that memory partially reconstructed, untested, and filtered through his mother's own recollection.[20] He acknowledges, just a few lines later, the uncertainty of what is genuinely remembered and what is imagined, and throughout this autobiography he asserts the autonomy and intangibility of the workings of memory as he talks of his memory as operating somewhat independently of himself:

> Memory is like a long broken night. As I write, it is as though I am waking from sleep continually to grasp at an image which I hope may drag in its wake a whole intact dream, but the fragments remain fragments, the complete stories always escape.[21]

*A Sort of Life* is as much Greene's attempt to navigate his own memory as it is an attempt to navigate his past. "Memory often exaggerates" he says at one point, before admitting that he abandoned a novel about a school because he could not endure living in that environment in his memory.[22] This consciousness of the vagaries and the sensitivity of memory leads him to create, in *The Captain and the Enemy*, a novel about the relationship between narrative, memory, and fiction in the construction of autobiography.

---

17 Robert Olen Butler, *Conversations with American Novelists: The Best Interviews from the Missouri Review*, eds. Kay Bonetti, Greg Michalson, Speer Morgan, Jo Sapp, and Sam Stowers (Columbia: University of Missouri, 1997), 201-16, p. 205.
18 James Olney, *Memory and Narrative: The Weave of Life-Writing* (University of Chicago Press, 1998), pp. xiv-xv.
19 Graham Greene, *The Captain and the Enemy*, p. 35.
20 Graham Greene, *A Sort of Life* (Vintage, 1999), p. 13.
21 Ibid., p. 25.
22 Ibid, p. 54.

Baxter warns us at many points throughout the *The Captain and the Enemy* that we ought not trust his memory, but he makes certain to defend his text. At points, he blames the nature of memory itself:

> I am doing my best to describe a typical lesson which I received from the Captain, but I realize only too well that my description cannot be factually accurate. It has passed through the memory and the memory rejects and alters [. . .].[23]

He abdicates responsibility from his alterations—they are an inevitable part of any narration of past experience. Elsewhere, though, he asserts that truth must take a subordinate role to his impulse to write:

> I cannot pretend that all these details which I am trying so hard to reconstruct from my memory are necessarily true, but I feel myself today driven by a compulsive passion now that we are separated to make these two people live before my eyes again, to bring them back out of the shadows and set them to play their sad parts as closely as possible to the truth. I am only too well aware of how I may be weaving fact into fiction but without any intention of betraying the truth. I want above anything else to make the two of them clear to myself, so that they will continue to live as visibly as two photographs might seem to do propped up on a shelf beside my bed, but I don't own a single photograph of either of them.[24]

Here, the creation of fiction is centered on reconstructing, excavating, filtering, retrieving, and is in this way related to what we know about how memory operates.

The functions and operation of memory demonstrate that Baxter's "recollection" is far more contrived than he would have us believe. There are three main functions to the information-processing element of memory: encoding (receiving information), storage (holding this encoded information in the form of internal representations), and retrieval (recalling the information, based on some prompt or cue, or recognizing something once presented with it again). In terms of memory, encoding means more than just experiencing or perceiving the information: it involves interpretation—converting the information from one form to another. We see a word not as a string of individual letters, but we recode it into a meaningful unit. In the same way, fiction encodes and recodes events semantically, making sense of them, forming them conceptually into a particular shape. Retrieval can be of short-term memories or of long-term memories. The former are stored and retrieved sequentially; the latter are retrieved by association. Recollections of long-term memories tend to be disjointed, out of chronological narrative sequence, apparently random but linked by affiliation. It would be apt, then, if Baxter's narrative—disjointed as it is—were a conversational, stream-of-consciousness recollection of events. As autobiography, though, the lack of order in his recollections is suspicious. He is content with merely recalling—or at least giving the impression of doing so—without imposing a narrative structure, not entirely plausible given his repeated assertion that his autobiography is a fulfillment of his desire to write.

None of this, however, explains the repeated attention that Baxter draws to his

---

23 Graham Greene, *The Captain and the Enemy*, p. 67.
24 Ibid, p. 51.

failed or misshapen recollections. There are four main theories of forgetting in psychology. Decay theory[25] holds that memories that are not used fade over time, but this theory is generally discredited as a factor in the forgetting of long-term memories. Benjamin Lahey asserts that

> Memory "traces" appear to be "permanent" once they make it into [long-term memory]. Forgetting does not seem to happen in [long-term memory] because of disuse over time but because other factors, particularly *interference*, make memories irretrievable.[26]

Interference theory asserts that other memories interfere with the retrieval of what the individual is trying to recall.[27] It seems, though, that this interference primarily affects the retrieval of information, rather than of experience. Freud believed in what psychologists now refer to as motivated forgetting, holding that the conscious mind often dealt with unpleasant memories by pushing them into the unconscious to repress them.[28]

More fitting to the problem of memory in *The Captain and the Enemy*, however, is reconstruction theory,[29] which suggests that the information stored in long-term memory is not forgotten, but just recalled in a distorted way. When Quigley tells Baxter about the credit that has been arranged for him at the Continental Hotel, Baxter's reconstructive memory jolts into operation:

> A great many years had passed since I last saw the Captain, but I remembered again that other chit which he signed after the smoked salmon and the orangeade.[30]

Baxter forgets (or neglects to mention) the pork chops that were also served at the meal, perhaps because it was the salmon that had made him thirsty and therefore impressed itself on his memory. His recollection of the event from his distant past that he relates in part one of the novel changes shape, albeit only slightly, in the retelling.

Psychologists have insisted that long-term memory stores meaning better than it does episodic detail, so we are likely to remember the substance of an event, but we may distort or add details to be consistent with the general idea of the memory. An experiment conducted by Johnson, Bransford, and Solomon in 1973 tested this theory. Research participants listened to the following passage:

> It was late at night when the phone rang and a voice gave a frantic cry. The spy threw the secret document into the fireplace just 30 seconds before it would have been too late.[31]

Later, participants were asked if they heard the following sentence:

---

25 Cf. Robert S. Woodworth, *Experimental Psychology*. Oxford: Holt, 1938.
26 Benjamin Lahey, *Psychology: An Introduction*, 11th ed., pp. 243-4.
27 Benton J. Underwood and Leo Postman, 'Extraexperimental Sources of Interference in Forgetting', *Psychological Review* 67 (1960): 73-95.
28 Cf. Sigmund Freud, 'The Aetiology of Hysteria,' in *The Standard Edition of the Complete Psychological Works of Sigmund Freud*, vol. III: 1893-99 (London: Hogarth Press).
29 Frederic Charles Bartlett, *Remembering: A Study in Experimental and Social Psychology* (Cambridge: Cambridge University Press, 1932).
30 Greene, *The Captain and the Enemy*, p. 115.
31 M.K. Johnson, J.P. Bransford, and S. Solomon (1973), "Memory for Tacit Implications of Sentences," *Journal of Experimental Psychology* 98 (1973): 203-05.

The spy burned the secret document 30 seconds before it would have been too late.

The original passage had said nothing about burning the documents, but most participants said that they had heard the second passage. The results of the experiment demonstrate that the subjects had based their memory on inferences that they created from the spy throwing the document into the fireplace. Subjects had retrieved the meaning of the sentence from their long-term memories, but had distorted the details because of their own inferences. It certainly seems that in *The Captain and the Enemy*, Baxter's recollections are influenced by association. For instance, when he sees the Captain and Liza kiss, he is reminded of another kiss he witnessed:

> They kissed each other at last—not the kind of passionate kiss which I had seen only once on the screen at *King Kong* and remembered ever after, but a small timorous kiss on either cheek, as though even that gesture was something which could be dangerous to the loved one, like an infection.[32]

This fictional kiss—the one that is part of Baxter's initiation into the experience of love that has previously been denied him—becomes the template against which he measures all other such expressions of affection. Having measured the kiss between the Captain and Liza against the love represented in the film, he concludes that their kiss is cold and tentative. But how are we to believe to be a credible witness a boy who perceives the world around him through the lens of either fiction or fantasy?

Later, however, Baxter reveals that it is not memory that gives rise to associations. He often recalls details not because of their occurrence but because he has crafted them into a meaningful text:

> It was a good many years since I had last seen the Captain, and I felt as though I were waiting for a stranger or indeed a character existing only on the pages of that youthful manuscript of mine, on which I am still working. He existed there better on paper than in memory. For example if I tried to remember the occasions when he had taken me to a cinema it was only *King Kong* which came to my mind because I had recorded that memory in writing. When I thought of his previous arrivals after a long absence—only too frequent during our life together—it was the unexpected one with a bearded face which I saw in my mind's eye, because I had described it in words, or the stranger talking to the headmaster, the one who had afterwards fed me with smoked salmon. It was again because I had tried to recreate this character in my sorry attempt to become a 'real writer'.[33]

The story of *King Kong* becomes a leitmotif in the novel, and although memory impinges upon its retelling, it shapes so much of our reading of the text. Even Baxter's memories of the film are tarnished. When he recounts his first viewing of the film he doubts even its title:

> it was I think called *King Kong* [...] King Kong, if it was King Kong, clambered about the skyscrapers with a blonde girl—whose name I don't remember—in his arms.[34]

---

32 Greene, *The Captain and the Enemy*, p. 59.
33 Ibid., pp. 125-30.
34 Greene, *The Captain and the Enemy*, pp. 43-4.

Not only does he have difficulty attempting to recall the title of the film and the name of its eponymous protagonist, but he also misremembers details. For most of the Empire State Building scene, Ann Darrow lies at the top of the tower. King Kong picks her up twice and gazes on her lovingly, before placing her down again on the relative safety of a ledge, out of the line of the machine-gun fire.[35] One of the key details to adhere to Baxter's memory is of the female lead kicking violently at the ape. At all of the points in the movie in which she is held, she kicks her legs in protest, but in a terpsichorean fashion, and never makes contact with the ape. Baxter's memory of the film has been shaped, like the spy story in the experiment performed by Johnson, Bransford and Solomon, by his interpretation of the kicking, rather than by the image of the kicking itself. But just as the narrative of *King Kong*, as it appears in the novel, is fashioned by Baxter's reconstruction of it to suit his frame of reference, so too does narrative come to fashion his memory: characters are more clearly drawn in his writing than in his imagination, and so his narrative serves as the cue for his recall.

Narrative shapes Baxter's memory, and it also allows him to make sense of past experience. The American psychologist, Donald E. Polkinghorne, writes:

> Narrative meaning functions to give form to the understanding of a purpose to life and to join everyday actions and events into episodic units. It provides a framework for understanding the past events of one's life and for planning future actions. It is the primary scheme by means of which human existence is rendered meaningful.[36]

For Baxter, then, the desire to write could be seen as a way of making sense of past events, and of making "these two people live before [his] eyes again, to bring them back out of the shadows and set them to play their sad parts" by structuring these past events into a broadly coherent shape. His consciousness of the problematic nature of memory could be a genuine expression of the frustration of the effect of time on the ability to recall.

But why Baxter should want to bring to life two characters to whom he has no emotional attachment is at first perplexing. He explains:

> It's not for any love I feel for them. It is as though I had taken them quite cold-bloodedly as fictional characters to satisfy this passionate desire of mine to write.[37]

His is a narrative in which the desire for recollection competes with the desire to make sense of the past. Making sense of the past involves both interpretation and interpolation: he can only understand by filling in some of the details. However, the suggestion of his "passionate desire" to write is ambiguous, and leaves us to wonder whether we should read the text as an autobiography with elements of fiction or as pure fiction within a fiction. As Brian Moore writes, in his *New York Times* review of the novel:

> The chronological setting is in the 1950s, but the atmosphere is like that of prewar England when the future held no promise and despair fell like rain on the grim

---

35 Merian C. Cooper, Ernest B. Schoedsack, David O. Selznik (Producers), Merian C. Cooper, Ernest B. Schoedsack (Directors), *King Kong* (United States: RKO, 1933).
36 Donald E. Polkinghorne, *Narrative Knowing and the Human Sciences* (State University of New York Press, 1988, p. 11.
37 Greene, *The Captain and the Enemy*, p. 51.

streets and squares. This fudging of precise dates is deliberate and heightens the dichotomy between what the narrator thinks he remembers and what he is inventing in his role as a writer. Thus, the unreliability of memory as a guide to our true feelings becomes one of the themes of the book.[38]

It is not only memory that is unreliable, though: the text as a whole is unpredictable and ultimately untrustworthy. Characters' identities are fluid: the Captain assumes a number of names, and signs his last letter "'The Captain, the Colonel, the Major, the Sergeant, Señor Smith'" with an exclamation mark after each name.[39] One's name sets the standard for one's life in the novel; Liza tells Jim how when she met the Captain he was called Colonel Claridge, but he changed it soon when he realized that he couldn't live up to it. Baxter notes:

> there is a strange importance about names. You can't trust them until you have tried them out.[40]

He is surprised by his own failure to have realized that he could easily have changed his hated name simply by adopting a new one.[41] He asks a question that could be as much on the reader's behalf as on his own:

> Would I ever cease to be a stranger in this region of the world where I was at a loss to remember all the names?[42]

We, as readers, are strangers in a text in which names are unreliable, and identity is fluid, constantly searching for signposts of meaning, indicators of truth, something solid within the text that we can use as a cornerstone for our interpretation. The novel repeatedly asks us to interrogate how we read it and how we extract or construct meaning.

Even language is shown by the novel to fail to stand up to any scrutiny of its reliability. The Captain uses words whose sounds he likes, but which he doesn't fully understand, and this quirk is attributed to a highly implausible story in which the Captain has in his possession in a prison camp only half of a dictionary. "The other half had been used as a bum wiper," [43] the Devil tells Baxter, perhaps echoing the cavalier attitude to language that permeates the novel. Meaning is defined in the novel by the speaker with no regard for the hearer (or reader), and so language becomes as fluid as identity, constantly shifting, always out of reach. We experience some of the problems of reading through Baxter's own attempts to engage with texts—whether those he has composed himself or those written by others. He uses reading to avoid his tedious Bible lessons with Liza, by choosing either inexplicable or unsuitable passages. He reads the letters written by the Captain and intended for Liza—she wants them destroyed lest they fall into the hands of strangers—while reassuring her that he has destroyed them without reading them. His readings are often superficial and unsystematic; he scours the letters for the word *love*, notes its absence, and remarks on the Captain's unusual use of language. But when he does engage with a text, it

---

38 Brian Moore, 'Father Lost me in a Backgammon Game,' *New York Times*. October 23, 1998.
39 Greene, *The Captain and the Enemy*, p. 168.
40 Ibid, p.36
41 Ibid, p. 28.
42 Ibid, p. 175.
43 Ibid, p. 98.

often creates a sense of disorientation for him because it does not tally with his own experience or perceptions:

> I read the letters several times. It was as though I was looking through someone else's eyes at the dying woman who had been my substitute mother, and as I seemed to peer at her between the lines, the mystery grew. [. . .] but when I read the Captain's letters I found myself in a foreign land where the language was totally strange to me, and even when a word was identical in my own tongue, it seemed to have a quite different meaning.[44]

The novel is largely metafictional: it uses self-referential narrative devices to repeatedly remind us that what we're reading—even Baxter's autobiography—is a fictional construct, and to ask questions about why writers write and how readers read. Yet, that the novel, and the autobiography contained within it, make such heavy demands of the reader, is hardly surprising. Obscurity, in this case, is key to compelling us to attempt to understand how, in a text that relies on the construction of memories and the tenacious connection between recollection and truth, that text itself constructs meaning.

The use of language in the novel is another device used to compound the self-reflexivity of the text. David Crystal, who bases an essay on his assertion that "Explicit reference to language is a major (albeit neglected) element in Greene's narrative artistry, inevitably conveying danger signals,"[45] notes that The Captain is an ambiguous character. He does not treat language with respect. He makes up words—a very bad sign. Not that the child is totally innocent. He has made up words too [. . .]. This is language as mystery. Language, for Greene, is a bit like a mysterious maze, which has an entrance but not necessarily an exit, and in which one might get lost forever.[46]

Language, names and identity are in a permanent state of flux in the novel, thereby enhancing the disconcerting nature of the eccentric narration, unreliable memories, and characters who are only shifting shadows without fully realized identities—just snapshots on a bedside shelf. Even the title of the novel is vague and ambiguous; Leopoldo Durán recounts his attempt to understand the title:

> Without ever having delved very deeply into this novel, I expounded my view about the Captain's 'enemy'. For me, it was both the 'Devil' and the Americans, as Pablo affirms in the novel. 'That's Pablo's view,' Graham said to me. 'It's more philosophical than that.'[47]

Greene revealed nothing more; through the novel the reader is left to mold these formless identities into some sort of shape—to read between the lines of Baxter's text, to attempt to determine truth from failed memory and fiction, and to try to decipher, as the epigraph puts it, the Captain from the Enemy.

---

44 Ibid, pp. 89-90.
45 David Crystal, "Going Especially Careful: Language Reference in Graham Greene," in *Dangerous Edges of Graham Greene: Journeys with Saints and Sinners*, eds Dermot Gilvary and Darren Middleton (Continuum, 2011): 128-48, p. 128.
46 Ibid, p. 136.
47 Durán, *Graham Greene: Friend and Brother*, p. 185.

The reader's task is not made any less complicated by Baxter's own insistence on the fictional elements of his writing. He often does not trust his own perception, let alone his own imagination:

> I thought he winked at me, but I could hardly believe it. In my experience grown-ups did not wink, except at each other.[48]

The novel is saturated with suggestions of self-consciously flawed interpretations, of half-truths and of lies—whether those of the narrator or those of the characters who surround him. Baxter repeatedly cautions us to distrust textual authority: he tells us how, as a child, he had always taken for granted that newspapers contained what he defined as "the gospel truth." Texts, this text cautions us, are where secrets are hidden (the newspaper containing the story of the jewelry robbery, for instance) and where lies are told. Baxter tells us of his first job as a newspaper reporter:

> having gained the job in spite of my youth by a very readable account of a bizarre accident which never really happened. Perhaps the title I gave the piece had caught the editorial attention—"The Biter Bit." I feared the editor might check up with the source which I falsely claimed, but I timed my piece well, the paper was just going to press, and the editor was anxious to get it in the first and only edition before the story could hit the headlines of the giants, the *Mail* or the *Express*. I had been innocent enough before then to share Liza's belief that what counted for a newspaper was truth rather than reader-interest, and my success helped to cure my innocence.[49]

Here, Baxter shapes his own metafictional text—the title, "The Biter Bit" refers not only to the unrevealed bizarre accident, but also to the gullibility of the reader of his story: the fictional reader of his journalism and the actual reader of his auto-fiction. Reader-interest, and not truth, he comes to believe, determines the nature of a text, and so he suggests that he is a master of creating the text that he thinks will most pique the reader's interest. Readers, Baxter insists, determine the level of the text's truth value—a truth, that he asserts is hidden "deeper than any grave"[50]—through what we demand from it; the author merely supplies what we want. Just as the reader may mistrust the fictional author, then, so too does he mistrust them.

Through Baxter's narration, even the sincerity of the Captain's letters to Liza become suspect. Baxter's perception mediates the Captain's spasmodic and indecisive composition of these letters from Panama, as though the latter is a schoolchild completing a particularly difficult exercise. Even Baxter's own partially formed narrative jars with him in part two of the novel, and he fails to recognize his own handwriting:

> I was taken a little by surprise when I came on this unfinished story—fiction, autobiography?—which I have written here. [. . .] There had been a period in my youth when I had nursed the vain ambition to become what I thought of as a 'real writer', and I suppose it was then that I began this fragment.[51]

---

48 Greene, *The Captain and the Enemy*, p. 10.
49 Ibid, p. 87.
50 Ibid, p. 128.
51 Ibid., p. 84.

We are continually reminded that this text is not to be relied upon, that it is a fiction within a fiction, and that our construction of its meaning is what will give the text its ultimate shape.

The text shifts from one literary mode to another: from fiction to autofiction, from epistolary novel to travel writing, from mystery to fabulation, and the reader is repeatedly called upon to help create meaning, as the reader is left to wonder whether there is any way to get to the essence of the text. Yet, in order to verify and validate our reading, we have to search for something within the text that is, in itself, verifiable. When, in part four, we step outside of Baxter's narration, we are left in the hands of an objective omniscient narrator, someone with no vested interest in the game of constructing meaning—a narrator we can trust. In part four lies the locus of meaning of the novel. Part four is again metafictional—about the act of reading, rather than the act of writing, as Colonel Martínez attempts to make sense of Baxter's discarded manuscript. Martinéz refers to the text as a novel, rather than an autobiography, suggesting that he is a far more astute reader than we. There is, though, one final puzzle to be solved:

> He touched the papers piled on his desk as though the mere feel of them might convey some answer to his question and then he spoke his thoughts aloud: 'King Kong. It haunts me that name King Kong. King Kong is the only clue we have. Could he be a name in some elementary book code which is all they would have trusted to an amateur like that? A character in Shakespeare, perhaps. Some famous line that even the gringos would recognize. Well, the boy's gone. He can do no harm to us. All the same... how I would like to break that code of his. King Kong.'[52]

The final line of the novel, narrated by Martínez, reads almost like a demand to the reader to supply the answer: "what or who is King Kong?" As readers, we are given the key to understanding the novel: we must decode what King Kong means to Baxter. In the fiction constructed around Baxter's autobiography, Greene has cautioned us against believing anything Baxter writes. The reference to the content of *King Kong* is true, though, because it lies outside of the fiction, and can be independently verified by us. It may be reshaped by Baxter's flawed memory or by the fictional tier of his narrative, but it remains independent from the text because it exists in the real world. Let us look again, then, at some of the details of Baxter's engagement with this fictional work.

Baxter's viewing of the film is dominated by his failure to comprehend, not understanding why the ape does not abandon the unwilling object of his affections. The Captain, who is brought to the brink of tears by the film, on the other hand, attempts to explain the interconnectedness of love and pain, but since only pain—not love—lies within the scope of Baxter's experiential frame of reference, he is at a loss to decipher the motif that he will forever associate with love. Indeed, much of the novel is Baxter's attempt to make sense of the peculiarities of human love. His knowledge of interpersonal relationships is shaped by his school experience of being an Amalekite: of being an outsider, picked on by the other students, having to remain constantly on guard. When the Captain tells him about Liza in advance of their meeting, Baxter can only understand her suffering in terms of his own:

---

52 Greene, The Captain and the Enemy, p.188
53 Ibid., pp. 24-25.

The word 'suffer' meant to me at that time the splashes of ink upon my face which still remained there [. . .], the visible sign of being an Amalekite, an outcast.[53]

Baxter reiterates throughout the text that the word *love* is meaningless to him. He questions whether he feels any love for either the Captain or Liza (and whether they do for each other,) but he does not have the experiential frame of reference to answer his own questions. As a child he equates love with fear: Liza is afraid of life without the Captain, and he of life without her. Love, for him, ought to be passionate:

> Even in later years, when sexual desire began to play its part, I would find myself wondering, do I love this girl or do I really only like her because of the pleasure that for the time being we share?[54]

His understanding of love is not experiential, but fictive, based on the martyology of King Kong for an unattainable and unrealistic love. All experience comes to be measured against this fiction, and so Greene creates a hermeneutic merry-go-round—a dizzying spinning of interpretation—where meaning is defined by fiction over experience, but where neither fiction nor memory of experience can be trusted. I write in "The Later Greene" that

> Jim's flaw is his blindness to, and disinterest in, the virtues that surround him; he refuses to believe in the Captain's love for Liza—a love that is poignantly proven in the final line of the novel. As he remains blind to the Captain's virtue—especially in his capacity for love—he spins for himself an intricate web of deceit from which he can only escape by attempting to determine where he stands in the Captain's affections. The second part of the novel—the part that echoes the tone and techniques of Greene's earlier entertainments—functions for the reader as a deliberate obfuscation of the theme of the redemptive power of human love that permeates it.[55]

Greene masks what I consider to be the true message of the novel—the ennobling power of love—because love, as the novel shows, is indefinable, impossible to pin down, and constantly shape-shifting. But the discussion of love in *The Captain and the Enemy* is for another speaker on another occasion. What matters in this discussion is that experience, recollection, and the shaping of meaning through textuality might overlie, but never fully conceal, the reader's search for meaning.

And so, Greene creates a narrative that is at times exasperating, where names are what Snyder refers to as "fictions of convenience," where identity is fluid, and where memories are untrustworthy.[56] This text shifts the responsibility of finding meaning on to the reader, and makes us toil to extract some kind of hermeneutic sense. We're made complicit in the obfuscation of meaning—reading is depicted in the novel as being a process shaped by subjectivity, by experience and perception, and texts are unreliable. But towards the end of the novel the author

---

54 Ibid., p. 47.
55 Frances McCormack, "The Later Greene: From Modernist to Moralist" in *Dangerous Edges of Graham Greene: Journeys with Saints and Sinners*, eds Dermot Gilvary and Darren Middleton (Continuum, 2011): 263-76, p. 275.
56 Robert Lance Snyder, "'What or Who is King Kong': Graham Greene's *The Captain and the Enemy*', Renascence 65:2 (Jan 2013): 125-139.

gifts us with a small token that can help us make sense of the whole. *The Captain and the Enemy* deserves a second reading, and a third. Greene's final novel may be frustrating, but what better prize could he have left us with than a novel that proves that meaning is made not just by the author, but by the author in dialogue with his readers?

**Dr. Frances McCormack** lectures at the National University of Ireland in Galway. She has published on a range of topics from Old English poetry to Graham Greene. Her monograph, *Chaucer and the Culture of Dissent*, was published in 2007, and she is co-editor of *Anglo-Saxon Emotions: Reading the Heart in Old English Language Literature and Culture* (with Alice Jorgensen and Jonathan Wilcox) and *Chaucer's Poetry: Words, Authority and Ethics* (with Clíodhna Carney). She was director of the Graham Greene International Festival in 2014.

# Graham Greene in Love and War: French Indochina and the Making of *The Quiet American*

## Kevin Ruane

The 2012 Graham Greene International Festival

Thank you very much for giving me the opportunity to talk about my research on Graham Greene, Vietnam and *The Quiet American*. Do bear in mind that this is still work in progress. I would welcome your comments and suggestions, as well as your questions, at the end. Perhaps I should say a little about myself and how I ended up here.

Many years ago, I took History and English Literature as my degree, but then took the fork in the career road named History, completed my doctorate on the French war in Indo-China, and went on to become what is known in the trade as an international, or diplomatic, historian. Over the years I have written a good deal on Vietnam, as well as on the Cold War. But the love of literature never left me, and a couple of years ago, I began a project that fused the two, history and literature. Greene, Vietnam, and *The Quiet American* were my points of departure.

But why? I think I was struck by the way that many readers seemed to look on the novel as fact–up to a point–as much as fiction. Not fact in that they believed the plot-line per se, but rather the background, the context, the big picture that Greene inserted, the real-life backdrop to the fictional tale. If at a certain level the novel was being read as history, had not the time come to see how it measured up as history?

For now, although I am sure that most of you are familiar with the story, a brief "barebones" outline of the plot of *The Quiet American* may still be useful. The two main protagonists are Thomas Fowler, a cynical and opiated British reporter working out of Saigon during the French war in Indo-China, and Alden Pyle, an idealistic and committed Cold War Warrior, the quiet American of the title, a member of the Economic Mission attached to the US Legation. Pyle is eventually exposed as a CIA agent secretly promoting a political-military Third Force between the French colonialists on one side and the communist-led Viet-Minh rebels on the other, a revelation which seals Pyle's fate. When a massive car bomb explodes in the center of Saigon killing and maiming innocent bystanders, Fowler recognizes the handiwork of General Thé, the leader of Pyle's Third Force. The bombing forms the backdrop to the climax of the novel, but it was also a real event, a case of fact and fiction fusing. It occurred on 9 January 1952, and its aftermath was captured as *Life* magazine's picture of the week.

In the novel, Pyle and Fowler are on the scene within seconds of the explosion. Pyle is stunned. "It's awful," he says surveying the carnage. He then glances down at his shoes.

> "What's that?" he asks, puzzled. "Blood," Fowler says. "Haven't you ever seen it before? . . . You've got the Third Force . . . all over your right shoe."

Fowler decides the time has come to do something about this meddling American before he does more harm. Fowler is also bitter because Pyle has stolen his Vietnamese mistress. So whether from political conviction or jealousy or a mixture of both, Fowler decides to use his contacts with the Viet-Minh to have Pyle assassinated. He was, "a good chap in his way . . . A quiet American," Fowler tells Vigot, the detective charged with investigating the murder. "A very quiet American," Vigot agrees with grim Gallic irony.

When it was published in 1955, the setting of *The Quiet American* would have been familiar to many of Greene's readers. The Viet-Minh victory over the French at the battle of Dien Bien Phu the year before, May 1954, had led to the settlement of this first Vietnam war. Vietnam was temporarily divided between a Viet-Minh north and an ostensibly noncommunist south, although the French retained significant political, economic and cultural influence south of the 17th Parallel. Nationwide elections were scheduled for July 1956 after which partition would end, the residual French presence would disappear, and the country would emerge reunited and independent. The elections, as we know, never took place.

Disillusioned, France withdrew ahead of schedule in 1955, leaving the United States to get on with building a separate anti-communist state in South Vietnam. The refusal of the North Vietnamese to accept this territorial cleavage as permanent was the catalyst for the second—American—war in Vietnam. By the time it ended in 1973 more than 58,000 US servicemen had died. The human cost on the Indo-Chinese side was anywhere between two and three million.

All of this obviously lay in the future when Greene's novel first appeared, but commentators have nonetheless remarked on his predictive power, in particular how the character of Pyle encapsulated the combination of American arrogance and naiveté that produced the awful US war in Vietnam. Through the character of Fowler, Greene appeared to condemn the USA's ability, born of ostensibly good intentions, to do great damage in the developing world. Given this leitmotif, one would not be surprised to learn that the novel, although well received in Britain, came in for fierce criticism in Cold War America, where reviewers bridled at the denigration of the US national character as personified by Pyle.

For all its supposed anti-Americanism, by the 1960s *The Quiet American* was essential reading for US journalists working in South Vietnam. Pulitzer Prize-winning journalist David Halberstam recently called it 'our bible.' Later, as the American war escalated, the novel became a standard text for the anti-war movement, which embraced it as a prophetic masterpiece about the perils of blind idealism run amok.

Leaving aside its cultural and contemporary political resonances, how then does *The Quiet American* fare as history? This question may seem inappropriate: as Greene himself remarked in the foreword to the novel, he set out to write "a story and not a piece of history." Yet Greene did muddy the distinction between fact and fiction by writing in the first person, and by including more direct reportage than can be found in any other of his novels. In so doing he underestimated the desire of his readers—and here I borrow from the critiques of others—"to make fiction fact," to have "fiction serving as history," and to accept the story as "real fiction." For those historians, however, as opposed to literary critics or cultural commentators, who have engaged with the novel, there is only one question worth asking: who was real-life model for Alden Pyle?

Over the years, Edward Geary Lansdale, ad-man turned CIA agent and later all-round Cold War celebrity, emerged as the "bookies' favorite" even though Greene always rejected the Lansdale/Pyle thesis. In the 1990's Greene's authorized biographer Norman Sherry demonstrated, to my satisfaction at least, that Pyle's views were a composite of attitudes the writer encountered in several Americans during his time in Vietnam in 1951–52. Of these, Leo Hochstetter, of the US Economic Mission, seems to have been the single greatest inspiration for Pyle's political outlook, though not his manner and bearing.

I want to ignore this Lansdale/Pyle non-debate. Instead I want to probe the novel's rendering of history from another angle and ponder whether the Americans really were working behind French backs to promote a Third Force. But in researching the US–General Thé relationship, I quickly discovered, to my surprise, that the British were also secretly fishing in Third Force waters too—and Graham Greene was in the fishing party.

The way I would like to do all this is to tell the story of Greene's first two visits to Vietnam, in 1951 and 1952, the period in which the novel is set and the period that in many other ways shaped the story. As I proceed, I will interweave with this Third Force business. To the extent that I quote Greene, it will be less from *The Quiet American* and more from his letters and journals, which I was fortunate enough to be able to look at in Georgetown, Boston, and Texas.

Greene went to Malaya in November 1950, where his brother, Hugh, was head of UK Information Services during the early phase of the Malayan Emergency. But Malaya bored Greene and he decided to return to England via Vietnam in order, so he said, to visit an old friend, Trevor Wilson, who was then "our man in Hanoi," British consul in Hanoi in North Vietnam.

It was to Saigon, the capital of Cochinchina, southern Vietnam, that Greene went first, arriving on 25 January 1951. Greene got very excited. "This is the country," he wrote in his diary. "What a sod place Malaya seems though this one is in greater danger." Then again, the danger was a large part of the attraction. Malaya had been a disappointment in that respect, but in Vietnam Greene discovered not one but two wars, each deadly in its own way. In the north, in Tonkin, was the big war, the business of armies. In Cochinchina the war was smaller in scale but still lethal, the business of assassins. On his second evening, Greene was invited to dine with General Jean de Lattre de Tassigny, who was both French High Commissioner and Commander-in-Chief of the French Expeditionary Force, the man, he noted, who had "stopped the rot" in Vietnam. And what a lot of rot there had been to stop.

(1.0 Greene, Phat Diem front, December 1951.)

The French war had begun in 1946 as a colonial conflict—the French attempting to reassert their imperial primacy in the face of determined resistance from the communist-led nationalists of the Viet-Minh under Ho Chi Minh. Five years on, however, with the United States supplying France with military assistance and the Chinese Communists providing similar aid to the Viet-Minh, the original colonial struggle had acquired a Cold War complexion. Meanwhile the Vietminh army, the People's Army of Vietnam (PAVN), commanded by General Vo Nguyen Giap, had developed into a formidable fighting force, and in autumn 1950, just a couple of months before Greene arrived, Giap's forces had won a stunning series of victories, wresting control of northern Tonkin and securing their supply lines to southern China.

In December 1950, Giap turned his attention to the Red River Delta, the hub of the French position in the north, launching a massive offensive to smash the French defenses. With Hanoi imperilled, the French High Command ordered the evacuation of French civilians, a precursor, it seemed, to the complete abandonment of the north and with it any prospect of winning the war. It was at this point that de Lattre arrived.

Dashing and debonair, the sixty-one-year-old general came to Indo-China with a reputation for firm leadership, strategic brilliance, temper tantrums, and great personal charm. He deserved the reputation. All the senior officers associated with the recent defeats were immediately fired, all talk of abandoning Tonkin was forbidden, and the French forces assured, "from now on you will be commanded," all of which had an electrifying impact on French morale. After successfully repulsing the threat to Hanoi, de Lattre went on to lead the French to victory in three more major battles in the first half of 1951. Meantime in his political role (he was also High Commissioner) he assured the Vietnamese that their independence was safe in his hands. What independence?

(2.0 Greene with French air force maintenance crew, 1951.)

Two years before, in 1949, the French had persuaded the ex-emperor of Annam, Bao Dai, to abandon the casinos and fleshpots of the Cote d'Azur to become chief of state of something called the "State of Vietnam." The State of Vietnam was given its independence but only within the framework of the French Union. What this meant in practice was that while the French relinquished control of much of the internal administration of the Vietnam, they retained control over foreign, defense and commercial policy. De Lattre spoke of perfecting Vietnam's freedom when the security situation allowed, but to many nationalists, and not just those involved with the Viet-Minh, the "Boa Dai solution" resembled a colonial con trick.

Let us return, then, to Greene's first meeting with General Jean de Lattre de Tassigny, their dinner date in Saigon on 26 January 1951. The general turned out to be anxious to win greater US support for the war and knowing that his guest was working for the influential, opinion shaping *Life* magazine, he was exaggeratedly attentive to his needs. Greene duly flew with de Lattre to Hanoi on 30 January 1951. The general immediately put a small plane and pilot at his disposal and encouraged him to overfly the delta defenses. That afternoon, accompanied by his friend Trevor Wilson, Greene set off, but in an entirely different direction, to Phat Diem, sixty miles south of Hanoi. Phat Diem was a largely autonomous city-state abutting the Gulf of Tonkin. It was controlled by a Catholic Prince Bishop, Le Huu Tu, and when melded with the adjoining diocese of Bui Chu, effectively exerted spiritual authority over 500,000 Catholics and wielded temporal power over much of the area's remaining, mostly Buddhist, population of half-a-million. In 1945, the Catholic Church in Vietnam had backed Ho Chi Minh's revolution but when the Franco-Viet-Minh war broke out, and as the Viet-Minh's communist outlook became more pronounced, the church shifted to a position of neutrality. In early 1950, the Vatican formally recognised Bao Dai's State of Vietnam. In Vietnam itself, the northern Catholic bishops, led by Bishop Tu, paid lip-service to the central government in Saigon, but in practice brooked no interference in their diocesan affairs. At the same time, Phat Diem's vulnerable geographical position on the edge of Viet-Minh-controlled Thanh Hoa province obliged the bishop to employ a combination of diplomacy and trade with the rebels, especially in rice abundant in his territory, to keep the war at a distance.

If all else failed, the bishop had his own army of some 3000 troops, which was just as well as a concomitant of Tu's pronounced nationalism was a refusal to allow the French base rights in his diocese. The Catholic Greene was captivated by Phat Diem, as was his friend and co-religionist Wilson. Greene also admired Tu's independence: "my number-one enemy is the French," Tu told him, "after which come the Communists." On this first occasion Greene spent just thirty-six hours in this "medieval Episcopal principality" before returning to Hanoi on 1 February. But it was soon clear that his unscheduled excursion had vexed de Lattre:

> 'Slightly picked on' and peppered with 'Godless anecdotes', he wrote of his next meeting with the general. At the time he attached little importance to the Frenchman's jibes but looking back he came to see the dinner as the moment when 'our relations began to cool', an 'inconvenience to me' but a 'disaster' for Wilson.

The nature of this disaster would not reveal itself until mid-1951. For now, after spending a fortnight in Vietnam, Greene returned home but he was determined to return as soon as possible—he had fallen in love with Indo-China—and thanks to *Life*, which commissioned a piece on the war, he was back the following October, this time for a ten-week stay. The interval between his visits witnessed two important developments. The first came in April when the bishops of Phat Diem and neighboring Bui Chu suddenly took sides in the war, declaring for Bao Dai. Mounting reports of Viet-Minh persecution of Catholics elsewhere in Vietnam seems to have persuaded the bishops to ally with Bao Dai and, by extension, the French. But Tu drove a hard bargain: the French agreed to provide financial subsidies to develop his armed forces, and meantime Tu was allowed to retain command of his troops and maintain his veto on French bases in his territory. At the end of May 1951, the inevitable happened– or inevitable once Tu had joined Bao Dai's side. The Vietminh attached Phat Diem as part of a wider offensive in the southern Red River Delta. After a month of fierce fighting, the French turned back the offensive.

(3.0 Greene with French troops, Phat Diem, December 1951.)

But de Lattre's satisfaction was tarnished by events involving Phat Diem. Tu's army had performed so poorly that it had to be rescued by French paratroopers at a cost in French blood. Afterwards an angry de Lattre accused Tu of withholding information about enemy troop movements in the build-up to the battle and insisted on the disbanding of the Catholic militia and its assimilation into the Army of the State of Vietnam. Grief for his son, Lieutenant Bernard de Lattre, who was killed in the fighting near Phat Diem, only intensified his anti-Catholic animus. The Vietminh offensive, and by extension Bernard's death, owed much to the "treachery" of the bishops.

The second development in the interval between Greene's visits was the rise to prominence of Trinh Minh Thé, a shadowy presence in *The Quiet American* but also, Greene tells us, "real enough." Indeed he was. At twenty-nine, Thé was Chief of Staff of the army of the Cao Dai, a southern-based religious sect that Greene had encountered at the start of the year. "They have a Pope, female cardinals, & their saints are Christ, Buddha, Mahomed, Victor Hugo & Auguste Comte," he wrote excitedly to his brother Hugh. "They number 2,000,000 & have a private army which at the moment is on the side of the French." The Cao Dai Holy See was in Tay Ninh, 60 miles north-west of Saigon, where Pham Cong Tac, the Caodaist pope, surrounded himself not just with cardinals of both sexes but sundry archbishops, bishops, and priests.

(4.0 'My nice bishop . . .', Le Huu Tu, 1951.)
(5.0 dedication by Tu ('souvenir') following Greene's time in Phat Diem.)

As for the sect's eclectic pantheon of saints, this reflected its blend of Buddhism, Confucianism and Christianity. "We succeeded," Tac maintained, "because we . . . perfected a first-rate religion. After all, what other can compete with ours, since we have picked the best points out of each and put them all together." Certainly Caodaism was a religion of substance. Founded in 1926, by 1945 it claimed perhaps as many as one-fifth of Cochinchina's 4.5 million people as followers.

The Cao Dai army meanwhile functioned both as the Holy See's defensive shield and, after the Franco-Vietminh war broke out, as an informal arm of the French expeditionary force. In return for French subsidies, Caodaist forces—some 15,000, with 20,000 reservists, in 1950 far bigger that the Catholic militia of the north—policed those extensive areas of Cochinchina where the faith flourished and provided the main source of popular resistance to the Communists in the south.

Then, in June 1951, Colonel Thé-he later promoted himself to general, suddenly deserted the Holy See, disappeared into jungle with 2,500 troops and a stockpile of weapons, and soon began advertising his credentials as a Third Force leader. Henceforward, he declared his policy would be "non-cooperation" with the colonial regime or its puppet Bao Dai or the Communist-dominated Viet-Minh. A number of unpleasant acts of terrorism followed, claimed by Thé's self-styled National Resistance Front, including the massive car bombing in Saigon of 9 January 1952.

In *The Quiet American*, it is Thé's violent actions which allow Greene via Fowler to arraign the United States for its idiocy in mistaking "a shoddy little bandit with two thousand men and a couple of tame tigers" for a legitimate Third Force candidate. But were the Americans really cultivating the real-life Thé in 1951-52? What we know is that US policymakers were undoubtedly worried that the stunted independence bestowed by France on Bao Dai would be insufficient to win over a majority of non-Communist nationalists to the anti-Viet-Minh cause. It was no good focusing exclusively on the military front, Washington believed; the political front too needed attention. Even as it recognised Bao Dai in 1950, the US government—the Democrat administration of Harry S. Truman—was looking for alternatives: an anti-Communist nucleus to build round if or when the French gave up the fight. Did this quest lead to Thé?

In *The Quiet American* Pyle belongs to the US Economic Mission, which gives him his CIA cover. Or to give it its real-life acronym, STEM, the "Special Technical and Economic Mission." The STEM files in the US national archives—oddly neglected by historians—confirm that the mission had numerous contacts with the Caodaists of Tay Ninh and thought highly of them, but the files contain no evidence of the USA's furnishing either the mainstream or dissident Caodaists with arms.

Intriguingly, British documents from the period, released after a Freedom of Information Act (FOIA) application, suggest that these denials may be too definite. The Foreign Office (FO) in 1951 was in receipt of a steady flow of intelligence suggesting that the Americans were "encouraging the formation of a separate Cao-Daist army" and officials agreed that the Saigon bombing was probably the unhappy consequence of US meddling. "I fear that there is nothing we can do about the foolishness of US Special Operations," minuted the Head of the SouthEast Asia Department. But there the paper trail dies. That the United States was potentially interested in a Third Force would not come as a total surprise to those familiar with the Vietnam story, but what has not been previously acknowledged is the extent to which the British were also actively seeking alternatives to Bao Dai. But why were they?

In the early 1950s Indo-China was a place where British national interests and international responsibilities converged. On the one hand, the preservation of a non-Communist Vietnam as a barrier to the spread of Communism to the rest of South-East Asia was a general Western Cold War objective. On the other, Tonkin was the forward defense of Malaya whose value to an ailing UK economy was considerable. The French, from a British standpoint, simply had to hold the line. But would they? If the French absolved themselves of responsibility, who would be prepared to lead the anti-Communist resistance? The FO doubted that Bao Dai, the playboy emperor, was up to the job. So did the Secret Intelligence Service—but where the Foreign Office could see no alternative to the wretched Bao Dai, MI6, it appears, had in mind a Catholic solution. And Greene would himself be involved in its promotion.

These shifts in the Vietnamese kaleidoscope in mid-1951 were witnessed by Greene at a distance. "I seem to have missed the bus in the last few weeks when Ho Chi Minh put on a big offensive," he wrote to Hugh at the end of June 1951. "My nice Bishop was completely surrounded in his diocese and had to be rescued by parachute troops. It would have been fun to have been with him and seen him in a crisis." He planned to return to Vietnam later that summer, but events got in the way.

In August he wrote again to Hugh: "De Lattre has become half crazy & wildly anti-Catholic since the death of his son." This was indeed the case. The general now looked on Catholics as potential quislings, none more so than Trevor Wilson, whose return to Hanoi at the end of his annual leave had been blocked by the French authorities who accused him of secretly encouraging the northern bishops to adopt anti-French attitudes.

Greene eventually returned to Vietnam in October 1951, but when he next met de Lattre—in Hanoi on 30 October—he was immediately struck by the contrast in his demeanor compared with the start of the year. The general was aloof, dyspeptic, even rude. Greene attributed this to a combination of grief for his son, hostility to all things Catholic, and a touch of Anglophobia. But there was also the Wilson factor. "He was sincerely convinced that in some obscure way, connected with the Catholicism of W[ilson] and myself and our interest in Phat Diem, we had been partly responsible for his son's death," Greene wrote later. As a result, "Trevor was thrown out of Indo-China and the FO lost a remarkable Consul and the French a great friend of their country." Trevor was innocent then. Or so Greene inferred. In fact, there is a lot more to the Wilson affair than Greene ever publicly revealed.

The first thing we must note in regard to the Greene-Wilson relationship is the espionage common denominator. Greene, as we know, had joined Secret Intelligence Services (SIS) Section V, Counter-Intelligence, during the Second World War, but resigned in May 1944 and claimed later that he never had anything more to do with the "old firm," as he called MI6. In actual fact he seems to have retained informal links to the intelligence service right through to the 1980s, passing on information gleaned during his many foreign trips, often in return for financial remuneration. As for Wilson, he is almost as elusive and enigmatic as his good friend Greene, but I have managed to piece something of a biography from his private papers and other sources.

Arthur Geoffrey Trevor-Wilson—note the hyphen, but I will continue to refer to him as Greene did in print, namely, Trevor Wilson—was born in East Molesey in the Surrey stockbroker belt on 12 August 1903. After school he went straight into business and banking and then, in 1939, at the outbreak of war, he joined the Territorial Army, and within two years found himself assigned to SIS as counter-intelligence operative. Malcolm Muggeridge, who worked with Wilson in Algiers in 1942, remembered him as "about the ablest Intelligence officer I met in the war, with an instinctive flair for the work, including all the deceits and double-crosses involved." In 1943 Wilson came back to England to work at SIS Section V's London headquarters, when and where his friendship with Greene dates from. Greene left SIS in 1944, and in 1945 Wilson joined Mountbatten's South-East Asia Command, SEAC, and it was through SEAC that Wilson and Vietnam first encountered one another. At the end of the war in Asia and the Pacific, SEAC forces oversaw the formal surrender of Japanese troops in southern Vietnam while the Chinese nationalists did the same in northern Vietnam—Japan had occupied Vietnam in and after 1941.

Wilson was sent to Hanoi in November 1945 to act as liaison between the British and Chinese forces, and over the next six months he met more-or-less weekly with a certain Ho Chi Minh.

A close bond developed between them, as Ho's surviving letters to Wilson confirm. But Wilson was also valued by the French for the way he represented their interests, and was even decorated by de Gaulle. Demobilized in 1946, he was immediately appointed to the diplomatic service, and presumably because of his intimacy with both the French and the VietMinh, he was sent back to Hanoi as British consul. Five years on, when Graham Greene arrived in Indo-China, he was still there.

As I have mentioned, Greene's publicly stated reason for visiting Vietnam in the first place in January 1951 was to see Wilson. But French security immediately questioned Greene's motives and warned de Lattre that Greene was probably still on MI6's books. On that first occasion the general let the matter ride, but by the time of Greene's second visit in autumn 1951, he was a changed man. "All these English, they're too much!" de Lattre complained. "It isn't sufficient to have a consul who is in the Secret Service, they even send me their novelists as agents and Catholic novelists into the bargain."

Whether de Lattre's charge against Greene is truly merited will be considered shortly, but in the case of the consul he was quite right: Wilson, as intelligence historian Richard Aldrich has confirmed, was an undeclared "stringer" for the regional SIS chief in Singapore. Having said that, Wilson was not the spy he once was.

Always a heavy drinker, by the early 1950s Wilson was exhibiting signs of incipient alcoholism and had developed an unfortunate habit when drunk of openly espousing views more in sympathy with the Viet-Minh than Bao Dai. Lucien Bodard remembered "a John Bull boozer—a living wine skin" who was fond of telling the French to their faces that the "whole people is Vietminh . . . you're going to be defeated!" Such outbursts irritated the colonial authorities, attracted the attention of the Sûreté, and militated against his effectiveness as an agent.

Further releases of Foreign Office documents under the FOIA mean that we can now "flesh out" the story of Wilson's downfall. In May 1951, Wilson was keen to gauge local reactions in Phat Diem to the Catholic hierarchy's declaration of support for Bao Dai's State of Vietnam and accepted a personal invitation from Le Huu Tu to spend three days in Phat Diem. Whatever he got up to there, de Lattre was soon on the warpath, denouncing Wilson to the UK Minister in Saigon for his "meddling with the Catholics." In July 1951, with de Lattre's fury showing no sign of abating, and with Wilson on the verge of being declared persona non grata, the FO decided to terminate his posting. But still the question remains ... what, exactly, had Wilson been up to at Phat Diem that so enraged de Lattre?

With MI6 files closed we are left to fill the gap. Even so, the clues point towards the encouragement of a Catholic Third Force. But what does that mean–Catholic Third Force? In 1950, although Vietnamese-born bishops accounted for only four out of sixteen Catholic bishops in total in Vietnam, they were responsible for more than half of Vietnam's estimated 1.2 million faithful and, to quote recent research by Charles Keith, they "embodied a growing desire among many Vietnamese Catholics not only for a Church freed from its missionary past but also for a Church in a nation freed from its colonial past." Phat Diem's Bishop Tu personified this nationalist outlook. And Wilson was friends with Tu. Whether of his own volition or encouraged by MI6, he encouraged Tu to assert his independence of Bao Dai and of France.

The neglected Wilson-Greene correspondence in the Burns Library at Boston College offers some further pointers. "I must not say much in an open letter," Wilson wrote to Greene in March 1951, a few weeks after Greene went home, "but events have moved swiftly since your visit ... [and] I find plenty of support ... for the Catholic solution from quarters where I should have hardly expected it." In May, Wilson wrote again of "fresh & interesting evolutions in Phat Diem & Bui Chu" and how the Catholic solution was "developing nicely."

But this was as far as Wilson got. De Lattre denounced him as a spy and deported him from Vietnam. De Lattre, we should remember, also believed that Greene was Wilson's co-conspirator, an accusation Greene vigorously denied in later years. However, as the Wilson-Greene correspondence shows, Greene was certainly aware of what Wilson was up to in Phat Diem. More tellingly, there is an intriguing hint in a Greene letter to his mistress, Catherine Walston, at the start of September 1951, six weeks before his second visit to Vietnam. Greene said he had been contacted by movie producer and one-time SIS agent Alexander Korda.

'The "old firm" have asked Korda if I'd do a job for them," Greene wrote to Catherine. "I don't know what. K's arranging a meeting...."

Short of gaining access to Greene's MI6 files, we can only guess as to what this job involved. It is tempting to suggest that it had something to do with Phat Diem and the Catholic solution. As for Wilson, he lobbied the French authorities to be allowed to return to Indo-China so he could put his affairs in order. Eventually, in November, he was granted a temporary visa.

Greene was already in Hanoi by then and, to start with, he looked forward to seeing Wilson again. But as the scale of de Lattre's anger towards the now ex-consul revealed itself, he began to wonder if it was wise to make contact. French surveillance of Greene's movements had become stifling and he was distressed that his freedom to operate as a journalist, never mind as an MI6 agent, was so circumscribed. Worse still, Wilson cabled that he was keen to go back to Phat Diem. "I wish to God T[revor] was not following that plan of his," Greene wrote. "I can see ... that he's only causing trouble not only to himself but to me & all his friends. Such a lot of trouble too."

On 18 November Greene dined with de Lattre for the last time. "Gen[eral] asked me if I was a member of the Secret Service & associated in it with Trevor," he wrote in his diary. "Felt he didn't believe my denial ... Said he had taken my part against the police but was worried by the reports they brought in. Accepted my word but does he? Felt I had not defended T[revor] enough, but the prejudices there are too great." The next day de Lattre boarded an aircraft for France. He would not return. Diagnosed with bone cancer, he went home for medical treatment but died on 11 January 1952.

(6.0, 7.0 Greene at orphanage, Phat Diem, 1951)

As he departed Hanoi, however, de Lattre insisted to an aide that Greene was a spy. "Why should anyone come to this war for four hundred dollars?" he asked, a reference to Greene's *Life* fee. The sardonic answer Greene gave his readers in later years was that de Lattre had mislaid a zero: $4,000 was well worth the effort. As to the idea he was a spy, this, Greene maintained, was a figment of de Lattre's grief-addled mind. Yet the denial does not fully convince, not when CIA veterans have attested that he took on "a short-term operational assignment because Trevor was gone," not when his journal for 1951 records a number of meetings with known members of the old firm, and when Norman Sherry is convinced that he was not only seeking information but talent-spotting local agents, "as any good spy would do."

I would like to close with a few words about the fate of the Catholic solution. When Greene first visited Phat Diem in January 1951 he had been moved and amazed. The strength of Tu and his flock "was an idea, and that idea love of their country. Christianity too is a form of patriotism. These Viet-Namese belonged to the City of God." By the time of Greene's next visit to Phat Diem, in November 1951, Tu and his Army of God had been humiliated and Greene's romanticized image of the bishop had been shattered. He now took issue with Tu's failure to address the social needs of his people: "Always money for Churches," he noted in his journal, "never for hospitals or education."

In Third Force terms, Catholicism and nationalism were all very well, but to compete successfully with the Viet-Minh, to win hearts and minds, as it were, Greene now recognized the importance of tackling poverty and other social grievances. But the bishop "was only interested in building more and more churches." He went back to Hanoi depressed.

But this was not quite the end of his Phat-Diem connection. Rumors soon abounded—well-founded—that Phat Diem had been over-run by the Viet-Minh. Sensing a journalistic scoop, he went back, arriving on 16 December 1951. The scene that greeted him was "shocking." Ever since he first went to Malaya, Greene had been desperate to experience war in the raw. Now he had his fill: "never have I seen so many corpses." After blundering into the no-man's-land between the French and Viet-Minh lines, exposing himself to grave danger, the local French commander decided that a tall, gangly, nosy British novelist was a liability in a war zone and ordered him back to Hanoi.

With this, Greene's interest in this particular Catholic solution ended.

Henceforth the Americans would be the exclusive proponents of the Catholic solution, eventually alighting on Ngo Dinh Diem in 1954 as the chosen one. Still, as I hope I have shown, there was a brief period when the British were also active in this regard, and when Greene himself was caught up in the kind of plot and entangled with a cast of characters—imperious French generals, Catholic warrior-bishops, British secret agents—that would not have been out of place in one of his own novels.

Fact in this instance was every bit as compelling as the fiction it spawned.

Photographs #1 and #3 courtesy of the Graham Greene collection, John J. Burns Library, Boston College, USA, of Greene in Vietnam 1951-1952.
Photographs #2,#4,#5,#6, and #7 courtesy of the Graham Greene collection, Georgetown University Library Special Collections, USA.

**Kevin Ruane** is Professor of Modern History at Canterbury Christ Church University. He has published widely on many aspects of modern international history, including the Cold War and the Anglo-American "special relationship." His most recent book is *Churchill and the Bomb* (Bloomsbury, 2016). He is now working on another book—a fusion of history, literature and biography—entitled *Graham Greene's Vietnam War* which amplifies the themes he outlined in "The Hidden History of Graham Greene's Vietnam War: Fact, Fiction and The Quiet American" in the journal *History* (2012). The story of Greene's real-life experiences in Indochina (involving espionage, opium, the CIA, exotic religious cults, the French secret service, a brutal war and an exotic location) is as compelling as anything in his fiction.

# "The Invisible Japanese Gentlmen:" Graham Greene's Literary Influence in Japan

## Motonori Sato

The 2014 Graham Greene International Festival

## Introduction

*May We Borrow Your Husband? And Other Comedies of the Sexual Life*[1] is a collection of short stories by Greene published in 1967. Contained within this collection, the first edition of which boasted a "swinging" dustjacket, is a short story entitled "The Invisible Japanese Gentlemen," which begins as follows:

> There were eight Japanese gentlemen having a fish dinner at Bentley's. They spoke to each other rarely in their incomprehensible tongue, but always with a courteous smile and often with a small bow. All but one of them wore glasses. Sometimes the pretty girl who sat in the window beyond gave them a passing glance, but her own problem seemed too serious for her to pay real attention to anyone in the world except herself and her companion.[2]

This is a charming example of the "mass-observation" of Japanese travelers, whose manners must have looked curiously foreign to the English eye. Significantly, however, the narrator's attention focuses more on "the pretty girl," who is a budding novelist, and her fiancé than on the Japanese gentlemen; indeed, the story revolves around the couple's discussion of their future, punctuated by short descriptions of the foreign group. Despite the fact that their seats are close to each other, the Japanese gentlemen remain "invisible" to the eye of the young female writer.

This short story is suggestive of prevailing attitudes toward race. On the one hand, the imagination of the female protagonist does not stretch beyond Europe, her first novel having been entitled *The Chelsea Set*, while her second is to be set in St. Tropez. On the other hand, the male narrator is not just a mass-observer, but also a novelist whose attention focuses on the English couple and the Japanese group alike. In a nutshell, the Japanese gentlemen are at least *visible* to the eye of the narrator and Greene, while they are invisible to the eye of the protagonist. This ambiguity is perhaps the hallmark of Greene's literature.

The question I would like to pose here is simply this: *Are we (i.e. the Japanese) invisible to your eyes?* If we are not, then I think I can end my discussion here. If you can see us, you can observe us and, moreover, this act of observation will lead you to acknowledge a foreign culture. If, however, the answer is in the affirmative, it will be necessary to press on with this paper since the aim of my discussion is to introduce to the reader certain links that connect Greene and his Japanese readership, and

---

[1] Greene, Graham. *Comedies of the Sexual Life*. London: Bodley Head, 1967. 137-141.
[2] Greene, Graham. "The Invisible Japanese Gentlemen." *May We Borrow Your Husband? And Other Stories*, 137.

to make Japanese gentlemen appear less invisible to your eyes. In the pages that follow I will focus on two writers whose works constitute precisely such links: Saiichi Maruya and Shusaku Endo.

## Saiichi Maruya

Maruya is a writer perhaps not well-known in English-speaking countries, but who has been one of the most important and influential in Japan since his debut in the 1960s. He studied English literature at Tokyo University in the postwar years and taught at Kokugakuin University in the 1950s and the early 1960s when he turned full-time writer, producing a dozen well-crafted novels. He was most productive, however, as a critic and essayist, writing about almost all aspects of human life. As a critic he was as somber and serious as T. S. Eliot, writing unashamedly about the great tradition of Japanese literature; as an essayist he was more relaxed, discussing humorously our daily lives, relations between men and women, drinking, and fashion. He was also a translator of English literature, and in particular of James Joyce, translating *Ulysses* and *A Portrait of the Artist as a Young Man* in the 1960s, and subsequently revising these translations in the later stages of his life. After his death in 2012, the complete works of Maruya were published (and the time has perhaps now come to discuss seriously his literary contribution).

Maruya was an academic-turned-writer, and his academic work consisted of writing essays and translations. The academic essays he wrote in the 1950s and the early 1960s demonstrate his shrewd understanding of modernist literature. For example, in "The Gentlemen from the Western Country," he claims that the essence of modernist writers such as Joyce, Eliot, and Pound lies in their experience of exile:

> Because they did not have their mother language, they could discover and present a new function of language; because they did not have tradition, they were able to gain an acute awareness of tradition; because they came from outside of Europe (or at least from the peripheral parts of Europe), they could capture the grandeur of Europe with such an extraordinary vividness. Namely, because of these positions, they could prove the thesis that the true avant-garde stems from classicism. Thus, their work became the most precise and beautiful expression of all the anxiety and aspirations of a Europe which was aware of its own decline in the wake of the fin de siècle and the First World War.[3]

What he learned from his study of English modernism was the thesis that the avant-garde and classicism are not mutually exclusive, but that they are two sides of the same coin. This is a point that he repeatedly emphasized in both his literary criticism and his literary creation.

Recently there have been plenty of independent translators of English literature in Japan, but the task has been chiefly assigned to those specialists whose choice of works to translate has determined the course of their academic careers. Maruya is now remembered as a translator of Joyce partly because of his commitment to modernism, and partly because of his definitive translations of *Ulysses* and *A Portrait of the Artist as a*

---

3 Maruya, Saiichi. "The Gentlemen from the Western Country." *Nashinotsubute*. Tokyo: Shobunsha. 1966, 218-242. 238; translation my own.

*Young Man*. However, in the 1950s when he started his career as an academic, the first writer that Maruya opted to translate was Graham Greene. He translated three novels consecutively: *Brighton Rock* in 1952, *Loser Takes All* in 1956, and *It's a Battlefield* in 1959. In addition, Maruya revised his translation of *Brighton Rock* in 1959 when it was included in the Selected Works of Graham Greene.[4] In short, the 1950s was the decade when the translation of Greene into Japanese took flight, and Maruya was part of the driving force behind this movement.

Interestingly, in the afterword to his revised translation of *Brighton Rock*, Maruya went so far as to suggest that this work was the best among all of Greene's novels:

> For it includes all the aspects of Greene: the plot of detective fiction, Joycean technique, Catholicism, his boyhood interests, feminism, the Persecutor and the Persecuted, exciting and poetic urban landscapes, cinematic influences, obsession with Evil.... This novel offers an archetype of "Greeneland."

Maruya's comment on *Brighton Rock* demonstrates his rigorous understanding of the novel and his keen attachment to "Greeneland." In fact, during his translation, he wrote three essays on Greene: "What is Entertainment?" (1953), "The Style of Graham Greene" (1959), and "Fatherless Family" (1958). His ideas appear somewhat half-baked; however, his passion is apparent here as in the afterword. It seems as if he were immersed in the world of Graham Greene, being at a loss as to what to say. Such a tendency is perhaps inherent in the nature of translation, with Maruya passing through an English landscape unknown to himself while trying to find his own voice as a novelist.

His translation of Greene, I would urge, served as an apprenticeship for Maruya the novelist. He made his debut in 1960 with *Fleeing from the Face of Jehovah*, and turned full-time writer with *Grass for My Pillow* in 1966. He also published *Singular Rebellion* in 1972, *Rain in the Wind* in 1975, *Tree Shadows* in 1988, and *A Mature Woman* in 1993. Moreover, Maruya would receive most of the most prestigious literary awards with these novels and, poignantly, proved fortunate enough to find a collaborator who was willing to translate his novels for an English audience. This accomplice was Dennis Keene,[5] a poet, academic, and translator who taught English literature at the Japan Women's University.[6]

The first Maruya novel that Keene translated into English was *Singular Rebellion*, which was published in 1986 to huge acclaim (Greene's comment was brief: "I liked it very much."); the second comprised a collection of four stories entitled *Rain in the Wind,* which was published in 1990 and awarded a special prize for the Independent Foreign Fiction Award in 1991; the third, *A Mature Woman*, was published in 1995; and the fourth and last, *Grass for My Pillow,* was published in 2002. The author's and translator's collaboration ended when Keene died in 2007.

---

4 Maruya's translation of *Brighton Rock* constituted the sixth volume in a fifteen-volume edition of *The Selected Works of Graham Greene*. Hayakawa-shobo was to update this edition with a twenty-five volume, definitive edition of the complete works of Graham Greene. For a bibliography of Graham Greene in Japan, see Iwasaki. Iwasaki, Masaya. *A Bibliography of Graham Greene in Japan.* Tokyo: Sairyusha, 2010.

5 For Dennis Keene's academic career, see Powell. Powell, Brian. "Dennis Keen: Poet and Translator." *The Independent* (London) February 26, 2008. 34.

6 Maruya, Saiichi."The Independent Foreign Fiction Award: In the Middle of the Rainy Season." *The Independent* (London) June 22, 1991, 28.

## *Grass for My Pillow*

Translations are destined to be overdue. It took fourteen years for Greene's *Brighton Rock* to cross the Oceans and reach the Japanese shore.[7] Likewise, it took exactly the same number of years for Maruya's *Singular Rebellion* to reach the English shore. It is perhaps ironic therefore that Maruya's last work to cross the sea was *Grass for My Pillow,* his first novel to be published subsequent to his becoming a full-time writer, a gap spanning some thirty-seven years.

I will discuss the novel in some detail later, since this work is to Maruya what *Brighton Rock* is to Greene, i.e. it includes all of his aspects and more importantly was written under the direct influence of Greene. Before doing so, however, I would like to argue that Greene's influence on Maruya is as huge and enduring as that of modernism. Let us begin by briefly examining *Rain in the Wind*. On receiving a special prize for the Independent Foreign Fiction Award in 1991, Maruya contributed an article to *The Independent*, speculating on the reason for his winning this award:

> I assume the prize has been awarded mainly to the title story, and that in itself gives me particular pleasure since the real hero of that work ... is Japanese literature itself. As a Japanese writer, it is part of my fate to write under the influence of European literature, a fate that I have always embraced with pleasure. But a much larger aspect of that fate is to be aware that one is still writing in the great tradition of the literature of my own country, a destiny which, I regret to say, few of our writers in this century, particularly nowadays, truly acknowledge.[8]

Maruya's philosophy, put simply, appears to be this: the key to successful writing is writing under the influence of European literature while being aware that one is still writing in the great tradition of the literature of one's own country.

At first glance, Maruya's ideas look conservative and anachronistic, especially when he mentions "the great tradition of the literature of my own country." However, his statement is corroborated by his insight into modernism, and the thesis that the true avant-garde stems from classicism. Through this, he obliges a new generation of writers to become modernists—this is a point to which I will return later during my treatment of *Grass for My Pillow*.

What traces then, one may ask, of the influence of European literature can one detect in *Rain in the Wind?* Certainly, Maruya is indebted to Nabokov's last novel, *The Gift*, for its metafictional framework. However, in the afterword to his own novel, Maruya reveals that a direct source of inspiration was an episode concerning Oscar Wilde that appeared in Greene's autobiography *A Sort of Life*. This is how an encounter between Greene's father and his friend George on the one hand, and the disgraced writer on the other, is narrated.

> Once—it was in Naples—they had a curious encounter. A stranger hearing them speak in English asked whether he might join them over their coffee. There was something familiar and to them vaguely disagreeable about his face, but he kept them charmed by his wit for more than an

---

[7] "Translator's Afterword." *Brighton Rock*. Trans. Saiichi Maruya. 1959. Tokyo: Hayakawa-shobo, 1979. 283-284.
[8] Maruya. "The Independent Foreign Fiction Award: In the Middle of the Rainy Season," 28.

hour before he said goodbye. They didn't exchange names even at parting and he let them pay for his drink which was certainly not coffee. It was some while before they realized in whose company they had been. The stranger was Oscar Wilde, who not very long before had been released from prison. "Think," my father would always conclude his story, "how lonely he must have been to have expended so much time and wit on a couple of schoolmasters on holiday." It never occurred to him that Wilde was paying for his drink in the only currency he had.[9]

Maruya incorporated this episode into his own narrative, working in a substitute for Wilde. According to a reviewer from *The Independent*, *Rain in the Wind* is "an extended literary adventure in which an academic tries to research and reconstruct an encounter, many years earlier, between his father and a celebrated poet."[10] Maruya chose Santoka Taneda, a Japanese poet famous for his free verse, as a substitute for Wilde, but let him pay for his drink, too, in the only currency he had. This episode set the tone and theme of the novella. On receiving the special award for this novella, Maruya must have been thankful to Greene for his influence: it was only a shame that the Japanese writer could not deliver an address of thanks to Greene who had died a couple of months before the award was announced.

Let us now turn to discuss in greater detail *Grass for My Pillow*. In his translator's introduction to the novel, Dennis Keene presents a summary of the story:

*Sasamakura (Grass for My Pillow)*, first published in 1966, is a novel about a man who successfully evades military conscription from October 1940 until the end of the Pacific War in August 1945, and the delayed consequences of this refusal to conform as he experiences them twenty years later, in 1965.[11]

The man in question, as a consequence, has a dual identity: In postwar Japanese society Shokichi Hamada is a middle-aged university administrator, living in peace with his wife in a small flat; during the war period Kenji Sugiura is a young sand artist, traveling all over Japan in order to escape punishment for the most serious of offenses. The novel alternates so seamlessly between the story of Hamada and the story of Sugiura that the readers are often lost in the vertiginous development of the plot.

As one can see from this brief introduction, Maruya is heavily indebted to Greene for his literary creation. As witnessed above, Maruya once enumerated the characteristics of "Greeneland": "the plot of detective fiction, Joycean technique, Catholicism, his boyhood interests, feminism, the Persecutor and the Persecuted, exciting and poetic urban landscapes, cinematic influences, obsession with Evil."[12] If one discounts Catholicism and replaces it with ethics, these characteristics all apply to Maruya's modernist thriller. In particular, Green's empathy with the Persecuted furnishes the basic tone and theme of the novel via a characterization of Sugiura, a fugitive on the verge of paranoia. To my mind, Sugiura

---

9 Greene, Graham. *A Sort of Life*. London: Bodley Head, 1971, 26.
10 Winder, Robert. "Foreign Fiction / A Far Cry from Kensington: Robert Winder Reflects on the First Annual Shortlist for the Pounds 10,000 Independent Award." *The Independent* (London) June 1, 1991. 29.
11 Keene, Dennis. "Translator's Introduction." *Grass for My Pillow*. Trans. Dennis Keene, New York: Columbia University Press, 2002. 1-14, 1.
12 Maruya, Saiichi. "Translator's Afterword," 283; translation my own.

is reminiscent of Conrad Drover, a character from Greene's *It's a Battlefield,* who is deluded into thinking that the Assistant Commissioner is persecuting him. Hamada also suffers from paranoia, with the stigma of being a draft resister, which slowly drives him into a corner.

Of particular poignancy is the way the story of Hamada is smoothly overtaken by that of Sugiura:

Hamada turned over the pages, and read aloud one poem that caught his attention:

Again this fitful
slumber bamboo
grass for my pillow
one night of dreams
alone to bind us

"Pretty difficult stuff, isn't it?"

Kuwano glanced over his arm at the page, and said: "Not all that difficult, you know. There's a certain amount of word play that perhaps requires elucidation, the bamboo associations, for example..." But he paused, looking slightly embarrassed....

"What does 'bamboo grass for my pillow' mean?"

"Well, I'm not absolutely sure, but I suppose it's much like the conventional pillow of grass on which the traveler always laid his homeless head, and is thus the same symbol of transience, etc. What's going on in this case is, presumably, a shared pillow; one night of love while traveling around, over as soon as begun.... It is perhaps conceivable that, in the Manyoshu period, people really did sleep while they were travelling in places where there was lots of bamboo grass. After all, it's a very tenacious weed. Luxuriates all over the country. Still, it couldn't have been comfortable, prickly stuff like that. Hardly the sort of thing for a pillow."

Hamada interrupted the flow of professional talk:

"That rustling it makes wouldn't let you sleep very well. Almost unbearable, with no place to rest your head. A restless journey."

Kuwano went suddenly silent, looking intensely at Hamada's face. The association he's made between the sound of bamboo grass and restless journeying had obviously been read as a direct reference to Hamada's wartime experience as a draft resister, and Hamada immediately regretted his own words since he didn't want to get back onto that subject again. Kuwano went on looking at him, and Hamada went on being looked at, for the phrase "bamboo grass for my pillow" had certainly meant something to him, but he couldn't think what. Could it be the sprigs of bamboo grass used for the Festival of the Weaver in July? No, surely not that.[13]

The answer to the question of what the phrase "bamboo grass for my pillow" means to Hamada is provided directly after his story has ended. In the case of modernism, including Greene's writing, this would be done by means of a "stream of consciousness," since the agent of remembrance is Hamada, not his alter-ego

---

[13] Maruya, Saiichi. *Grass for My Pillow*. Trans. Dennis Keene. New York: Columbia University Press, 2002., 154-155.

Sugiura. However, Maruya gives a new twist to this modernist technique; the story of Hamada is to be hijacked by the story of Sugiura without any break occurring between the two narratives. Thus, the next paragraph starts as follows:

> The town of Wakayama was full of soldiers, and Sugiura, the sand artist, lived with an oppressive awareness of them, feeling a peculiar shock one morning when he saw a group of them, who'd spent the night in the same lodging house as himself, going off to join their division.[14]

This sudden change in the time scale is what makes *Grass for My Pillow* distinctively modernist. David Lodge describes the modernist handling of temporality as follows:

> [M]odern fiction eschews the straight chronological ordering of its material, and the use of a reliable, omniscient and intrusive narrator. It employs, instead, either a single, limited point of view, or multiple viewpoints, all more or less limited and fallible; and it tends toward a complex or fluid handling of time, involving much cross-reference back and forward across the temporal span of the action.[15]

Maruya's fluid handling of time is, however, double-edged. On the one hand, the smooth transition from one narrative to another embodies the continuity between wartime and postwar Japanese society in which the nationalist mindset remains intact. On the other hand, the shuttling back and forth that takes place between the two narratives is not as smooth as is typically exhibited in the stream-of-consciousness technique. In fact, the transition is rather abrupt and disjunctive, which serves to make his readers pause and think about the links between past and present. This effect acts as a challenge that Maruya invites his readers to take up. Indeed, it is ironic that the only point concerning the English-language edition with which I would take issue concerns the handling of precisely this transition: either Dennis Keene, or the editor of the Columbia University Press dared to put the image of the mushroom cloud produced by the explosion of an atomic bomb on the front cover, which ruined Maruya's brilliant avant-garde strategy by regularly separating the two narratives using a double spacing.

To conclude, Maruya's *Grass for My Pillow* is a modernist novel whose narrative is peopled with the Persecutor and the Persecuted, the villains and heroes of "Greeneland". Furthermore, the novel also employs and updates a modernist handling of time through a simultaneous attempt to maintain and disrupt the natural flow of the narrative; the readers are compelled to pause and consider the relationship between past and present, wartime and postwar societies and mindsets. The final element I would like to add to these modernist techniques concerns a dimension of paradoxical modernist heritage. As a critic, Maruya had been adamant that the true avant-garde stems from classicism. This belief he set out to put into practice by embedding a medieval poem about "grass for my pillow" into the text and encouraging his disgraced anti-hero to embrace it. Thus, Maruya embodies an ideal author,

---

14 Ibid., 155.
15 Lodge, David. "The Language of Modernist Fiction: Metaphor and Metonymy." *Modernism: A Guide to European Literature 1890-1930*. Ed. Malcolm Bradbury and James McFarlane. 1976. London: Penguin Books, 1991. 481-496. 481.

writing under the influence of European literature while being aware that he is still writing in the great tradition of the literature of his own country.

## Shusaku Endo

Shusaku Endo is perhaps one of the most popular and accessible Japanese writers for an English-language readership. Since having been baptized a Christian at the age of twelve, he immersed himself in Christian writing. In the postwar years he studied French literature at Keio University, and in the early 1950s he went to France to study French Catholic literature. On returning to Japan in 1953, he began to establish himself as a novelist, while regularly contributing literary criticism pieces to journals. In spite of his ill health, Endo was a prolific writer. To name only his most ambitious, successful novels, he published *Umi to Dokuyaku* in 1958 (*The Sea and Poison* in 1972), *Chinmoku* in 1966 (*Silence* in 1969), *Samurai* in 1980 (*The Samurai* in 1982), *Sukyandaru* in 1986 (*Scandal* in 1988), and *Fukai Kawa* in 1993 (*Deep River* in 1995). He was able to find collaborators who were keen to translate his major novels into English before they became long overdue. Moreover, the short interval between the Japanese and English publications is evidence of his global popularity.

Thanks to his translators' enthusiasm, Greene was able to read Endo's novels in English; in fact, Greene was to send his comments on *Silence* to Endo, the two men being mutual admirers. In his essays, Endo mentioned Greene as often as François Mauriac, almost as if Greene were his friend.

Interestingly, the following encounter between these two men is said to have taken place. In 1985, when Endo visited London, he came across an old English gentleman in a three-piece suit in the elevator of the hotel he was staying in. The gentleman asked him "Which floor?" When Endo replied, he pushed the third floor for Endo and the fifth floor for himself. As soon as they parted, Endo called the reception and made sure that the gentleman was Graham Greene. Endo left a message and Greene called him back and asked him out for a drink in the bar. One can only imagine what their encounter was like: the English gentleman was 81-years-old, the Japanese gentleman 62. It was an encounter between two of the greatest writers of the twentieth century. This is, in fact, Endo's favorite story, and there are several variations on it. Endo tailored his story, depending on his mood. My favorite version is a comical one in which Endo reveals an awkward situation in the bar where he talked to Greene in French and could not make himself understood.[16] Imagine the silence which must have fallen upon the two old gentlemen, shaking hands yet incapable of understanding each other. Endo was quick to call the interpreter who was accompanying him, and ended this embarrassingly awkward situation. In this essay, Endo confesses that after they started to exchange letters about their works, he started to read Greene's novels seriously either in Japanese or in French.[17] My guess, however, is that he always read Greene in Japanese.

Perhaps Endo could neither speak nor read English, in which case he was trying to fathom the depth of "Greeneland" through translations. However, this does not mean

---

16 Endo, Shusaku. "An Encounter." 1985. *The Collected Works of Shusaku Endo. Vol. 13.* Tokyo: Sinchosha, 2000. 381-383, 382.
17 Ibid.

that his reading experience was impoverished for having done so. In 1954, when he turned novelist, Endo published a collection of essays entitled *The Problems of Catholic Writers,* and devoted one chapter to Greene, in which he demonstrated his serious commitment to Catholicism and his sympathetic understanding of Greene's religious writing.

## Silence

This chapter on Greene bears the curious title "The Sin of Pity," and is a piece of writing that shows brilliantly what Endo, a budding novelist, had learned from reading the elder Catholic writer. This essay provides a context in which to discuss Endo's masterpiece *Silence*, and in the remainder of this paper I would like to furnish a summary of this as yet untranslated essay and link it with the major theme of the novel in question.

Endo's point is crystal clear: in the novels of Greene, pity is the cause of a chain of sins:

> It is intriguing to ask why Greene started to explore seriously the theme that an excess of pity would not still a sadness in others, nor help alleviate their agony, but [would] lead his protagonist to [commit] horrible sins. *The Heart of the Matter* is a further exploration of this theme, a world of the hell of pity.[18]

Endo claims that The *Heart of the Matter* is a case in point and quotes Scobie's bitter observation on life and love to support his insight:

> When he was young, he had thought love had something to do with understanding, but with age he knew that no human being understood another. Love was the wish to understand, and presently with constant failure the wish died, and love died too perhaps or changed into this painful affection, loyalty, pity . . . [19]

Endo thus points out five sins that Scobie has committed because of an excess of pity: borrowing money for Louise's journey to South Africa, adultery with Helen, receiving Communion without making a Confession, Ali's death, and the worst of all: Scobie's suicide.

However, Endo here is not criticizing Scobie for his sins, but is describing Scobie's sins with compassion. What is intriguing about his argument is the way he is torn between his devotion to Catholicism and his commitment as a writer of humanity. On the one hand, Endo explains to his Japanese readers what Scobie's pity means in terms of Catholicism:

> The Church orders a human being to do his best for the happiness and salvation of others. But it does not mean that he should put his own eternal salvation at risk to do so. Charles Péguy let Jeanne d'Arc cry out "Oh my Lord, if there is any human being condemned to Hell, condemn me instead to burn in Hell for eternity." Catholicism would criticize this aspiration while regarding it as a sublime prayer. That is, it means that it disregards the grace of God working on the destiny of each individual.[20]

---

18 Endo "The Sin of Pity," 42; translation my own.
19 Greene, Graham. *The Heart of the Matter*. 1948. London: Vintage, 2004, 236.
20 Endo, "The Sin of Pity," 46; translation my own

Scobie's pity leads him to take the place of God and to disregard the grace of God, which is a fatal mistake.

As a Catholic writer Endo is, however, more sympathetic to Scobie. He claims that "a Catholic writer, being a Catholic, will pray furtively that the soul of his own character, in spite of his sins, should be saved in the world of eternity."[21] Endo, while being aware of Catholic viewpoints, sticks to the point that we are human, not divine:

> It is God who judges Scobie, not us humans. As Scobie thought, we cherish the last part that neither we nor others can understand. And it is this secret chamber of our souls to which God sends the light of grace.[22]

Endo thus emphasizes the double-edged nature of Scobie's pity. While it results in numerous mistakes and sins, there are moments when it elevates Scobie almost to the height of a saint. Endo gives an example of Scobie praying to God for a dying girl. Endo ends this chapter with a question, which seems to me to be asked of God: "Why can we not think that God wiped the tears from Scobie's eyes and touched his tired face when he departed from the earth?"[23]

As for the plot of *Silence,* I can find no better synopsis than the one given by Martin Scorsese, whose film adaptation of this novel is long overdue.

*Silence* is the story of a man who learns—so painfully—that God's love is more mysterious than he knows, that He leaves much more to the ways of men than we realize, and that He is always present . . . even in His silence. For me, it is the story of the one who begins on the path of Christ and who ends replaying the role of Christianity's greatest villain, Judas. He almost literally follows in his footsteps. In so doing, he comes to understand the role of Judas. This is one of the most painful dilemmas in all of Christianity.[24]

The man in question, Rodrigues, a Portuguese Jesuit, is betrayed by a Judas figure, Kichijiro, and, being tested in extremely cruel and painful ways, begins to identify himself with Christ only to realize ultimately that he is not a Christ, but a Judas. He ends up finding himself a traitor, stamping on the image of Christ, as Kichijiro does, in order to prove that he has renounced his faith. Briefly stated, this is the main plot of the novel.

Will the soul of Rodrigues be saved in the world of eternity? This is perhaps the question which Endo is asking his readers, for Rodrigues is the Portuguese Scobie, as Endo is the Japanese Greene. In his essay on Greene, Endo once claimed: "It is God who judges Scobie, not us humans . . . [W]e cherish the last part that neither we nor others can understand.[25]" We can replace Scobie with Rodrigues, and believe that "it is this secret chamber of our souls to which God sends the light of grace." In the climax of the novel, encouraged by Ferreira, a respected Jesuit who decided to apostatize in order to save some Japanese Christians from suffering, Rodrigues follows in his senior's footsteps.

---

21 Ibid., 47; translation my own.
22 Endo, "The Sin of Pity," 47; translation my own.
23 Ibid., 48; translation my own.
24 Scorsese, Martin. "Foreword." *Silence*. London: Peter Owen, 2007. 1-3. 2.
25 "The Sin of Pity." *The Collected Works of Shusaku Endo*. Vol. 12. Tokyo: Sinchosha, 2000. 41-48,47; translation my own.

The priest raises his foot. In it he feels a dull, heavy pain. This is no mere formality. He will now trample on what he has considered the most beautiful thing in his life, on what he has believed most pure, on what is filled with the ideals and the dreams of man. How his foot aches! And then the Christ in bronze speaks to the priest:

"Trample! Trample! I more than anyone know of the pain in your foot. Trample! It was to be trampled on by men that I was born into this world. It was to share men's pain that I was born into this world. It was to share men's pain that I carried my cross."

The priest rested his foot on the fumie. Dawn broke. And far in the distance the cock crew. [26]

God was no longer silent. It does not matter whether the voice was internal or external. What matters is the fact that Rodrigues could bask in "the light of grace" which God had sent to him. In addition, his soul was saved precisely because of the pity he showed to the suffering Japanese Christians. In fact, it was Rodrigues who found himself shouting "Trample! Trample!" when Kichijiro complained that he would be put to the test of stamping on the image of God.[27] He had acted on instinct, out of "a feeling of pity."

As we have seen, for Endo, pity is a double-edged emotion. On the one hand, it sets in play a chain of sins. Rodrigues's pity will bring about his own downfall since Kichijiro, having been released, goes on to betray Rodrigues. On the other hand, this most human feeling elevates Rodrigues to the height of a saint and allows him to hear the internal voice of God when he is most in need of it. I would like to interpret this as a moment of grace and argue that Endo is a Catholic believer as well as a Catholic writer. In *Silence*, Endo shows a benevolent consequence of pity as well as its malicious consequence. And ultimately, it is when Endo embraces its duality that he comes closest to Greene.

---

26 *Silence*. Trans. William Johnson. 1969. London: Peter Owen, 2007, 271.
27 bid., 95.

**Motonori Sato** is Professor of English at Keio University in Japan, where he teaches modernism, film studies, and film production. His research interest lies primarily in British modernism and British cinema. He is the author of numerous articles and Book chapters as well as his monograph *The Poetics of the British New Wave: British Cinema and the Genealogy of Social Realism* (Kyoto: Minerva Publishing Company, 2012). His book, *Graham Greene and the Cinema,* is forthcoming from Keio University Press. He is currently researching the legacy of modernism in contemporary literature.

# "All Writers Are Equal but Some Writers Are More Equal Than Others:" Some Reflections On Links and Contrasts Between Graham Greene and George Orwell

## Neil Sinyard

The 2011 Graham Greene International Festival

The title of this paper is somewhat frivolous and of course indebted to, and a variation on, one of Orwell's immortal slogans in *Animal Farm*. Yet all writers *are* equal in the sense that all of us are potential writers with stories to tell and, at the point of entry, i.e. the blank page or blank screen staring at you, we are all equal. It is at that point, though, that *equality* ends and *quality* starts. There are two relevant quotations I would like to cite here.

Firstly, from Greene's introduction to a book by the brother of the actor Charles Laughton, Tom Laughton, called *Pavilions by the Sea: The Memoirs of a Hotel-Keeper* (1977), where Greene writes "Rashly I encouraged him to write a book—rashly, because that hackneyed phrase everyone has one book inside him is deceptive and totally untrue. Everyone has the material in his memories for many books, but that is not the same thing at all." Secondly, at the end of "Fielding and Sterne," Greene quotes T.S. Eliot: "At the moment when one writes ... one is what one is, and the damage of a lifetime ... cannot be repaired at the moment of composition."

In *Speaking to Each Other, Volume Two* (1970), Richard Hoggart said of Orwell that "he was one of those writers who *are* what they write," and I think Greene was the same. He and Orwell did not just write for a living; they lived to write. I think one of the reasons that both of them were resistant for a long time to the idea of a biography—and it is curious that they should share one biographer, Michael Shelden—was that both felt that their books told more about them than an account of their lives would. And what made them "more equal" than most other writers of the last century was their ability to cross the cultural divide: to write in a manner that commanded the attention and study of the academic community—for I would guess that collectively, the number of books written about Greene and Orwell would total well over one hundred—but to write also in a manner that was accessible to a mass readership and has entered the public consciousness. Think only of Orwellian phrases and concepts like "Big Brother" and "Room 101" from *Nineteen Eighty-Four* and how they have been used and abused and what they now portend. In Greene's case, hardly a week goes by without coming across some reference to a Greene-like phrase—"Our Man in somewhere-or-other," or "a *quiet* American." Even Peter Mandelson lifted the title of "The Third Man" for his political memoirs, presumably in the full knowledge that the central theme of Greene's screenplay is betrayal.

They were born within a year or so of each other—Orwell in 1903 and Greene in 1904—which meant that, when they came to artistic maturity more or less at the same time, the mid 1930s, they were essentially reacting to the same set of social and political circumstances in what was a vital decade for both men personally, politically, and aesthetically. Orwell, of course, died at a much younger age than Greene, but one of the reasons that their work transcends their times is that both were unusually prophetic writers, not simply in the sense that they anticipated the future but that they were novelist/prophets: they wrote books with a strong moral sense, they wrote novels of warning.

I find that there are links both trivial and significant between the two writers. They were both very tall. Greene was well over six feet and Orwell was six foot three inches with size twelve feet. How significant that is to their personalities as writers would be difficult to say, though Orwell did actually comment that one of its consequences for him was that to see what was in front of his nose was a constant struggle. I would say that the essence of his writing credo is there: to look beyond the obvious.

They both had blue eyes. Orwell had sea-blue eyes; Greene's blue eyes were, to a lot of people, his most striking physical feature. Apparently they struck terror into Norman Sherry; they fascinated Stravinsky, when the two men met; and in Paul Theroux's novel *Picture Palace* (1978), in which Greene makes an appearance, Greene's eyes are said to give the impression "of a creature who can see in the dark . . . they gave away nothing but this warning of indestructible certainty." In his autobiography, Greene says one of his favorite childhood games was hide-and-seek in the dark, and now we know why: he had an unfair advantage. More fundamentally, piercing perception into the dark recesses of the human psyche was to be a prime characteristic of his writing.

They also share biographical coincidences. Their professional names differed from their birth names. George Orwell's "real" name was Eric Blair and the change of name was a conscious determination to take on a change of identity and, as it were, reject his heritage and upbringing. He disliked the name "Blair" and chose "Orwell" after the name of a river in Suffolk. He chose "George" as his first name because it sounded very English, he thought, and also he hated the name "Eric": he said he always had the feeling that people grew into their names, and, as he did not want to grow into an "Eric," he decided to do something about it.

Graham Greene was born Henry Graham Greene. I am not sure at what point he became "Graham" but I have always thought that "Graham Greene" is a wonderful name for a novelist, because it is so strong and alliterative. Intriguingly, Greene once slipped back into his original identity calling himself "Henry Graham" in his cameo as an insurance executive in Francois Truffaut's film, *Day for Night* (1973), a sort of practical joke on Truffaut who didn't immediately recognize him.

Another odd coincidence: on different occasions they were both treated by the same physician, Dr. Andrew Morland, a consultant at University College, London, who was a specialist in tuberculosis and who had treated D.H. Lawrence in his final illness as he was also to do with George Orwell. Morland was a very cultured and highly respected man. When he died in 1957 it was said of him in the British Medical Journal: "He had a strange power to unify antagonisms, to reconcile contradiction and to merge thought into action.... He was a good physician and a good man." Substitute "writer" for "physician" and that could almost serve as an obituary for both Orwell and Greene.

On a more serious note, one finds similarities of literary motivation. In 1947 George Orwell wrote an essay entitled "Why I Write," and in 1948 Graham Greene participated in a published work entitled *Why Do I Write? An Exchange of Views Between Elizabeth Bowen, Graham Greene and V.S. Pritchett*. There are certain passages in the Orwell essay about his literary motivation that reveal striking parallels between his and Greene's writing inspiration and personality. Early on in the essay Orwell wrote of his "lonely child's habit of making up stories" and sensed that his "literary ambitions were mixed up with the feeling of being isolated.... I knew I had a facility with words and... I felt this created a sort of private world in which I could get my own back for my failure in everyday life."

There are two more things relevant to Greene's motivation for writing than anything he himself says in *Why Do I Write?*, which give his thoughts on the relationship between writer and society. The writer, he says, "should accept no special privileges from the State" and about the relationship between literature and morality, "Literature has nothing to do with edification... a novelist must tell the truth as he sees it... literature presents the personal morality of an individual and that is seldom identical to the morality of the group." He begins to go deeper into his literary motivation in *A Sort of Life*, which turns out to be remarkably similar to Orwell's view.

When Orwell refers to writing as a way of "getting my own back," that phrase would undoubtedly have struck a chord with Greene. In his 1939 essay "Man Made Angry," Greene quotes with approval that statement of Paul Gauguin, "Life being what it is, one dreams of revenge." Some of his fiction serves as a means of paying off old scores—what the psychiatrist Edmund Bergler, in his book *The Writer and Psychoanalysis* (1950), called "injustice collecting." Bergler's definition of a writer was "a person who tries to solve an inner conflict through the sublimatory medium of writing." That seems suggestive of what both Greene and Orwell were seeking to achieve.

Connected with this are two matters that Orwell mentions and again which might also apply to Greene: his childhood feeling of being, as Orwell put it, "isolated and undervalued" and his reference to his unpopularity at school. In Greene's case this similarly perceived "unpopularity" at school arose from being the son of the headmaster and the bullying he received at the hands of two fellow pupils whom he referred to in his autobiography as Carter and Watson. As part of Greene's avenger strategy when he became a writer—and he had a particular interest in Jacobean Revenge tragedy—Carter would turn up in various unsavory guises: he is explicitly referred to in Greene's introduction to Marjorie Bowen's novel, *The Viper of Milan*, as having the same "genius for evil" as the novel's villain, Visconti; it is the name of the intended assassin in *Our Man in Havana* whom the hero will kill. Yet there is an extraordinary moment in *A Sort of Life* when Greene recalls running into Watson by chance in Kuala Lumpa in 1951 and being quite disarmed by Watson's recollection of their school days and how inseparable the three of them had been. Like Gauguin, he had been dreaming of revenge all these years and planning to humiliate them in public, only to find the reunion a total anti-climax because Watson is nostalgic and Carter is apparently now dead. Actually, Norman Sherry was to discover that Carter was not dead at all and did not die until 1971, the year *A Sort of Life* was published.

The key is Greene's reflection on this encounter and its meaning in relation to his writing:

> I wondered all the way back to the hotel if I would ever have written a book had it not been for Watson and the dead Carter, if those years of humiliation had not given me an *excessive* [my emphasis] desire to prove I was good at something, however long the effort might prove.

I have always been struck by the use of the word "excessive" there, as if Greene knew that this might be an over-reaction to this childhood trauma, as if it provided the spur for writing rather than the reason, that the trauma served a particular need. I do think it signals Greene's hypersensitivity at this stage of his life, and how writing came to his rescue in the way it did for Orwell too. In both cases, writing became inextricably bound up with their self-esteem: in both cases it was when they were writing that they felt completely themselves. A mutual friend, Michael Meyer wrote: "Every good writer I know hates the actual process of writing... Orwell did, so does Greene. I know one or two bad ones who enjoy it." That greatest of all Hollywood screenwriters, Billy Wilder, said the same thing: "Show me a writer who enjoys writing and I will show you a bad writer. This does not mean that every writer who doesn't enjoy writing is a good writer..." Towards the end of "Why I Write," Orwell says: "Writing a book is a horrible, exhausting struggle, like a long bout of some painful illness. One would never undertake such a thing if one were not driven on by a demon whom one can neither resist nor understand." Orwell and Greene wrote not out of pleasure, but out of necessity: it was in their veins. When asked by a television interviewer in Moscow in 1987 what made him write, Greene replied: "I don't know. It's like an illness. It's like a boil on one's cheek and at a certain moment you feel you have to scratch it off. Life would be impossible for me if I knew that I would never write another book."

There are two career similarities. Both of them, at different stages in their life and for different lengths of service, were policemen, which, given the instinctive anti-authoritarianism of both men, is remarkable. Of course, Orwell's anti-authoritarianism actually stemmed from his experience as a policeman for six years in the Indian Imperial Service in Burma, and his growing hostility to Imperialism in all its forms.

This is memorably expressed in "Shooting an Elephant," which is an incident that comes to symbolize for him the futility of Empire, when the man turns tyrant it is his own freedom he destroys and ends with his typically honest reflection that he had only done it to avoid looking a fool. Greene had become a Special Constable for a few months in 1926 during the General Strike, which was completely out of character in terms of his later political sympathies, but I have sometimes wondered whether the experience fed into his later work, as it did with Orwell, and gave him a different slant, for example, on his portrayal of the Lieutenant in *The Power and the Glory*, who is a very interesting character and quite sympathetically observed, as if Greene saw in him something of his own younger, more conservative, self.

I will pass over the fact that they were both members of the Independent Labour Party in the 1930s and were both employed in the Ministry of Information in the 1940s, and they were both film critics for a while. On the surface, this highlights their differences. Although both of them were ahead of their time in writing seriously about popular culture, Orwell's approach was essentially sociological whereas Greene's was more aesthetic. Orwell much preferred book reviewing to film reviewing: he hated having to tramp to a preview theatre to see the film and then attend a reception afterwards with the makers or distributors where, as he put it, "you are expected to sell your soul for a glass of inferior sherry." Greene would never sell his soul for an inferior sherry, and he quite liked getting out of the house and postponing the problems he was having with his current novel. He really appreciated the cinema, delighted in its mass appeal, and wrote about it better than any other film critic of the time.

Interestingly, though, their tastes coincided in one particular area: they both liked Charlie Chaplin. During his twenty-six-week stint as a film critic for *Time and Tide*, Orwell raved about *The Great Dictator*, the film in which Chaplin satirized Hitler and which was controversial at the time because America was not yet in the war. In 1940, filmmakers in Hollywood were under great pressure to refrain from attacking the Fascist threat in Europe. Chaplin also exerted a great influence on Orwell: indeed both *Animal Farm* and *Nineteen Eighty-Four* owe a great deal to the example set by Chaplin in *The Great Dictator*. The satirical vein that Orwell adopts for the first time in *Animal Farm* has definite similarities with *The Great Dictator*. Chaplin is wiser than the intellectuals, Orwell said, "just as animals are wiser than men." Perhaps the germ of the idea for *Animal Farm* starts there. In the Chaplin film, Hinkel becomes Hitler and Napolini/Mussolini; in Orwell, Snowball/Trotsky, Napoleon/Stalin, etc.

Confusion of identity closes both works. Chaplin's ferocious attack on totalitarianism and the cult of The Great Leader anticipates *Nineteen Eighty-Four*, as do numerous details of the film: countries called Tomania and Bacteria in Chaplin are re-named Oceania and Eurasia in Orwell; Chaplin's state ordered "Happy Hour" in *The Great Dictator*, which is transformed into Orwell's "Hate Week" in *Nineteen Eighty-Four*.

I think what confirms this connection for me finally is the most contentious aspect of the film, which then and now divided the critics but which Orwell deeply admired: namely, the film's final speech, when Chaplin departs from the Tramp persona for the last time and for the first time speaks to us in his own voice, urging the common people to unite in the name of democracy, "to fight for a new world—a decent world that will give men a chance to work—that will give youth a future–and old age a security." The speech is quoted in full in Chaplin's autobiography. The language Chaplin uses is very similar to the kind of language Orwell uses in his essay "Looking Back on the Spanish War," written in 1943, in which he asks "Shall people be allowed to live the decent, fully human life which is now technically achievable, or shan't they?" Orwell was deeply moved by this film, and its style, tone, and ideas were profoundly influential, I believe, in shaping Orwell's approach to *Animal Farm* and *Nineteen Eighty-Four*. So, even though their approaches to cinema were miles apart, Greene and Orwell both found something in Chaplin to which they could respond in the enrichment of their art.

About half-way through his essay "Why I Write," Orwell becomes more specific about his writing intentions, which in turn clarifies for him where he had previously been going wrong and the essential ingredient his work had lacked; and Greene had a similar revelation that would change the direction of his writing in a significant way. For Orwell, the turning-point was the Spanish Civil War. "Every line of serious work that I have written since 1936," he writes, "has been written, directly or indirectly, against totalitarianism and for democratic socialism, as I understand it . . . What I have most wanted to do throughout the past ten years is to make political writing into an art." And at the end of the essay, he underlines the point: "Looking back through my work, I see that it is invariably where I lacked a political purpose that I wrote lifeless books and was betrayed into purple passages, sentences without meaning, decorative adjectives, and humbug generally." Just as Greene was to suppress his early novels, *The Name of Action* and *Rumour at Nightfall*, it is possible that Orwell, if he had lived long enough to supervise a collected edition, would have done the same and omitted *The Clergyman's Daughter* and *Keep the Aspidistra Flying*.

Just as politics came to Orwell's rescue and helped to define his distinctiveness as a writer, in Greene's case it was the cinema and Catholicism. In the *Arena* documentary on Greene in 1993, Anthony Burgess claimed that Greene had it in him to be a great writer but that he had sold out and become merely a good one; that he had made a Faustian pact with commerce and betrayed his talent. In earlier works like *It's A Battlefield* and *England Made Me*, Burgess argued, Greene was reaching for greatness through wrestling with significant social themes in an advanced experimental style, but he sold out to the commercial blandishments of the thriller, which could be turned profitably into movies, and which Greene coated with Catholicism, "for sensational effect." "He could have been a great novelist," Burgess said, "but opted to be a good one—and this was a sin," which, Burgess implied, might have been the attraction.

My own view is more or less the diametrical opposite of Burgess's. Works like *It's a Battlefield* and *England Made Me* demonstrate to me that Greene had not yet found his voice. He dabbles with modernist effects in *England Made Me* more out of a sense of literary duty than with any great enthusiasm. If he had continued along the path that Burgess prescribed, he would have remained a good writer in an accomplished but relatively impersonal vein. He became an exceptional writer when he came upon the moral, emotional and narrative terrain that was his alone—Greeneland, if you will, though he hated the term—and when he found the style that could unlock all his gifts as a novelist. The cinema vitalized his style and Catholicism deepened his themes; the turning-point came roughly fifty pages into *Brighton Rock* in which a crime story about right and wrong moves into a spiritual allegory about Good and Evil and a hoodlum's struggle against the law and rival gangs turns into the story of a lost soul wrestling with God and the Devil.

What did they think of each other? A mutual friend, Michael Meyer had introduced them and they had all met at *Rules* restaurant some time in 1947, and apparently had got on well; Meyer's only disappointment was that they talked more about politics than literature. It led to further meetings which were conducted on friendly terms. They were very different personalities, though, and it would be fair to say that they were not unconditional admirers of each other's work. Greene did like *Animal Farm* and wrote a favorable review of it in the *Evening Standard*, and indeed recommend it as a possible film subject for Walt Disney—"But is it perhaps a little too real for him?" he wondered. Greene not only liked it but stood up for it when the Ministry of Information, which had received a copy, took a dim view of the satire. Apparently one leading official complained to Orwell, "Couldn't you have made the leaders some other animal than pigs?" That did not bother Greene, because he had a soft spot for pigs, but his championing of the book is interesting because it is a reminder that, incredible as it might seem today, *Animal Farm* had a great deal of trouble getting published. T.S Eliot had turned it down on behalf of Faber, essentially for political reasons. Greene also thought that *Nineteen Eighty-Four* was very good, "except the sex part," he said. "That's ham."

Orwell's most extended critique of Greene came in a rather notorious review he wrote of *The Heart of the Matter* for *The New Yorker*. It is a fascinating piece because it really does highlight fundamental differences of outlook between the two men, however many other things they might have agreed on. In fairness, it is worth noting that Orwell might have felt a bit guilty about the review because he said to a mutual acquaintance, Anthony Powell, "If you happen to see Graham Greene, could you break the news to him that I have written a very bad review of his novel for *The New Yorker*?" Whether the advance warning was a sign of regret, or to cushion the blow, or to encourage Greene to cancel his subscription to *The New Yorker*, is unclear; and it is likely that Greene was unconcerned because adverse criticism seemed not to bother him and because the book had been a huge seller and made him financially secure as a writer for the first time. Coincidentally the same thing was to happen to Orwell the following year with *Nineteen Eighty-Four,* so at least he had a taste of success before his death in 1950: it is astonishing to think that even a classic like *Homage to Catalonia* had only sold 800 copies by the time Orwell died.

Orwell's review is witty, well written, combative, and defiantly prejudiced but with some acute observations. His main objection seems to be basically that it is not *Burmese Days*, i.e., that it does not square with Orwell's own experience of serving as a policeman in a colonialist situation and community. Consequently, he finds the plot "ridiculous," and because Greene does not really address racial tensions, which would have been a dominant emotion in that community, the setting becomes irrelevant: "the whole thing might as well be happening in a London suburb," he writes. Orwell also cannot understand the hero Scobie because he seldom seems to think about his work and hardly ever about the war, even though it is 1942. "All he is interested in," writes Orwell, "is his own progress towards damnation." Given that this is the main focus of the novel, it seems fairly reasonable; and as Henry James might say, one must surely allow the author his basic idea—one's only criticism should be directed towards what he has done with it.

Orwell was a marvelous critic when he was on a writer's wavelength, as in his magnificent essay on Dickens. But in *The Heart of the Matter* he underestimates the skill and importance of Greene's evocation of the setting; he also underestimates the colonialist theme; it is not emphasized but is nevertheless there. In *The Art of Fiction* (1994), David Lodge has written a masterly analysis of the opening of the novel, in which he teases out some of the undercurrents of colonialist prejudice embedded in the style; he suggests that even the title of the novel might be a conscious allusion to one of the most devastating critiques of European colonialist exploitation in literature, Joseph Conrad's *Heart of Darkness*.

Probably the most provocative part of the review, though, is his commentary on the novel's Catholicism. Orwell was brought up in a Catholic school, which does not seem to have been a happy experience and no doubt colors his response. He dislikes what he calls a "sort of snobbishness" in Greene's attitude, that, as Orwell interprets it, "it's spiritually higher to be an erring Catholic than a virtuous pagan" and that, as he puts it, "ordinary human decency is of no value." It is intriguing that the word "decent" or "decency"—which the *Oxford English Dictionary* defines as "generally accepted standards of behavior and morality or propriety"—is a word that Orwell returns to again and again, whereas the word seems to be completely absent in Greene—I cannot recall an occasion when he ever uses it.

Individual morality interested Greene more than general morality and conformity to accepted standards of behavior interested him not at all. Orwell goes on: "Hell is a sort of high-class night-club, entry to which is reserved for Catholics only, since the non-Catholics are too ignorant to be held guilty." *The Power and the Glory* excepted because at least the struggle "between the worldly and the unworldly values," as Orwell puts it, is split between two characters, and makes for an interesting character conflict and contrast between the priest and the Lieutenant. But he finds *Brighton Rock* incredible because, he says, "it presupposes that the most brutishly stupid person can, merely by being brought up a Catholic, be capable of great intellectual subtlety." I would not have thought Pinkie's upbringing was a particularly good advertisement for Catholicism. Orwell sometimes does have a somewhat prescriptive, monolithic view of character. Greene never found contradictions in character at all surprising, drawn as he was to 'the honest thief' and "the tender murderer" that Robert Browning wrote about.

But for Orwell, those kinds of character ambivalences do not seem to register. "Scobie is incredible," he concludes, "because the two halves of him don't fit together. If he were capable of getting into the kind of mess that is described, he would have got into it years ago." One asks why? Orwell continues, "If he believed in Hell, he would not risk going there merely to spare the feelings of a couple of neurotic women." Surely it is more complicated than that. "And one might add that if he were the kind of man we are told he is that is a man whose chief characteristic is—a horror of causing pain—he would not be an officer in a colonial police force." Now there he might have a point; and it was the one point that Greene responded to in his "Congo Journal," when he said that he had known a Commissioner in Freetown who was humane and sensitive. Still, it is notable that, for all its success, Greene always thought *The Heart of the Matter* was one of his weaker novels, good on description, but exaggerated in its portrayal of the hero's dilemma. I sometimes wonder whether Orwell's critique affected him in some way and influenced him against the novel.

To conclude, the importance of the impact of their childhoods and their public and private school experiences on their artistic development cannot be overstated. Greene's experience at Berkhamsted School had profound ramifications; Orwell always said that his experience at his boarding school, St. Cyprian's, which he immortalized in his essay "Such, Such Were the Joys," gave him an insight into what living in a totalitarian state must be like, which became invaluable when he wrote *Nineteen Eighty-Four*.

Their artistic characters were formed in the 1930s; Greene and Orwell can provide a sense of the whole decade, particularly in terms of its social and political upheavals. Both wrote their Spanish Civil War books: Orwell, *Homage to Catalonia*; Greene *The Confidential Agent* and, almost by default, *The Power and the Glory*, which, although not set in Spain, addresses religious persecution and dictatorship, which dominated Greene's perception of the conflict. Their respective novels of 1936, Orwell's *Keep the Aspidistra Flying* and Greene's *A Gun for Sale*, although ostensibly about other things, are peppered with prophecies of war and foreboding for the future. Greene even uses the word "holocaust" at one moment in his novel. Greene and Orwell are also the least insular of writers—Greene travelled to Liberia, Sweden, Mexico etc., during the decade for the material of his books, and Orwell was down and out in Paris as well as London, fought in Spain, and found Wigan to be a foreign country. Ironically, this makes them peculiarly aware of English insularity.

When Orwell died in 1950, Malcolm Muggeridge, who knew both men well, wrote in his obituary that "Orwell's writing, like Graham Greene, expressed in an intense form some romantic longing." When Muggeridge wrote those words, Greene was actually about to embark on the novel that, more than any other, expressed an intense romantic longing, *The End of the Affair*. "Romantic longing" seems less obvious in Orwell, but I think Muggeridge was using the idea of Romanticism in the way that T.S. Eliot used it of Henry James: not in the sense of romantic love but in the sense of a romantic view of life's potential, to convey the intensity of his idealism, the capacity to see the possibility of an ideal society, and to cling to that possibility however many times he is made aware of the disparity between hope and fact. An attitude of cynicism was alien to both men.

Richard Hoggart referred to Orwell as "the conscience of a generation;" William Golding described Greene as the ultimate "chronicler of twentieth century man." When they sat down to write, they were afraid of nothing and no one. They relished their freedom in belonging to no literary clique or party line or artistic movement or anything that might inhibit their capacity to speak the truth as they saw it. They saw through propaganda and cant and occasionally had enormous fun in satirizing their absurdities. Their consistent theme was sympathy for the underdog: standing up for the poor against the rich, the weak against the powerful, the outsider against the Establishment, the oppressed against the dictatorial, the individual against the State.

It would be hard to think of two more coruscating yet compassionate chroniclers of the last century nor two voices more urgently needed in our present time, to speak out with eloquence and moral authority against injustice, hypocrisy, and the abuse of power. When Orwell reviewed Chaplin's *The Great Dictator*, he concluded: "the allure of power politics will be a fraction weaker for every human being who sees this film." He linked Chaplin with what he called "one of the basic folk-tales of the English-speaking people, Jack the Giant Killer—the little man against the big man." There is something of that in both Greene and Orwell. There are Big Brothers at large and they take many forms—social, political, bureaucratic, governmental—but an individual can still nibble away at the base, can still be a piece of grit in the State machinery, to use Greene's phrase; and, in so doing, give hope to those who are downtrodden or simply tired of being lied to. And occasionally—just occasionally—the Giant falls.

**Neil Sinyard** is Emeritus Professor of Film studies at the University of Hull, UK. He is the author of 25 books on film and over 100 articles on film, a number of which relate either to film adaptations of literature in general or screen adaptations of Greene in particular. He is the author of *Graham Greene: A Literary Life* (Macmillan 2003); contributed a chapter to *Dangerous Edges of Graham Greene* (Continuum, 2011); is the Literary Editor of the *Graham Greene Newsletter*; is a former Director of the Graham Greene International Festival; and has been an invited lecturer on Greene at a number of international universities, including the Sorbonne in Paris.

# Darkest Greeneland: *Brighton Rock*

## Cedric Watts

The 1999 Graham Greene International Festival

## On Greeneland

The term "Greeneland," with an "e" before the "l," was apparently coined by Arthur Calder-Marshall. In an issue of the magazine *Horizon* for June 1940, Calder-Marshall said that Graham Greene's novels were characterised by a seedy terrain that should be called "Greeneland." I believe, however, that Greene, who enjoyed wordplay on his own surname, had virtually coined the term himself. In the 1936 novel, *A Gun for Sale*, a crooner sings a love song featuring a flower from Greenland. The song offers a flower; Greene offers a lyrical interlude. There the word has the normal geographical spelling, but the author is clearly being slyly self-referential. By 1972 Greeneland had been granted the accolade of an entry in Volume 1 of the *Supplement to the Oxford English Dictionary*. There the definition is this: "A term used to describe the world of depressed seediness reputedly typical of the setting[s] and characters of the novels of Graham Greene." You may agree that in numerous works of fiction that he published, particularly between 1931 and 1951, whether the fictional location were ostensibly London or Liberia, Mexico or Brighton, the author transformed it into Greeneland: a distinctively blighted, oppressive, tainted landscape, in which sordid, seedy and smelly details are prominent, and populated by characters who include the corrupt, the failed, the vulgar, and the mediocre. In *Brighton Rock*, when the moon shines into Pinkie's bedroom, it shines on "the open door where the jerry stood": on the Jeremiah, the chamber-pot.[1] Later Dallow, standing in the street, puts his foot in "dog's ordure": an everyday event in Brighton but an innovatory detail in literature. So far, so familiar. But Greene characteristically resisted the term he had helped to create. In his autobiographical book, *Ways of Escape*, he writes:

> Some critics have referred to a strange violent 'seedy' region of the mind (why did I ever popularize that last adjective?) which they call Greeneland, and I have sometimes wondered whether they go round the world blinkered. 'This is Indo-China,' I want to exclaim, 'this is Mexico, this is Sierra Leone carefully and accurately described. I have been a newspaper correspondent as well as a novelist. I assure you that the dead child lay in the ditch in just that attitude. In the canal of Phat Diem the bodies stuck out of the water . . .' But I know that argument is useless. They won't believe the world they haven't noticed is like that.[2]

This passage offers a standard artistic defense of the strange. "I am simply being truthful," says the artist; "I see more clearly than you." But one objection to Greene's defense is obvious. He has selected his world. He chose to go to exceptional regions: dangerous, violent, and sometimes sordid regions. He repeatedly sought what others

---

[1] The Jeremiah was widely used in England until the 1950s but was soon rendered extinct by central heating, by the elimination of the 'outside' lavatory, and perhaps by greater sensitivity or prudishness in such matters.
[2] *Ways of Escape*. London: Bodley Head, 1980, p. 77.

would choose to avoid: warfare, oppression, crisis, vice, and squalor. For instance, he had chosen to travel to Phat Diem in Vietnam during the war between the Vietnamese and the French. Greene's journal for 16 December 1951 records that child dead in the ditch and the canal "thick with bodies," while bombs and mortar shells exploded nearby. If you ask *why* he chose such regions, there are many answers. One is that such regions are newsworthy, so Greene was often paid by newspapers and magazines as a reporter.

Another answer is that such regions are sometimes politically important, so Greene might be paid by the British Secret Service for investigating them. He liked being paid several times for the same job, and once remarked that the British Secret Service was "the best travel agency in the world." He seems to have been involved with that travel agency from the 1930s until the 1980s. A third answer is that such regions provided exciting material for works of fiction. As in the case of two of Greene's literary heroes, Joseph Conrad and R. B. Cunninghame Graham, it sometimes looks as if the adventurous travels had literary motivation. The need to find material for subsequent literary creation was an incentive to roam.

A fourth answer is his imaginative responsiveness to literary works which described regions both blighted and perilous. Greeneland is part of a vast territory that was explored by Dickens in *Bleak House*, by Baudelaire and by British decadent poets of the late 19th century, by Conrad in *The Secret Agent*, and by Eliot in "The Waste Land." In traveling and describing the world's surface, Greene was extending an imaginative and cultural empire. And a fifth answer is psychological. In his autobiographical works, Greene repeatedly claims that he found danger an antidote to boredom, and by "boredom" he often seems to mean depression. One psychological explanation of Greeneland, therefore, is that the vistas are partly those seen by a rather depressed person, and partly those seen by a person who is seeking danger as an antidote.

To explain, however, is not to explain away. Many people have been depressed, but only Graham Greene produced that abundant, brilliant and diverse array of literary work. In any case, in his later years, as his Catholicism evolved unevenly and inconsistently towards agnosticism, in 1978 he termed himself a "Catholic agnostic." Greeneland gave way to a brighter, more cheerful, even comic landscape. One is reminded of the gentleman who told Dr. Johnson, "I have tried too in my time to be a philosopher, but, I don't know how, cheerfulness was always breaking in." There are happy endings for the heroes of *Loser Takes All, The Potting Shed,* and *Our Man in Havana*. Some of the stage plays are replete with comedy, even farce at times: notably *The Complaisant Lover, The Return of A. J. Raffles,* and *For Whom the Bell Chimes*. Some of the later novels are not only lighthearted, but also revisit earlier themes and regions in a spirit of blithe picaresque regeneration: examples are *Travels with My Aunt* and *Monsignor Quixote*.

Arguably, one of the gods served by Greene was the Roman god Janus, the two-headed god who looks in opposite directions at the same time: the tutelary deity of January, janitors, thresholds and paradoxes. Greene loved paradoxes large and small. Whether as Catholic Communist, as British secret agent who aided Fidel Castro, as anti-Semite and pro-Israeli, as creator of Greeneland and its mocker, he reveled in the paradoxical.[3] And no novel is more paradoxical than *Brighton*

*Rock*. But perhaps I should rather say, "No novel is more paradoxical than the novels called *Brighton Rock*."

## The *Brighton Rock* Variations and the Vanishing Jews

The first *British* edition of *Brighton Rock* has a character called Prewitt and a range of anti-Semitic details. This Heinemann volume is the ancestor of the British Uniform and Library Editions of Greene's work. The first *American* edition of *Brighton Rock* has a character called not Prewitt but Drewitt, and it lacks most of the anti-Semitic details. That Viking hardback volume is the ancestor of the Viking, early Penguin, and Bantam paperbacks. For the Collected Edition, published by Heinemann and Bodley Head in 1970, Greene revised the British text, removing various Jewish allusions. Later Penguin paperbacks follow the Collected Edition text. In my book *A Preface to Greene,* I always quoted the British first edition texts of his novels, because it is politically and critically important to quote the text that fits the attributed original date and the majority of its early reviews; but I often drew attention to significant textual differences which were to appear in later editions.[4] One general reflection is obvious. Graham Greene's literary output is even larger and more varied than appears to be the case. A particular text may have very significant variations, silently entered by Greene over the years. Eventually, there will be scholarly editions of his works, editions with endnotes, glossaries, and variant readings, and the significant differences will at once become apparent. At present, readers and critics may sometimes be at cross-purposes as one or another cites a phrase or passage which does not exist in the text that others have read.

For example, in the 1938 British text of *Brighton Rock*, Colleoni, the wealthy gang-boss, has "an old Semitic face;" in 1970 it becomes "an old Italian face." In 1938 his gang was "a group of Jews;" in 1970 they were "a group of men." In 1938, "Down the broad steps of the Cosmopolitan came a couple of Jewesses with bright brass hair and ermine coats and heads close together like parrots, exchanging metallic confidences;" in 1970, "Jewesses" became "women." In 1938, while Pinkie waits to meet Colleoni at the Cosmopolitan, "A little Jewess sniffed at him bitchily and then talked him over with another little Jewess on a settee." In 1970, the phrase "little Jewess" becomes "little bitch." We can guess what is probably happening here. Probably the later Greene, writing long after Belsen and Dachau, is regretting the occasional anti-Semitism of his pre-war novels and is revising *Brighton Rock* accordingly.[5] The revision, however, was not thorough. In both 1938 and 1970, we are told that Crab "had been a Jew once, but a hairdresser and a surgeon had altered that," presumably by dyeing his hair and reshaping his nose.

Anti-Semitism is evident in several of

---

3 He visited and corresponded with the disgraced traitor, Kim Philby, who had betrayed numerous British agents, and described Philby as "a good and loyal friend;" but his correspondence with the traitor was "passed on to MI6 through his brother-in-law Rodney Dennys'." See *Graham Greene: A Life in Letters*, ed. Richard Greene. London: Little, Brown, 2007, p. 401.
4 Textual variations are discussed in my *A Preface to Greene* (London: Longman, 1996), pp. vii, 118-21. Incidentally, around 1950 the Invincible Press, Sydney, Australia, published *Brighton Rock: An Entertainment* in an undated paperback edition which drastically condensed various parts, so that (for example) the final chapter was reduced to less than one page. The book gives no warning that the text is thus abridged. It seems virtually certain that the publishers and not the author bore the responsibility for these alterations.

Greene's early novels, notably *The Name of Action*, in which the villain, Kapper, is a Jew associated with sexual depravity, revolution, and hatred of the Madonna of the Roman Catholics. Greene later suppressed this novel, forbidding re-publication. In *A Gun for Sale*, the plot centers on a conspiracy by wealthy Jewish industrialists to start World War II so as to boost their profits. *Stamboul Train* is perhaps the oddest novel in this respect, for there the hero, a Jew called Myatt, repeatedly encounters anti-Semitic prejudice, which is depicted as brutal and harsh; yet Myatt himself eventually conforms to stereotype because he is a shrewd businessman who finally sacrifices love on the altar of cash profits. Thus, one of the darkest features of darkest Greeneland is the anti-Semitic theme.

We are all sinners, and therefore I hesitate to cast a stone. Instead, I emphasize that in *The Confidential Agent*, 1939, the depiction of Forbes *alias* Furtstein is broadly favorable, and that after World War II, during the conflicts of Israelis versus Arabs in the 1960s and 1970s, Greene's sympathies lay mainly with the Israelis; and he was on friendly terms with General Moshe Dayan, who became the Israeli Defense Minister. In 1981 Greene was awarded the Jerusalem Prize, which included a sum of $5000, in recognition of "an author who has contributed to the world's understanding of the freedom of the individual in society."

## Brighton and *Brighton Rock*

I think that *Brighton Rock* is not the *best* of Greene's novels, for *The Power and the Glory* deserves that accolade; but it is probably the most striking, provocative, and extreme. It is corrosively negative, grotesquely nightmarish, and cynically black-comical. It is a thriller, a detective novel, and a moral-cum-theological paradox. It offers realism, expressionism, and satiric stylization. It is hauntingly memorable rather than fully convincing. But it takes us deeper into darkest Greeneland than any other of Greene's novels. The real Brighton is repeatedly inflected into a Brighton which is a garish hell-gate.

Greene was remarkably accurate in his topographical details. Montpelier Road, Brighton, still stands. No. 56, a terraced house divided into flats, is where Pinkie lived. To this day there remains the tunnel beneath the race course. You can still drink in Dr. Brighton's pub, where Pinkie met Hale.

Brighton does indeed still offer a combination of the bright and the sleazy, the hedonistic and the violent, the exuberant and the sordid. Among other requests, Norman Sherry asked me to trace Black Boy, the racehorse that is crucially important in the novel. Ida has a bet on the horse at odds of ten to one against, and the horse wins, so she has enough money to stay in Brighton and pursue Pinkie. Without Black Boy, Pinkie might never have been caught; in a telling irony, Black Boy was the tip given to Ida by Hale, Pinkie's victim. I therefore spent many fruitless hours in Brighton Public Library reading the racing results in the local *Evening Argus* for the 1930s. But then I discovered that there was a horse called Blue Boy which won the Balcombe Stakes at ten to one in June 1936. At once you see that to compare is to contrast. To see sameness is to see difference. By changing the horse's name from Blue Boy to Black Boy, and then by letting Tate call it

---

5 Satan assumed the form of a black dog in the subsequent films entitled *The Omen*, which appeared in 1976 and 2006.

Black Dog, Greene plays a theological joke. A black dog may be the form assumed by the devil, according to old literary works such as *The Witch of Edmonton*, the play which supplies the novel's epigraph.[6] *Black Boy* was also a nickname for Satan: as Shakespeare reminds us (in *Titus Andronicus*, *Othello* and *Macbeth*, for instance), in the past the Devil was often depicted as black. In short, the change of the horse's name reveals the quality of sinister theological humor that runs through the novel. The horse backed by Spicer, which comes second, is called *Memento Mori*; Spicer doesn't know what that name means, but it foretells his own death at Pinkie's hands. The mordant theological humor is perhaps at its most blatant when Pinkie tells us his phone number: 666, the number of the evil Beast in the Book of Revelation, Chapter 13, verse 18. Pinkie comes from Paradise Piece. You might think that an unlikely address, too heavily ironic, but there was a real Paradise Street in the east Brighton slums in the 1930s.

Another task that Norman Sherry gave me was to find documentary proof that in the 1930s razor gangs operated at Brighton race course. I thought that would be easy. Older residents of Brighton assured me that such gangs had indeed operated there. But when I studied the pages of the *Evening Argus* for year after year, I found that those razor gangs, so well-remembered in Brighton, had apparently arrived not in a car from Montpellier Road, not in a train from London, but by air: on a diverted flight of, or arranged by, Graham Greene's imagination. In that local newspaper, I found not a single account of a gang fight involving razors in Brighton in the 1930s. The battle which had prompted the fracas described in the book had actually taken place at Lewes race course, not Brighton, and Greene had transferred it. Not one of the real gang used a razor. The gangsters used a hatchet, a crowbar, an iron bar, and half a billiard cue. The police were waiting in ambush, and sixteen gang members were arrested and jailed; whereas in the novel, Colleoni's mob is *not* arrested. It serves Greene's purposes to suggest some collusion between Colleoni and the forces of law and order. On the other hand, what happened at Lewes was that the Hoxton Mob from London attacked two bookmakers allegedly controlled by Darby, or Derby, Sabini, a gangster based in Brighton; so there was some territorial similarity to what happened in the novel. Furthermore, the Hoxton Mob was seeking revenge because one of their members had had his throat cut by Sabini's gang at Liverpool Street Station: clearly a source for the murder of Pinkie's patron Kite, who also had his throat cut at a London station—in his case, St. Pancras. Kite's death had first been described in *A Gun for Sale*, 1936: the initiation of what is now called a "transtextual narrative."[7]

Pinkie is seventeen, and you may deem

---

6 Some years after I had written those words, a relevant letter appeared in *Graham Greene: A Life in Letters*, pp. 398-9. Greene in 1988 responds thus to an enquirer:
Yes, the changes in *Brighton Rock* and *Stamboul Train* and if there is one in *A Gun for Sale* were made by myself. After the holocaust one could not use the word Jew in the loose way one used it before the war. Myatt is in fact one of the nicest characters in *Stamboul Train*, both brave and sympathetic. In the case of Colleoni I think I was wrong to have made him a Jew in the first place with such an Italian name. The casual references to Jews at one particular hotel is a sign of those times when one regarded the word Jew as almost a synonym for capitalist. Big business seemed our enemy [. . .].
(Some readers may doubt that "casual" is the correct term for those references.)
7 Transtextual narratives (and covert plots) are defined and discussed in my book *The Deceptive Text: An Introduction to Covert Plots* (Brighton: Harvester, 1984).

that an implausibly early age for a gang boss. But I found an issue of the *Evening Argus* in 1936 which reported the arrest of a local gang leader, and his age was seventeen. Again and again, Greene, in *Brighton Rock,* has used actual events and locations, but the material is repeatedly inflected in distinctive ways. Consider this quotation:

> Brighton in the red fusing light looked like a wonderful imagined place, and the lights on the sea just played about, and me, I played with them, and the wind ruffled the water back, and right up in the sky were two ruddy clouds flung together, and they were perfect, like two lovers at last met in a kiss.

This is wonderful: lyrical affirmative romanticism. And, of course, that quotation is not from Greene. It is from a letter that D. H. Lawrence wrote in 1909, describing the beauty of Brighton.[8] This, in contrast, is Greene in *Brighton Rock*:

> The sun slid off the sea and like a cuttle fish shot into the sky the stain of agonies and endurances [...]. An old man went stooping down the shore, very slowly, turning the stones, picking among the dry seaweed for cigarette ends, scraps of food. The gulls which had stood like candles down the beach rose and cried under the promenade. The old man found a boot and stowed it in his sack and a gull dropped from the Parade and swept through the iron nave of the Palace Pier, white and purposeful in the obscurity: half-vulture and half-dove.[9]

Yes, that is Greene, offering a description that's vivid, distinctive, somewhat nightmarish, observing the poverty behind Brighton's facade of fun. There is a touch of Metaphysical poetry in the conceit or odd simile. As a cuttlefish squirts its purple ink, so the setting sun squirts its redness, and that red resembles blood: it is the stain of "agonies and endurances;" therefore, subliminally, Christ's suffering is evoked. If some writer notes that there are seagulls around the Palace Pier at Brighton, that may be mere realism; but there is no mere realism about that gull noted at the end of this description: it is half-dove, suggesting the dove of peace and its biblical associations; but it is also half-vulture: like the old man, it is another scavenger, but this one seeks carrion. In such descriptions, Brighton becomes Greeneland. And Greeneland is an Eden blighted and polluted by fallen humanity.

## The Paradoxes of the Plot

In his early years as a novelist, Greene was constantly trying to square the circle. He was seeking to write novels which would approach in merit the works of authors he admired, notably Conrad and James; but he was also seeking commercial success. One result was his notion of producing not only relatively demanding works, each of which would bear the subtitle *A Novel*, but also relatively popular works, each of which would bear the subtitle *An Entertainment*. Eventually, he scrapped this distinction, which became unmanageable. And *Brighton Rock* shows why. There he had managed to put the two kinds of work together in one narrative. *Brighton Rock* was subtitled *An*

---

8 *The Letters of D. H. Lawrence*, Vol. 1 (London: Heinemann, 1979), p. 127.
9 *Brighton Rock* (London: Heinemann, 1938), pp. 187-8. Some subsequent editions misprinted "shot into the sky the stain" as "shot into the sky with the stain," thus making the evening sun soar upwards like a rocket when it should actually be vanishing below the horizon.

*Entertainment* in its first American edition but subtitled *A Novel* in its first British edition, a fact which nicely sums up its ambiguity and its dual appeal. It is a crime thriller and a detective story. It is also a theological melodrama of a very subversive kind.

Greene told his literary agent that in *Brighton Rock* the central thematic tension is between the ethical outlook and the religious outlook. The concepts of "right and wrong" are challenged by the concepts of "Good and Evil." You can easily see how the secular, ethical plot works. Charles "Fred" Hale is murdered by Pinkie and his gang, though there is later a verdict of death by natural causes, because when the stick of rock is forced down his throat, as we may infer, he suffers a heart-attack.[10] Ida Arnold is suspicious of the circumstances and investigates. Trying to protect Rose from Pinkie, she pursues him, saves Rose from suicide, and brings about the destruction of Pinkie. Ida feels that a good job has been well done: a double killer has been punished. Right has prevailed over wrong. In this plot, the ethical outlook prevails.

Against Ida's secular ethic, however, the novel obviously invokes a religious frame of reference. Here the novel's appalling paradox is generated. Pinkie, the killer of Hale (and later of Spicer), has had a Roman Catholic indoctrination, and is still, in his perverse way, a believer. Thus, for all his evil, and indeed largely because of his sense of evil, he inhabits the religious dimension. As Pinkie puts it:

"These atheists, they don't know nothing. Of course there's
Hell. Flames and damnation, [...] torments."
"And Heaven too," said Rose with anxiety, while the rain fell interminably on.
"Oh, maybe," the Boy said, "maybe."[11]

In the characterization of Pinkie, Greene seems to be conducting a taxing literary experiment: to see whether the reader's pity can be won for a person who seems to be irredeemably callous and ruthless. Pinkie's cruelty is carried to almost ludicrous extremes: "She loves me, she loves me not," he says, tearing the wings off a fly. He wields a razor, carries a vitriol bottle, and jests crudely about his victims. He is a Judas to Spicer, his accomplice, and even to Rose, who remains loyal to him even though she knows his wickedness. Yet, in various ways, Greene seeks to elicit some pity for him.

Firstly, Ida Arnold's world of secular right and wrong is made to seem superficial. She's an English Mae West with a blowsy appeal, a resilient courage, a hearty optimism; but she is associated with carnality and vulgarity. Pinkie's Catholicism is warped: it's partly Manichaeism, sometimes almost Satanism; ""Credo in unum Satanum," the Boy said."[12] Greene was fascinated by Manichaeism, by the notion that the world, particularly the material and carnal, is almost entirely the territory of Satan. He said he found in Dickens' *Oliver Twist* the "alluring taint" of the Manichee. Pinkie is an instinctive, intuitive Manichaean. He

---

10 Greene loved covert plots: plot sequences that are so obliquely or elliptically presented that only on a second or subsequent reading of the novel are we able to fill the gap. One such gap is the mystery of what the gang tried to do to Hale in the rock shop under the Palace Pier. If we look carefully at the references to Brighton rock in the novel, we are able to solve the mystery. In *The Power and the Glory*, the manner of Coral Fellows' death is another covert plot.
11 *Brighton Rock*. London: Heinemann, 1938, p. 71.
12 His Latin, though remarkable, is faulty: the last word should be "Satanam."

is disgusted by the world and is attuned to the transcendental, to an eternity, even if an eternity of hell fires.

In 1930, in a notorious passage in an essay on Baudelaire, T. S. Eliot wrote

> [T]he possibility of damnation is so immense a relief in a world of electoral reform, plebiscites, sex reform and dress reform, that damnation itself is an immediate form of salvation—of salvation from the ennui of modern life, because it at last gives some significance to living ... Baudelaire was man enough for damnation.[13]

"I have always believed that there are two levels [of experience]:

> One that of science and common sense, and another, terrifying, subterranean and chaotic, which in some sense holds more truth than the everyday view. You might describe this as a satanic mysticism. I have never been convinced of its truth, but in moments of intense emotion it overwhelms me.

That is Bertrand Russell, the eminent rationalist. So Pinkie, gripped by the paradox of the virtue of evil, is in very distinguished company.

In contrast to Pinkie's sense that he may be hell-bound, Pinkie's victim, Fred Hale, is cremated at an Anglican Service that is fiercely satirized for its wishy-washy theology; and what happens to poor Fred then? Presumably he does not deserve Hell, or even Purgatory[14], for we are told that he becomes merely "part of the smoke nuisance over London." Meanwhile, Pinkie resembles a blighted candidate for priesthood: he recoils from alcohol, feels nostalgia for the Mass and the choir, and says that priests are quite right to avoid the horror of sexuality. "When I was a kid, I swore I'd be a priest," he tells Dallow. The novel's events unfold around the time of Pentecost; and in this case, it is Pinkie, a rather diabolical apostle, who receives "the gift of tongues" when praising the priesthood; the novel quotes the biblical phrase. He has at least elicited the selfless love of Rose, a fellow Catholic; whereas Ida Arnold's love life is a matter of brief hedonistic encounters. Pinkie, furthermore, retains the notion that he might one day repent and gain salvation. He repeatedly half-recalls William Camden's lines, "Betwixt the stirrup and the ground / Mercy I asked, mercy I found." The manner of his death may seem designed to rule out any last-minute penitence. His own vitriol suddenly burning his face, Pinkie throws himself into the sea from the cliff-top at Telscombe Cliffs. Nevertheless, after his death, when Rose visits her Catholic church, the priest tells her: "You can't conceive my child, nor can I or anyone—the .... appalling .... strangeness of the mercy of God."

Thus, briefly, the text raises the truly appalling prospect that the villainous Pinkie may be granted salvation and eternal bliss. Greene here and elsewhere entertained the notion of a self-subverting Catholicism, that is to say, a Catholicism which, by stressing that God transcends human understanding, subverts official ecclesiastical attempts to legislate theologically on God's behalf. Anyway, Rose is doubly consoled, thinking not only of Pinkie's possible salvation but also that she may be pregnant and may therefore produce, as the priest says, "a saint—to pray for his

---

13 Eliot, T.S. *Selected Essays* (London: Faber & Faber, 1932), pp. 375, 377.
14 Alighieri, Dante. *The Inferno*, III, 41-2.

father." But she then proceeds towards "the worst horror of all": the gramophone disc on which Pinkie has recorded the message "God damn you, you little bitch, why can't you go home for ever and let me be?" It is one of the cruelest endings in literature. In the film, as we have seen, divine intervention, it seems, causes a crack in the record, so that she hears only an apparent message of love. We do not see whether she eventually moves the needle forward to the subsequent words "I hate you, you little slut." Logically, she would.

To challenge a simple hostile verdict against Pinkie, Greene deploys not only a religious case, but also a secular case of the kind that would appeal to liberals and socialists. "Roman Catholics are working together with the Communists," Greene assured the Russian leader Gorbachev in 1987, postulating a happy alliance of believers and atheists. But already, in *Brighton Rock*, you can see Greene's attempt to blend the religious and the left-wing cases. Greene said later of Pinkie: "His actions arose out of the conditions to which he had been born."[15] There is one world for the rich, and a harsher world for the poor. Along the coast at Roedean, the daughters of affluence play hockey on the grassy terraces overlooking the sea; but the novel stresses that Pinkie's early years were blighted by harsh conditions in the slums. In the squalid setting of Paradise Piece, he shared the room in which, on every Saturday night, his parents brutally copulated; hence, in part, his recoil from sexuality. Wordsworth's "Immortality Ode" says "Heaven lies about us in our infancy;" in *Brighton Rock* this becomes "Hell lay about him in his infancy." But it is largely a man-made Hell. Like the sixteen-year-old Rose, Pinkie is the child of poverty: both have known the drabness and squalor of the Carlton Hill area of East Brighton. The novel notes the chaos of the slum-clearance work there; naturally, it does not describe the new council estates in which the former slum-dwellers gained decent houses with gardens.

There is, however, an additional case that Greene enlists in order to win a grain of sympathy for Pinkie. And that case is, alas, the anti-Semitic one that I mentioned earlier. Ranged against the two shabby young Brightonians are the rich and powerful and, according to the first British edition of the novel, the Jews. There is no room at the inn for Pinkie and Rose; or at least no room at the Cosmopolitan Hotel, where they are refused accommodation on their wedding night. The Cosmopolitan is the stronghold of Jews, it seems; particularly of the affluent gangster from London, Colleoni. He is at home there, in his luxurious suite; his henchmen are Jews, and in the hotel lobby the Jewesses sit at ease, sneering at the shabby local boy. The real Bedford Hotel becomes in the novel the Cosmopolitan, and the Cosmopolitan is true to its name: it has a Louis Seize writing room, a Pompadour boudoir, and an American Bar. The implication is that the aliens are invading Brighton. The shabby local Catholic is hopelessly outnumbered by wealthy and powerful Jews from the City; that is one of the themes.

In the battle to control the protection-racket in betting at Brighton, Colleoni, who already controls slot-machines, is bound to win. The forces of law and order purport to be neutral, but in practice side with Colleoni. The local police advise Pinkie to give way to the greater rogue: "He's got the alibis." And Colleoni is buying his way

---

15 *The Other Man: Conversations with Graham Greene* (London: Bodley Head, 1983), p. 159.

to even greater power: he is set to become a Conservative MP. "He'll go in for politics one day," we are told. "The Conservatives think a lot of him—he's got contacts." Consequently, with "his old Semitic face,"

> he looked as a man might look who owned the whole world, the whole visible world that is, the cash registers and policemen and prostitutes, Parliament and the laws which say, 'This is Right and this is Wrong'. [16]

Perhaps the most insidious part of the special pleading on Pinkie's behalf is implicit in the narrator's descriptions. Pinkie's disgust at life often seems to be shared by the narrator in his repeated observations of the drabness, the tawdriness, and the sleaziness of the world. "Why, this is Hell, nor are we out of it," says Prewitt, misquoting slightly the words of Mephistopheles in Marlowe's *Doctor Faustus*; and the narrator gives potent support to that near-Manichaean sense of the Hellish lurking beneath the superficial pleasures of Brighton. At Nelson Place, where Rose's parents live, the front door's pane is broken, the passage stinks "like a lavatory," and the staircase is carpeted with old newspapers which report rape and murder. The parents, sitting amid unwashed dishes by an unlighted stove, agree to sell Rose to Pinkie for fifteen guineas, whereas Judas required thirty pieces of silver for his act of betrayal. By repeatedly noting the sordid, the narrator evokes in us a distaste which overlaps Pinkie's.

The novel's title, *Brighton Rock*, refers to confectionery, the sticks of rock sold in the shops on the sea-front. It also refers to the stick of rock used in the murder-attempt on Hale. And the title certainly refers to human nature. Ida Arnold says to Rose:

> "Look at me. I've never changed. It's like those sticks of rock: bite it all the way down, you'll still read Brighton. That's human nature.... 'Confession... repentance,' Rose whispered 'That's just religion,' the woman said. 'Believe me. It's the world we got to deal with.'" [17]

Human nature is reassuringly consistent in Ida's view and is tainted with original sin, according to the Catholic view. Confession and repentance may briefly clear that taint for the world at large, the corruption remains. After his secular, and therefore theologically sinful, marriage to Rose, Pinkie feels that he is capable of faint tenderness towards her: he feels "the prowling pressure of pity." In the car, driving with her towards death, he even has to ward off "an enormous emotion" which "beats on him like something trying to get in: the pressure of gigantic wings against the glass. *Dona nobis pacem*." "Yes, give us peace," he thinks, as the car drives towards the blighted landscape of Peacehaven, a township established after the Great War. He actually wards off, as though they were dangerous temptations, the intimations of pity and grace. But, for all his viciousness, at least he is aware of such intimations.

In such ways, Greene develops the central paradox of *Brighton Rock*. Ida's decency prevails and Pinkie dies; but Pinkie, though wicked, is attuned to the eternal. Near the end of the novel, the priest refers to a remarkable Frenchman.

---

16 *Brighton Rock*, 88.
17 Ibid., 288.

"This man decided that if any soul was going to be damned, he would be damned too. He never took the sacraments, he never married his wife in church. I don't know, my child, but some people think he was—well, a saint."

The Frenchman was Charles Péguy (1875-1914), a poet who was killed in the Great War. It's he who provides the French epigraph to *The Power and the Glory*, an epigraph which in English reads:

The sinner is at the very heart of Christianity. Nobody is as competent as the sinner in the matter of Christianity. Nobody, unless it is the saint.

In Greene's work, the shocking and dangerous paradox of the sanctified sinner is hinted at in *Brighton Rock*, is developed splendidly in *The Power and the Glory*, and reaches its extreme in *The End of the Affair* when we discover that the adulterous Sarah has become a miracle-working candidate for canonization. And these are works by the author who later said on various occasions:

I dislike the word [God] with all its anthropomorphic associations. I don't like the term "sin." I don't believe in hell. With the approach of death I care less and less about religious truth. With age [...] doubt seems to gain the upper hand. It is my own fault. I've never been much of a religious person.[18]

## Conclusion

To conclude, *The Revenger's Tragedy* is a play written around 1607 by Cyril Tourneur or Thomas Middleton or both. Greene knew it well. The central character is Vindice, an avenger who becomes part of the corruption he excoriates. He moves amid a debased world, denouncing sexual vice and invoking the purity of death. Pinkie is a modern Vindice, part of what he detests; a deranged Puritan who, looking at Spicer, notes the stink of whisky, the eruption around the mouth, the corn on the yellowed foot; and who, when Sylvie awaits him open-legged in the back of a car, recoils, choking in nausea: "I'd rather hang," he says.

Like a Jacobean revenge drama, a piece of Swiftian satire, or a lurid expressionist film, *Brighton Rock* is a minor masterpiece in a highly stylized mode. It is a well-paced melodramatic thriller with metaphysical ambitions; a vivid, intense, bizarre, sardonic crime novel. Considered in an appropriate context of rather stylized literary works, or in a context of intelligent thrillers, it succeeds. If you seek sober realism, you may be disappointed. An inquisitorial critic could argue that Pinkie is a rather artificial character, an auxiliary to a vile and striking thesis, rather than a fully plausible villain. The *dénouement* of the plot depends on coincidental meetings, lucky timings and unlikely sightings, not to mention a policeman who can throw his truncheon with amazing speed and accuracy. Through the garish and blighted landscapes move some grotesque, caricatured, and pathetic characters manipulated by a narrator who sometimes seems to be a connoisseur of nastiness. *Brighton Rock* remains Graham Greene's most memorable exploration of darkest Greeneland and of the appalling paradox of the virtue of evil.

---

18 Quoted in *A Preface to Greene*, pp. 85-6.

**Professor Cedric Watts** served in the Royal Navy before reading English at Cambridge University (having won an Open Exhibition, a college grant), taking a B.A. (First Class) and a Ph.D. there. He is Emeritus Professor of English at the University of Sussex. His twenty-five books include *A Preface to Greene; R. B. Cunninghame Graham; The Deceptive Text: An Introduction to Covert Plots; Literature and Money; Shakespeare Puzzles; and Final Exam: A Novel* (by 'Peter Green'), praised by Ian McEwan as 'a stimulating blend of high-energy intellectual and sexual tease.' He has written poetry, tales, and satiric essays, and, for Wordsworth Classics, he has edited 21 plays by Shakespeare.

# Travels with Graham Greene

## Bernard Diederich

Graham Greene had a divine habit of turning up when a place was about to break into the news. He really did not need my help. He knew how to sniff the air and while not endowed with language skills except English, in which he became a master, he had a sixth sense and extraordinary clairvoyance about people and places. I had the pleasure of accompanying him on some of his forays in the Caribbean and Central America and can be accused of placing him at the center of controversy in the 1970s and 1980s by opening his passage to Panama and introducing him to the country's strongman, Brig. Gen. Omar Torrijos Herrera.

Even in Graham's later years, during the last of his trips to Central America, he was able to march through the area's political quicksand sorting out its labyrinth of intrigue. Undaunted, the author of *The Quiet American* looked for some familiar faces from Indochina days as the Contras' not-so-secret "secret war" with its CIA handlers heated up. On his last trip to the region in December 1985, he went to Nicaragua and, with U.S. President Reagan's words ringing in his ears—that the anti-Sandinista Contras "are our brothers and these freedom fighters we owe them our help...they are the equivalent to the founding Fathers and the brave men and women of the French Resistance..."—Graham received a decoration from the Sandinistas, who were grateful to have a friend in the famous British author.

Since his death, Greene and his writings have been the object of concentrated analysis, which would have amused him. Some of the allegations are outrageous and unfounded. If Graham could stand up in his grave he might shout a word he learned in his travels in Spanish America: "basta!"—enough!"

When I first met him, I realized that he was really a shy man. But over the years I also learned just how committed he was in his incessant quest. Greene was proud of an ancestral connection to the beautiful islands of the Caribbean. In fact, I often wondered whether his ancestors had not communicated their love for the islands and adventure to him.

In 1963 when dictator Francois ("Papa Doc") Duvalier was at the height of his terror in Haiti, Graham went back to Haiti to test that terror. At the beginning when I first met him, in Haiti in 1954, he was to me just a famous writer on vacation, very English and very quiet. Much later I saw him as a literary sword (he preferred a long bow and a full quiver of arrows) striking at Papa Doc, whom we both equated with fascism of the Hitlerian strain. Graham needed no prodding. In targeting Papa Doc in the novel *The Comedians* and later the movie version of the book, Graham gave poor Haitians a voice when they had no voice. And this voice was heard around the world. For his effort he came close to becoming another of Papa Doc's victims.

Greene's elimination, which was seriously considered by Duvalier and his aides, attested to the effectiveness of *The Comedians*. It was only after he died, and while researching my book in Haiti, that I learned how infuriated Papa Doc was, not so much by the book but by the movie version of it, which was the last script Greene wrote. Duvalier was prepared to take extreme action against the writer. Graham suspected, but never knew, the true danger he had faced. Ultimately, Papa Doc decided on an alternative plan to strike at Graham, spending thousands upon thousands of dollars from the Haitian state treasury to have the film banned in France.

Panama and Central America were to be his last hurrah, and what a pleasure it was accompanying him. It helped him produce two more books—*Getting to Know the General* and *The Captain and the Enemy*. The "*Viejo Ingles*," the "Old Englishman," as he was known affectionately in Spanish-America did not win the Nobel Prize but he was honored by men in those countries whose causes he supported. His cause was not always Washington's cause, but then in the '80s there were many Americans who did not agree with Washington fanning the fires of the Cold War in Central America.

Some of the anecdotes he told me along the trail still enliven my memory. He was a great raconteur. The Graham Greene I came to know often reminded me of my own father who had a similar sense of humor, love of pranks, and enjoyment of applying a little shock treatment during a dull moment.

Who was Graham Greene? Like all complex human beings, and perhaps all of us, he was not one person, but many. Greene himself once told a newsman in Haiti that he was pursued by an adventurous, rather indiscreet man by the name of Graham Greene. I knew him best as an inexhaustible voyager who detested boredom. From time to time I reported on his travels in snippets for *Time* magazine's "People" section.

One of the most fascinating stories of that time never made it to print: *The Forgotten Hostage*. Greene's efforts to save a kidnap victim in El Salvador were complicated and required massive amounts of time. I had agreed to Graham's request to embargo the story until the kidnapped victim went free.

He died.

In the early years of our friendship in the mid-1950s, I helped introduce Greene to what was then the pleasantries of Haitian life. Later, in the early 1960s, I helped navigate him through the Byzantine labyrinths of the Duvalier dictatorship of the early '60s. During these latter years, I took him to meet a band of Haitian guerrillas hibernating in an old insane asylum in the Dominican Republic. The group had failed to overthrow Papa Doc and had been forced into exile. Greene, in fact was to have more impact on the Duvalier regime than the guerrillas and all the many attempts to dislodge the Haitian tyrant. But our relationship was not one of reporter and invariant subject.

As noted, the Graham Greene I knew did indeed enjoy living on the "dangerous edge of things," as he put it, and the closer to the edge the better. No one could have loved more than he the thrill of a Volkswagen "bug" skirting the edges of a sheer precipice along the Dominican-Haitian frontier, or flying in an old Cessna with a seemingly mad Panamanian poet. Greene scorned movie-formula heroes and villains. He detested mediocrity. Nor did he actively seek public acclaim. He didn't consider himself a news story when he occasionally "escaped" from England, and later from Antibes during the crowded tourist season on the French Riviera, but instead preferred a low profile, avoiding public attention and interviews. From his perspective, the Americas offered him one of the last frontiers to live and explore as he chose. At times, he spurned his friends' advice and appeared to be swimming against the tide. He was a man who, when all was said and done, relied on his own instinct.

My book, *Seeds of Fiction*, is about Graham Greene and how he drew inspiration to write seven of his books. Greene's first important book, *The Power and the Glory*, was the result of his first trip to Mexico in spring of 1938, and his last, *The Captain and the Enemy*, published in 1988, ended a few hundred miles to the south in Nicaragua. Though Graham Greene is associated with Indochina, (*The Quiet American*) and the Cold War intrigues of Europe (*The Third Man*) and Africa, the fact is that seven of his books (conspicuously also including *The Comedians, Our Man In Havana, The Honorary Consul, The Lawless Roads, Travels with My Aunt, Getting to Know the General* and *The Captain and the Enemy*) were drawn from his odysseys through the Americas encompassing—in addition to Mexico, the Caribbean, Central America and South America.

The "*Viejo Ingles*" will be sorely missed by those who loved and respected him. To salute his memory, and to imbue his historical persona with accuracy it deserves, I rummaged through my old notebooks and unearthed some 130 odd letters I received from Greene over years of our friendship. My book, *The Seeds of Fiction*, is the product of that friendship.

## In Greene's Footprints

It was May Day 1968. The old town of Villahermosa, the capital of the Mexican state of Tabasco, was paralyzed by students demanding the removal of their governor. On one side of the main city plaza, before the Catholic *Templo de la Concepcion,* militant students stood their ground expectantly. One held a sign, "No dispares"[don't shoot].

Rifle-bearing soldiers prepared to fire bristled on the other side before the plaza's largest building *Palacio de Gobierno.* They were not the sloppy, grubby, uniformed soldiers that Graham Greene described after his 1938 trip here, but smartly uniformed elite paratroopers from Mexico City. What had not changed were the black vultures that Greene so hated. Gliding above, their ugly little heads peered down on us, sensing that there would be "carrion" that day. From the time, three decades ago, when Greene had stood in the same old city main *Plaza de Armas*, and written "If I had moved a camera all round the edge of the little plaza in a panning shot it would have recorded all the life there was in the capital city." The *Templo de la Concepcion,* partially destroyed in 1925 during the religious persecution period, had been rebuilt with a new imposing façade, seven years after Greene's visit. This had been the fief of governor-dictator, *Jefe Máximo*, Tomás Garrido Canabal (1920-35) the vicious anti-clerical leader in Mexico who created the Red Shirts, a fascist paramilitary group to hunt down Catholic priests and shout at Garrido's command, "God does not exist, nor ever has existed!" He was finally booted into exile in 1936 by President Cárdenas. One foolish act, a single stone, could trigger bloodshed as the two groups faced off across the plaza in a high noon scenario.

The students were standing firm next to a flag draped coffin. It would be an ideal photograph to illustrate my *Time* magazine story. Earlier, a student running from the police had drowned. Students said he had been swallowed up by the smelly, muddy Grijalva River below the town's plaza. They swore that he had been running from the governor's "corrupt police." I lifted my camera and focused on the students surrounding the coffin.

"No, no puede tomar fotos."

A soldier had suddenly materialized next to me and barked the order, "No, you can't take photos."

I looked down into a very Indian face and saw angry eyes. Ignoring the soldier's order I snapped away with my little Leica camera. The soldier pushed me behind the Army líneas. When I gained my balance, I demanded in Spanish; "Take me to your general!"

"I am the general," the soldier snapped.

It was then I recognized the angry soldier. He was the short, barrel-chested Gen. José Hernández Toledo, commander of the paratroopers, and scourge of the students protesting that year across Mexico against their government's "corrupt one-party rule."

The general was furious. Hot and sweaty Tabasco heated tempers. He demanded my film. "One moment please," I said, "Excuse me but on what authority?" adding that I was a newsman with government credentials. Had he, I asked, declared martial law and taken over the town? He did not answer. His orders were to crush student protests. The government in Mexico City did not want bad publicity. It was the year Mexico City would host the Olympic Games and they did not wish the role of the Army in squashing dissent to become a story.

Checking my papers and searching my camera bag, the General held up a small book.

"Qué es esto?"
"What is it? "Nada," ["Nothing"] I replied. Then I added, "It is an old guide book."

Graham Greene's 1939 non-fiction tome *The Lawless Roads* was to me still relevant as a guide to this area of southern Mexico. It was a good read and filled with good quotes for a story on the region. General Hernandez dropped it (published as *Another Country* in the U.S.) as if it were contaminated. I would have liked to ask the General if he had read *The Power and the Glory* but he shooed me off like a vagrant.

Villahermosa proved to be only a curtain-raiser for the bloody government clamp down on the students at Tlatelolco's *Plaza de la Trés Culturas* in Mexico City five months later. As in Europe and elsewhere, students in Mexico in the 1960s were out to change their world. They marched out of the autonomous universities shouting every known leftwing revolutionary slogan against social injustice, repression, and one-party monopoly on power, and paratroopers marched into the centers of learning, violating their prized autonomy and it became bloody. President Gustavo Díaz Ordaz had become paranoid, and had convinced himself that it was all a communist conspiracy.

As the Tabasco student protest fizzled and their flag-draped coffin proved to be empty—only symbolic, I made a note to write a report on "The Beautiful City" to Greene. I recall how Greene described the Villahermosa police chief's welcome, telling him he was home, that the place was populated by Greenes and Grahams. I could report to Graham that the Mexican Greenes of Villahermosa were prospering, having opened a motel. In my brief note to him I had enclosed an updated brochure of Villahermosa. Graham replied with his usual whimsy, "I was delighted to have details of the Motel Greene which I feel I must visit one day. The Maria Dolores seems to be exactly as I remember it!"

A month earlier, reporting on Mexico's main archeological sites for a *Time* "Modern Living" cover story (10 May 1968) designed to set the scene for the 1968 Olympics in Mexico City, I had taken a two-seater puddle-jumper light plane to Palenque from Villahermosa.

"I think there were only two classes of men I really liked in Mexico—the priests and the flyers," Graham writes in *The Lawless Roads*. "They are something new in Mexico," he recounts, "with their pride in history, their dash, their asceticism; non-drinking and non-smoking...."

My pilot had insisted on finishing his lunch. I waited impatiently. Finally we were airborne. The sun beat down on our cockpit. He flew in a steady line over the plains that were dotted with basins of water flashing silvery in the sun. His large belly was wedged against the controls. The combination of that overloaded plate of enchiladas and the heat had my pilot fighting an airborne siesta. Over the roar of the little plane's engine, I did my best to question him about the history of his state where Hernán Cortés had landed to conquer Mexico, only to receive a series of grunts. When we approached the mountains he was wide awake and carefully guided the plane down to a dirt strip where a thin little girl holding a faded red umbrella acted as the Palenque control tower.

Graham recounted in *The Lawless Roads* riding a mule from Salto de Agua to Palenque and eventually to his "very Catholic city" of San Cristóbal de las Casas. Any trip by mule back, especially in Tabasco's heat and humidity and cold nights on the high mountains on that slow-moving animal, I imagined the ordeal as a form of torture. Nevertheless, the ruins at Palenque, called the Athens of Mayan civilization, were worth the trip. Greene had been more interested in the fate of the Catholic priests than ancient Mayans. As we arrived, workers were digging out more of the ruins from the encroaching jungle. Of all the ruins of a bygone civilization I visited in Mexico, Palenque was definitely the most impressive. Its murals had been restored. The temple of Inscriptions loomed across from the palace, whose four-storied tower archaeologists believed was an observatory built about A.D.692. They were digging, hoping to find other pyramids buried in the mountainside. Young children hocked pieces of pottery and small figures they claimed were the genuine articles found in the dig.

With sufficient notes, interviews, and "color" for our editors in New York, my pilot was happy to take off as the mist descended down the mountains like a heavy blanket. The little Indian girl smiled and unfurled her umbrella as I blew a kiss to her. The City of Snakes quickly disappeared into its shrouds.

For Graham dare-doing paid off in raw material for his masterpiece which had won critical acclaim the world over. *The Power and the Glory,* about personal salvation and the human condition in the person of a Mexican priest, had been read by every Roman Catholic priest and nun I ever met. My eldest sister, a Nun whose faith was strong and unremitting, found the book a triumph of her faith.

Returning to the land of the fugitive "Whisky Priest" did make me ponder Greene's faith and my own. Personally, I preferred not to discuss religion. It was a private affair, especially as I had become a fugitive from my Irish Catholicism pumped into me as a child. As the underdog minority religion in my native New Zealand, we defended it with our fists when necessary. Graham, as a convert and writer, knew more about theology and did believe in God, whereas I respected the belief of others and their many Gods.

In our correspondence during the late 1960s, Graham and I discussed his visiting Mexico again. In a 19 April 1969 letter he was seriously thinking about returning:

"I'd very much like to visit you, but probably late July or August would be the only time and I should imagine the weather would be rather unbearable then? Another problem is that I would have to pay for my journey by arranging an article in one of the Sunday papers on the situation in Mexico and I could hardly stay with you or be connected with you if I did that as I suspect my report would not be very favorable!"

I assured him that he need not worry about getting me into trouble, as I already was on President Gustavo Díaz Ordaz's black list for my sympathetic coverage of the student demonstrations, and especially the Tlateloco Plaza massacre on the eve of the Olympics. I was one of the lucky ones. Along with thousands gathered to hear a student speaker, we stood amid the remains of Aztec ruins next to a colonial church and surrounded by high apartment buildings. Having recognized secret service agents among us, I warned my *Sports Illustrated* colleagues in Mexico to cover the Olympics to leave the area, as there would be trouble. When the flare signal that launched the shooting went up, it was the Aztec ruins that saved many of us from the fate of the students killed that night. The army and plain clothes agents, in an organized ambush that ran amok, began shooting in all directions precisely as a student began to speak from high up on the Edificio Chihuahua. Who was in command? None other than Gen. José Hernández Toledo, and he was wounded leading his troops, and wounded by a government agent, not a student. My eye-witness *Time* story, "Noche Triste", did not endear me to government officials, nor did my coverage of the students' protests in *Life En Español*:

"I still very much want to visit you in Mexico, but the winters are not so easy for me," Graham wrote on 2 July 1971. "Who knows though—I might be able to make a brief two-week visit around Christmas. Would that be an impossible time for you? I am afraid it's too late for me to make any very definite plans."

He went instead to Chile to meet with President Salvador Allende, as the Marxist chief of state was the other major hemispheric story in the making.

Years later atop a helicopter landing pad on a high Sierra Madre peak the author met General Toledo again. Happily the General was in charge of an anti-poppy (opium) campaign.

## Red and Black Greenes of St. Kitts

In the winter of 1993, I found myself on the island of St. Kitts. I was sailing as a lecturer through the eastern Caribbean on the four-mast bark *Sea Cloud*—it had been built sixty-one years earlier for Mrs. Marjorie Merriwether Post and later became Dominican dictator Rafael Trujillo's yacht, the *Angelita*—and I had not forgotten that afternoon in 1956 on the verandah of the Oloffson, and Graham Greene's telling of his tropical relatives in the Caribbean. When we anchored off Basseterre, the tidy capital of St. Kitts, I decided to pursue the Caribbean Greenes. It was as if I were prolonging our journeys together.

My genealogical research proved fascinating. Graham's Great Uncle Charles, it turned out, as Graham said, died on the island of fever at age nineteen after having sired thirteen children! Charles' prolific performance had occurred after the emancipation of the slaves on St. Kitts. Two years before Charles died, Graham's paternal grandfather, William Greene, then fourteen, had joined "Uncle Charlie" on the island to help the latter run the family plantation. Grandfather William went back to England after his brother's death in 1842. Much later, William Greene returned to St. Kitts where he himself died.

"Look in at St. Kitts under its strange dictator. There's an excellent hotel there on a black volcanic beach called The Golden Lemon kept by two Americans . . . they give good food and local food and the rooms are charming, furnished mainly from Haiti," Graham had written to me in 1977. He also wanted me at the time to pick up the trail of the Caribbean Greenes. Later, reporting for *Time* about St. Kitts and its longtime premier, Robert Bradshaw, there was no time to pursue Graham's tropical relatives. Now, on a break from my lecturing voyage, I had the chance to do so. Graham had traveled to St. Kitts once with his brother Hugh and encountered a Greene that Graham was satisfied was a grandchild of Charlie Greene and therefore his cousin. During a 1977 visit in the company of his friend Yvonne Cloetta, they had discovered Charlie's tomb and met another cousin called Victor.

Like many of the other Caribbean islands, St. Kitts was fought over by the British and French, who left a mixture of English and French names of places and people. At St.Kitts and Nevis Telecommunications Company (Nevis being the adjoining island), the twin nations' 142-page 1993 telephone directory revealed, on Page 64, a listing of 21 Greenes. Later my taxi driver said, pointing down Fort Street, "Down there is a Greene."

"Greene's Boutique & Musiquarium" had one of the best locations in town. And it was more than a boutique—it offered music, andincluded the "Why Not Bar: Good Times Bar." Three attractive young shop girls were arranging rows of T-shirts adorned with either parrots or a vernacular Caribbean warning: "Tak you mouth out of me Damm business." I asked to see Mr. Greene. A young, well-built mulatto emerged, a gold chain dangled from his neck.

"You are Mr. Greene?"
"Lorenzo Greene."
"Could I ask you about your roots? Look, I had a friend, a writer named Graham Greene. He is dead now. He has the same last name as yours. Have you ever heard of him?"
"Yes I think so.
"Well I wonder if you are any relation."

Lorenzo Greene was not sure of his family's genealogy. "There is a tomb of an old Greene in the Christchurch cemetery they tell me," he said, adding, "My grandfather was Benjamin Greene and he lived in Sandy Bay. He was an estate [the local term for sugar plantation] manager for the Lamberts six miles west of Basseterre. My grandfather was high-color; he had very light skin like you. My Uncle Clarence Greene, he is 65-years-old and works at St. Kitts Sugar Manufacturing Company, in the electric department. He might be able to tell you more."At the sugar mill's electric workshop they said Clarence Greene had retired to run a grocery shop in Sandy Point. On the main road running through Sandy Point town I found the shop, despite the fact that it bore no name. Mrs. Clarence Greene came to the counter and summoned her husband from the back. Standing behind the counter, Clarence Greene was as tall as Graham. Clarence had hazel eyes and a reddish tinge to his hair. He did not mind discussing his roots.

"I've heard of that Englishman, the one who writes," he said. Yet like his nephew

Lorenzo, Clarence didn't know where their family had acquired the name Greene. "My grandfather was the same color as you," Clarence continued, "No; I've not read his books." "They say my grandfather was Irish," interjected Clarence's wife, who was a shade darker. They lived upstairs in what appeared comfortable circumstances. On a little "Coke is it" blackboard appeared the day's special written in chalk: Pig snout and bags drink (cordial drinks sold in plastic bags).

"At work they used to tease me that I was Portuguese," Clarence explained. (During the 1840s after the abolition of slavery on St.Kitts in 1838, local planters imported some one-thousand, five hundred workers from Madeira to work their sugar plantations. Most returned home after fulfilling their contracts but some stayed and went into business.) Clarence suggested I go back down the road to Basseterre to the village of Challengers. "There is an elder Greene sister there; she might be able to help."

But the house of the elder Greene woman on the main road through Challengers was boarded up. The villagers said she had died two years earlier—Clarence had evidently been unaware of the fact. When I told the villagers I was looking for Greenes, they directed me to another Greene, an older woman who was black.

"That Greene lady died two years ago, she was a red Greene. I am a black Greene," was how the woman identified herself. ("Red" is used widely in the Caribbean to denote a person of lighter skin.) She confessed that she had not the slightest idea how the black Greenes had come by their name. A small group of villagers had gathered and were sympathetic to my search. The 1840s were a long time ago, they reminded me, but they agreed that Uncle Charlie's thirteen offspring could have produced a lot of Greenes.

## Stolichnaya for a Bon Blan

The young University students craned forward in their seats. They shared an eagerness, a thirst, for knowledge of the lost decades when dictatorship had turned their country into an intellectual wasteland. The scene in Port-au-Prince on the afternoon of Friday, 26 May 1995, was a rare official homage to British author Graham Greene—this particular tribute being offered by grateful Haitians. Greene's 1966 novel, *The Comedians,* and the film version for which he wrote the script, had lifted the shroud and exposed Dr. Francois "Papa Doc" Duvalier's tyranny in Haiti to the world. Greene had also won the enmity of Papa Doc, who at one point contemplated having Greene tracked down abroad and physically eliminated.

At the May 1995 *hommage* in French and Creole-speaking Haiti, the Caribbean republic's new Minister of Culture, Jean-Claude Bajeux—former Roman Catholic priest, and exile, who had accompanied Greene and me on our 1965 border trip, a victim of Duvalier's tyranny—was well qualified to lecture on *"La Metaphysique du Mal Chez Graham Greene"* (The Metaphysics of Evil as Seen by Graham Greene"). And Bajeux's audience was all too familiar with the metaphysics of evil, their country having only just emerged from three bloody years of post-Duvalierist military repression during which many of these same students were forced to flee for their lives in boats or to seek refuge in rural Haiti, becoming exiles in their own country. Some of their fellow students had been killed.

The white walls of the newly established non-governmental Info-Service lecture hall, located in an old, renovated Port-au-Prince gingerbread mansion, were covered with posters (provided by the London-based British Council) illustrating Graham Greene's long and productive life. While carrying out his book research at the height of Papa Doc's terror in August 1963, Greene, traveling by taxi, often passed this house on Avenue Charles Sumner in Turgeau, a residential section of the capital, while returning from the Hotel Sans Souci to the venerable Grand Hotel Oloffson. He spent many an afternoon writing up his notes at nearby Hotel Sans Souci where foreign newsmen were staying during the crisis. Now, after thirty-two years, a Greene had returned. Graham's niece, tall, handsome red-haired Louise Dennys, had been invited as the representative of the Greene family. Among the guests was Haiti's best known radio announcer, Jean Dominique, who was later assassinated.

Haiti was no longer Greene's nightmare republic. Haitians were enjoying—at least for the moment—some hope of a better future. A force of twenty-two thousand American troops had made a "soft landing" in Haiti in September 1994 and restored democratically elected President Father Jean-Bertrand-Aristide to power, after he had spent three years in exile. On 31 March 1995, U.S. President Bill Clinton, from a reviewing stand in front of the National Palace, had watched the change of command from U.S. to United Nations peacekeepers. It was an historic sight: an American president seated on a reviewing stand on the steps of what was once a palace of terror. As the bagpipes of a battalion of peace-keepers from Bangladesh wailed, the regimental colors and country flags of the various foreign troops and nations involved in the peacekeeping mission fluttered like colorful *Vodou* flags [beaded *Vodou* flags carry images of their gods in many colors] on the palace lawn.

Of Haiti and *The Comedians* Greene had written, "I would have liked to return yet a fourth time [to Haiti] before completing my novel, but I had written in the English press a description of Doctor Duvalier's dictatorship, and the best I could do in January 1965 was to make a trip down the Dominican and Haitian border—the scene of my last chapter [of *The Comedians*]—in the company of two exiles from Haiti. At least, without Doctor Duvalier's leave, we were able to pass along the edge of the country we loved and to exchange hopes of a happier future."

Bajeux and I were the two exiles from Haiti and Graham's traveling companions. The former priest knew his subject well. During his 23 years in exile, now-Culture Minister Bajeux had been professor of European and Caribbean literature at the University of Puerto Rico, and Greene had been a favorite writer since the ex-cleric's youth. In his ninety-minute lecture Bajeux traced Greene's literary form and emphasized the author's belief in human value and purpose. He defined at length the famous writer's treatment of good and evil. Bajeux stressed that Greene, through his anti-heroes like the whisky priest in *The Power and the Glory* [1940] and Pinkie the murderer in *Brighton Rock* [1938], showed that good and evil coexist within all of us. It is a lesson to all of us, Bajeux said, to be reminded that good and evil coexist in our own souls and that is where we have to look, not outside ourselves. In stating that he had found evil [hell] in Duvalier's Haiti the famous author meant, Bajeux explained, that he (Greene) had found some evil characters in Haiti— whom he later portrayed in *The Comedians* [1966]. The lecture ended with a discussion among professors attending the *hommage* on the origins of violence in Haiti, without reaching any conclusive point. Nevertheless,

Bajeux made reference to the suggestion that a "*Makout* lies in all of us." [The name *Makout* by 1995 had become a Haitian generic term for an evil person.]

On the Monday following the lecture, Louise Dennys, her husband Ric, an American priest friend, and I were escorted to the palace by Minister Bajeux. I couldn't help thinking how pleased Graham would have been–a Greene in Papa Doc's palace! Graham had requested an interview with Dr. Duvalier in 1963 but the then-President-for-Life had refused. The closest Graham had come to the palace was the *Casernes Dr. Francois Duvalier*, the forbidding police headquarters across the street from the alabaster-white presidential offices and residence.

There were no military sentries at the palace gate that Monday. In fact, Haiti no longer had an army. President Aristide had dissolved it upon his return from exile. The country's traditional arbiter of power since independence from France, in 1804 after a long, bloody revolution by Haiti's slaves, was no more. The palace itself had undergone several transformations since the hurried departure of Francois Duvalier's anointed heir to power, his son Jean-Claude "Baby Doc" Duvalier, nearly a decade earlier. One short-lived, military-backed president had called in a *Vodou* priest to exorcise the place of Duvalier evil. When the "Little Prophet", as Father Aristide was known, was swept to power by his *Lavalas* (flash flood) movement, orchids replaced guns in the palace. However, despite the elaborate presidential chair that street children he had rescued made for Aristide, which they presented to him when he entered the National Palace February 1991—the children wanted to cover all bases as an old Haitian legend has it that the presidential chair is "*range*," (bewitched)—the military dragged Aristide out of the palace, came close to killing him, and eventually booted him into exile.

At our meeting with him that Monday following the homage to Graham Greene, President Aristide talked amicably and enthusiastically to Ms. Dennys about his hopes for a literacy campaign (Haiti's illiteracy remains high at 87 percent). A self-described voracious reader, Aristide said he had read *The Comedians* while studying at a seminary in La Vega, in the neighboring Dominican Republic. (Actually, I had presented him with a first edition copy of *The Comedians* in Washington D.C. while he was in exile and he promised to read it.) The meeting went on longer than the allotted time. When Aristide, himself an author, learned that Ms. Dennys had once had her own publishing business and currently represented a prominent American publishing firm in Canada, where she resided, the president invited us into his adjoining workroom to show off his books and to present her with a beautiful painted box–a modest but simple tribute to Greene. There was nothing in the decorative box, just the air of Haitian freedom, Aristide joked.[1]

With the homage concluded, while we were relaxing on the balcony of the Grand Hotel Oloffson, I mentioned to Louise, Ric, and Father Alberto Huerta, a professor of literature from the University of San Francisco who had corresponded with Greene over his religious beliefs, how I had left a bottle of Stolichnaya vodka at a *Vodou* temple as a tribute to Graham, following

---

[1] But Aristide himself put that precious air of Haitian freedom to the test. What many suspected about the violence-prone little priest manifested itself. Exhibiting characteristics not unlike Papa Doc Duvalier, he was overthrown, and today lives in exile in South Africa.

his death in Switzerland on 3 April 1991. After attending Greene's memorial service at London's Westminster Cathedral, at which Louise had delivered a warm and simple eulogy, I had returned to Haiti and left Graham's favorite midday martini at *Mambo* Lolotte's *hounfor* (temple), located on the Cul-de-Sac plain some dozen miles north of Port-au-Prince.

*Mambo* Lolotte and the other women of her family, I recalled, were sorting freshly harvested yams in her *peristyle* (central part of the temple) the day I motored out into the countryside to see her. I wanted to leave a bottle for Graham at a *Vodou* temple, in the *Vodou* manner for the departed. "It is for a *bon blan* [good white man"], I explained to the *Vodou* priestess. She interrupted her labors and unlocked the door to a small thatched hut, the *callie mysteres*, home of the *lwas*—the spirits. It was late afternoon. There was no embarrassment on my part. It seemed like the natural thing to do. I did feel she should know that the bottle was for the spirit of a writer "who did what he could to help Haiti."

The priestess's muscular arms and legs were caked with mud from harvesting yams. It had been a good harvest. She was a strong and handsome woman, who did not live off her religion, *Vodou*, but instead worked the land and never failed to pay dues to her gods, in the form of a rich ceremony to them. She traditionally celebrated the *manger-yam Vodou* ceremony in her sanctuary. It did appear to pay off. Most years she had a bumper crop. Graham would have liked her.

As she opened the door of the hut enough sunlight peeped in to guide me to the altar dedicated to the *lwas*. I chose a little space between the dust-laden bottles of liqueurs, wines and spirits, discernible only by their shapes, in which to place Graham's bottle of Stolichnaya. It would, I was confident, remain there and gather its own coat of dust from the neighboring fields.

There was no need for a bottle of vermouth. Graham used just a drop of vermouth when mixing a gin martini but never with vodka. Lolotte asked no questions. "It is for a good *blan*," I repeated. "He did what he could for the Haitian people." The priestess murmured a prayer and called upon *"Bon Dieu"* to look after his spirit. "He wrote a book about Haiti; it was called *The Comedians*," I added, explaining briefly and as well as I could in this spiritual setting what Greene meant by *"Comedians"*. *Mambo* Lolotte understood, exhibiting surprising sophistication. As she left to return to preparing her yams for market, she stood for a moment in the doorway of the little hut, in thought. "We are *les Komedyens*," she said, using the Creole word." We Haitians are all actors. We must be to survive." Unlike Catholicism, *Vodou* has no heaven or hell. Graham's soul would be free to wander—he would like that—and even return to Haiti. After she left I remained for a long, reflective interval in the cool *Vodou* sanctuary. As had occurred at Graham's memorial Mass in London's Westminster Cathedral, memories of the man flooded back. Paradoxical as he often was, Graham, the Catholic convert, would have been more at home with this simple *Vodou* tribute in Lolotte's *hounfor* than high Mass at Westminster. The *Vodou* priestess's prayer would have been less embarrassing for him and he was easily embarrassed. Yet the Westminster service was in the Latin he loved.

A remarkably independent human being, Graham had continually challenged his adopted faith (He had been born into the Church of England.) This constant questioning had made him, I believed, a better

Catholic than most. I left the offering of Stolichnaya to repose in Lolotte's *bagui* and then worried that I should have gotten a larger-size bottle. The *Vodou* gods liked to be abundantly pleased.

The light was fading. I took leave of Mambo Lolotte, bidding her a generous farewell. Ironically, Lolotte's *peristyle* was a neighbor to Pont Beudet, Haiti's ancient but still functioning insane asylum. Not far down the road was what remained of Jean-Claude Duvalier's ranch. The entrance gate to the walled-in property was broken and hanging on its hinges. The unmanned, rusty guard turrets and high concrete wall were all that were left standing of the once-elaborate country retreat of Baby Doc Duvalier. Peasants in the area said that the army had looted the ranch residence and then set it afire, blaming the local people. Even the mounds of lead from spent bullets on Jean-Claude's private shooting range had been collected for scrap. (In Haiti, a poverty-ridden nation of automatic recycling, very little goes to waste.) As I passed Baby Doc's ranch on my return to Port-au-Prince, vegetation rotted in the swimming pool and cows and goats grazed in his ex-wife Michele's garden. I thought to myself: How quickly can disappear the trappings of power.

When I finished the story of my memorial pilgrimage, Louise asked me to take them out to meet Lolotte. I agreed. We arrived unexpectedly at Lolotte's sanctuary to find the priestess officiating with a group of faithful at prayers. We were given chairs and waited until the prayers ended. *Mambo* Lolotte greeted us and graciously agreed to open her *bagui* with its offerings. To my pleased surprise, Graham's bottle of Stolichnaya had been elevated to repose on a red cushion on a miniature rocking chair. Father Huerta asked the *Vodou* priestess whether he could say a prayer, and she readily acceded. We four visitors stood before the small altar with the Mambo as Father Huerta led us in a silent prayer. It was an ultimate ecumenical act. Graham would have understood.

**Bernard Diederich** is a journalist and biographer who has devoted much of his career to covering political events in Central America and the Caribbean. He founded Haiti's English language newspaper, the *Haiti Sun*; he also served as a correspondent for The Associated Press, *The New York Times*, Time-Life, and the *Daily Telegraph* in London.

Diederich was with Fidel Castro on his victory march to Havana in 1959. In 1963, because of his news reporting, Diederich was imprisoned by the Haitian dictator, Papa Doc Duvalier, and was eventually expelled from the country. He is the author of many books, including *Seeds of Fiction: Graham Greene's Adventures in Haiti and Central America 1954-1983*, which chronicles events in his long-term friendship with Graham Greene. His recent memoir is *Pamir: Sailing the Pacific in World War II*.

# Traveling in Greeneland

## Quentin Falk

More than thirty years after the publication of my first book, *Travels in Greeneland: The Cinema of Graham Greene* (and even more poignantly at the Silver Anniversary of Greene's death,) I now find myself in, of all places, America's Deep South, heart of the Bible Belt, writing the great man's name and dates on a white board in a classroom at the campus of the University of North Georgia (UNG), about seventy or so miles from Atlanta.

Writing and talking about Greene, with whom I had a short but fascinating acquaintance in 1983/84, has not only brought me here, for the third time, to this rather beautiful institution, sited picturesquely near the start of the 2,150-mile-long Appalachian Trail, but also helped to introduce me to the wider Greene "family" of friends, fans, and academics who have kept the flame lit for, arguably, the finest of twentieth—century English novelists.

That "family" became further, and very happily, extended for me in these halls of academe with the arrival as Spring began of Bernard Diederich, this year's Visiting Author at UNG (I had that honor in 2013), whose brilliant and revealing—albeit much too belated—memoir, *Seeds of Fiction*, about "Greene's Adventures in Haiti and Central America 1954-1983," to coin the book's subtitle, gave me new and revealing insights into the great man's colorful life and times.

I had the privilege of moderating three Q&As for Diederich, whose amazing recall and quiet humor belied a man on the cusp of ninety (he actually passed the milestone three months later), including one with my Creative Non-Fiction Writing class, who were clearly fascinated by his life as a journalist in some of the world's hottest spots as the bullets were flying. For his part, you could see how, in between teenager stories of four-masted ship voyages during wartime and a recital of various dictator oppressions, he still retained perhaps his fondest memory for his long friendship with Greene.

As Greene's latest biographer, his namesake Professor Richard Greene, puts it in an elegant Introduction to *Seeds of Fiction*: Diederich was "a guide and political adviser" to the author, more than 20 years his senior, as well as being, in Greene's words, "a figure of quiet heroism" who endured imprisonment and exile on account of his fearless journalism.

Although I did not realize it at the time, my first association with Graham Greene's more immediate family actually began when I was about fourteen or fifteen. Concerned especially about my lack of height, my father took me to see the country's leading endocrinologist, Dr. Raymond Greene, none other than Graham's older brother. Possibly taller than his younger brother, the good doctor—also a very accomplished mountaineer—was very encouraging, said something about slow-maturing bones, told us "not to worry," and sent us on our way. Some pills may also have been involved. At 17, I grew seven inches in the next year and a half.

I cannot remember whether I ever told his brother this either when we first met in Antibes in 1983 or, eighteen months later, at our brief reunion for an interview on stage at the National Film Theatre (NFT) on London's South Bank to celebrate both the publication of my book and Greene's impending 80th birthday. Also neither of us knew that the NFT occasion was being secretly if crudely filmed—flagrantly without Greene's permission—from the projection booth for, eventually, a wider television audience around the writer's Centenary in 2004, thirteen years after his death.

As for maintaining any sort of association after our collaboration on *Greeneland*, that never really seemed to be even remotely in the cards, remembering that Norman Sherry was still—to Greene's increasing annoyance—dogging his footsteps before the publication nearly five years later of what would be the first of three huge volumes of authorized biography.

As I wrote in the fourth and most recent edition of *Greeneland*, serendipitously published a couple of years ago by the University of North Georgia Press (now with the addition of a new chapter and a thoughtful Afterword by my latest boss, UNG English Department Head, Dr. Joyce Stavick), if I had hoped for "some obvious sign of approval [for my book], I was to be disappointed." In a polite but fairly terse letter about arrangements ahead of our NFT date, Greene added in a P.S., "Please, if your book is to be reprinted in paperback, correct the mistake on page 4 or it will be endlessly repeated. *Brighton Rock* sold 8,000 not 80,000 copies." Clearly the British taxman, who had apparently driven Greene into his French exile from 1966, still cast a very long shadow.

Happily, the book enjoyed some decent reviews at publication and, sometime later, even inclusion on a major Film Book of the Year Award shortlist—no, it did not win, sadly—before it began to recede from my memory as I took on, irregularly, new book projects, principally more conventional, showbiz-related biographies in between the bread-and-butter of film reviewing and various magazine editorships.

Then, in 1998, a summons arrived out of the blue from the organizers of the inaugural Graham Greene Festival asking if I would like to introduce a screening of *The Third Man* (incidentally, two years before it would be voted The Greatest British Film of the Century in a new millennium poll of film critics arranged by the British Film Institute (BFI); *Brighton Rock* was number 15). The venue, in the impressive 22-story Kodak UK headquarters, situated just off the town's famous "Magic Roundabout," was the first—and actually smallest—of a number of theatres, which would, over the succeeding years, host Festival screenings.

The following year, we were back in Hemel Hempstead where I introduced a screening of . . . well, perhaps not surprisingly, *Brighton Rock*, part of a four-pronged focus on the novel at that Festival, including talks on "Darkest Greeneland" by Professor Cedric Watts and "The Making of The Film" by Maire McQueeney, who also led a guided day visit of the town itself.

Over the next fifteen years, in a variety of venues ranging from the Elgiva Centre, Chesham to The Civic Centre, Berkhamsted via The Rex Cinema and the school's own Deans' Hall, I had a succession of ever delightful late autumn Festival assignments, introducing various films in the Greene canon. These included the remakes of *The Quiet American, The End of the Affair, The Honorary Consul, Across the Bridge, Dr. Fischer of Geneva*, and *England Made Me*.

Even more memorable, certainly from my point of view, were various close encounters with articulate filmmakers who had embarked on their own travels in Greeneland, explaining to me in front of very appreciative audiences, the pleasures and potential pitfalls of adapting Greene's work for the cinema and television:

writer-director Peter Duffell (*England Made Me*), the late writer-producer Richard Broke (*Dr. Fischer*), and, on two occasions, separated by more than a decade, producer Stephen Woolley (*The End of the Affair*), not to mention fine British actors such as Ian Hart and Greta Scacchi.

Away from the Festival, our paths would indirectly cross again some years after Greene had died when I was commissioned to write a new biography of Alfred Hitchcock. The more I researched Hitch's life, desperately trying to find something to say that had not been said a hundred times before in numerous previous memoirs, the more I kept thinking what a perfect fit he and Greene would have made, and not just because of their shared Catholic faith.

It was probably something to do with what another filmmaker, Neil Jordan, had sagely opined in his generous Foreword to the 2000 3rd edition of my book when he linked "those two poets of English criminality and bad conscience," while bemoaning their "lack of contact." Writing about the so-called "Master of Suspense" gave me a chance to re-examine Greene's "strange miasma," as Jordan put it, about the work of Alfred Hitchcock which began when he was reviewing some of Hitch's work in the Thirties: "How unfortunate it is that Mr. Hitchcock, a clever director, is allowed to produce and even write his own films. Though as a producer he has no sense of continuity and as a writer he has no sense of life . . . ." Years later, Greene would admit to me that he actually did like some of Hitchcock's later work (after he went to Hollywood).

But clearly he had not quite yet acquired that more forgiving retrospect when, in the late fifties, Hitchcock approached him about acquiring the rights to *Our Man in Havana*. "I refused to sell them to him," Greene told me. "I felt the book just wouldn't survive his touch."

However, I personally still like to fantasize from time to time just what Hitch might have fashioned from titles like *The Ministry of Fear*, *A Gun for Sale*, or even *The Tenth Man*. Criminality and conscience, indeed.

I write this during my final days of lately acquired academe in North Georgia wondering what Greene, with his often mordant views of many matters American, might have made of the current "Race for the White House," which day-by-day more resembles a chillingly tacky Reality TV show. Yet, the dawning possibility that America's next Commander-in-Chief might conceivably be a ruthless international businessman with strange hair, whose even stranger policies make *The Quiet American*'s Alden Pyle seem like a boy scout in comparison, is, happily for me at least, temporarily eclipsed—trumped?—by one of Greene's most outrageous creations, Augusta Bertram.

I am "teaching," as they say, both the book and film of *Travels With My Aunt* as part of a Film and Literature course I have called 'The Absurd'—an excuse for me to punctuate appropriate texts like Swift's *A Modest Proposal*, Kafka's *The Trial*, and Carroll's poem *Jabberwocky* with some favorite movies such as *Dr. Strangelove*, Woody Allen's *Love And Death*, and the Marx Brothers' *Duck Soup*. *Travels* is the only specific book-to-film example I have chosen, not just to introduce second-year American college students probably for the first time to a playful Greene but also to highlight graphically how Hollywood could so fatally mangle such an exhilarating text.

Ironically—befitting elements of my course subject—some of the students seem to find the screen adaptation rather beguiling, perhaps to do with the fact that the then 38-year-old Maggie Smith appeared to be auditioning for the ancient Dowager Lady Grantham from *Downton Abbey,* which has been a huge hit in the States and exposed the now officially veteran Dame Maggie to a whole new generation who know absolutely nothing of her earlier and much younger, Oscar-winning performances.

For me, this latest stopover in Greeneland brings to mind—maybe fulfills is a better word—not one of Aunt Augusta's more extravagant claims but rather the words of the Brighton fortune-teller Hatty when she predicts: "You are going to do a lot of travelling. With another person. You are going to cross the ocean. You are going to have many adventures." My travels in Greeneland have helped me have all that, and more.

**Quentin Falk** is the author of nine books including *Travels in Greeneland: The Cinema of Graham Greene*, shortlisted for the Mobil BFI Film Book of the Year, and biographies of Anthony Hopkins, Alfred Hitchcock and Albert Finney. He has also been a film reviewer for the *Daily Mail*, *Daily Telegraph*, *Sunday Telegraph*, *Sunday Mirror*, and *Catholic Herald*, as well as Editor of the trade paper *Screen International and Academy*, journal of the British Academy of Film & Television Arts (BAFTA). In 2016, he was a Visiting Professor of English at the University of North Georgia.

# 'Dr Fischer of Geneva' Or There's so Much More to Christmas Crackers

## David R.A. Pearce

### The 2009 Graham Greene International Festival

In 1931 Graham Greene was playing Honegger's *Pacific 321* on his gramophone as he contemplated the writing of *Stamboul Train*. In the urgent drumming of the wheels, he imagined himself steaming towards Istanbul, caught in an adventure involving frontiers. It was, said Vivien, one of their favorite records in their cottage in Chipping Campden.[1] Forty-eight years later, in 1979, it was Mozart's *Jupiter Symphony* that had caught Greene's mind. This record provided a point of reference in *Dr. Fischer*, and Greene celebrates the violinist Heifetz, who was almost exactly his contemporary.

Greene liked music, and this symphony is an important strand in *Dr. Fischer of Geneva*. The music of Mozart is the antithesis to Greene's spiritual quest. The music resolves uncertainties, is complete in itself, and soothes the edges of our lives. Perhaps that is why Greene is drawn to it, for he, in his writing, is intent more on exploring than on resolving. In his exploring he takes us with him and that is, perhaps, the reason why we read Greene and find his work enduring. But in the end he, and we, all seek some resolution to life's uncertainties. About God we cannot absolutely know. In Love we do not quite achieve. With Power we may for a while divert ourselves. With Death we become increasingly familiar. Greene rubs these themes between thumb and finger.

Death sits at the center of *Dr. Fischer*. In Jones's company, we and Graham sit in our reflective later days (Graham was 75), with our coffee and our memories—a photo or two, and a chair once sat in—"as often as you do these things you shall do them in memory of me." Who is the "me"? We shall explore that "me." The music plays. In it we find some comforting completeness. Woody Allen is reported to have said that this symphony proved the existence of God. Possibly Greene found the same to be true.

*Stamboul Train* was an earnest of what was to come with Greene. With novel after novel the same ingredients are taken out and dusted. In *Dr. Fischer*, 1980, they are rehearsed again, but the urgent movement has gone; the story is simplified; it is all compact and ritualized. There is the same bright-eyed interest, the same glint of humor, but there is a greater economy, a composure. It is a novella—shorter, tight, only 140 pages long. The ideas still twist and turn. What else should we expect of Greene—the fidget over words, semantics, theology; but the storyline is simple, uncluttered, almost static. Plot is less extravagant and demanding. We may see Greene's thoughtful, honest face, and that of Fr. Leopoldo Duran, his Jesuit confessor, to whom ideas were tossed. We can feel at home here in a room as simple and as bare as Greene's flat in Antibes: Minimalism, but never of the mind—that is until the music lends composure.

---

1 Sherry, Norman. The Life of Graham Greene, Volume I: 1904-1939. New York: Penguin, 1989, *408*.

The great power, the great attraction of a Greene novel is in engagement. The novel and the author interrelate, react. Greene is writing about his time, about his ideas at that moment when he feels age is creeping, and about the scenes. Scenes that he knew intimately well, and that his daughter remembered years later. The novel and Greene are compellingly synonymous and personal. Reality and symbolism merge, and there is always the deeper, longer intellectual vertebration that draws you onwards. Something allegorical, mythical, arresting lurks in the spare and focused narrative.

*Dr. Fischer of Geneva* can be viewed from different perspectives. The double title is intriguing. Already the possibilities of dialectic. *Dr. Fischer of Geneva*—the distinguished public figure! And *The Bomb Party*—Terrorism, or a hoax? What is the association? The nexus poses questions. Playfully Greene engages his reader. It's a martini, a fix—cocaine, opium—and much more legal. With this in mind, it is a surprise that this little book has not been more considered. Here is a mature Greene statement. We can be even more amazed that that omnium—gatherum biographer, Norman Sherry, does not even mention the novel.

Because the story is so pared down and focused, we have time to mull over the implications of its components: love, two house parties, two deaths, humiliation, and ultimate power of (one sort or another.) A reader may come to the novel from all Greene's previous work and be aware of his patterns of thought and predilection.

It is always fun to know how a story was born. Greene's daughter, Caroline Bourget, was present at that creative moment, and is our source of information. The occasion was a Christmas Eve dinner at her house in Vevey. Greene was there with his grandsons, Andrew and Jonathan. At the end of the dinner the boys pulled the crackers, and Graham conceived the idea that one of the crackers might not just bang, but explode. The other crackers might hold jewels or something of value. The boys joined in with suggestions of what they would like from their crackers. But one cracker was to be explosive. Greed is weighed against fear. We are back to Russian roulette[2] and that frisson of excitement to which Greene returns again and again. Suddenly, he has the focus for the story—the Bomb Party.

The instigator of this party is Dr. Fischer. He is immensely wealthy, his money coming from world-wide sales of Dentophil Bouquet. His wife, Anna, has died. Embittered Fischer, dead to Pity, now takes a sadistic delight in humiliating a few rich "Toads," as his daughter calls them, obsequious time servers. How far will greed overcome a sense of humiliation? He sees it as a research project.

Alfred Jones (whose story it is and through whose eyes we see everything) has a humble position translating letters for a Chocolate Company. Chocolate ruins the teeth, but Dentophil Bouquet keeps teeth white and sparkling. The two men are opposites in many ways, but not entirely. Always, with Greene, one must watch out for the similarities of opposites. Jones marries Fischer's daughter, Anna-Luise, and it is through her that the two opposites are brought together.

Fischer throws lavish parties for the Toads, and almost by chance Jones is included in the guest list. The parties center on the willingness of the guests to be humiliated for material gain. The Toads, rich already, are hooked, but will Jones, the ordinary man with the ordinary name, sell his dignity? Anna-Luise begs him not

---

2 Ibid., 121, 126.

to accept the invitation to the party that becomes, in this first instance for him, the Porridge Party. Fischer tries to humiliate Jones, but Jones remains aloof and scornful. He preserves his independence of will. He cannot be bought. Then, Anna-Luise is killed in a skiing accident. The final party is the Bomb Party. The guests dip into a bran tub for crackers. Five of the crackers contain checks worth two million francs; one contains a bomb—so we are told. Greed versus Fear. Jones is different. Out of misery for lost love he now might be bought by Death; he can be swayed by Grief. The others simply want the loot. That is the brief résumé of the plot.

The setting is important. Greene is always good on that envelope of reality. He sets this story in and around Vevey, in Switzerland. Fisher is spelled in the Swiss way—Fischer—and the name is important—Greene was very adamant that he wanted that particular name. He always chose names carefully and asked his daughter to check that there was not a real Dr. Fischer in the Geneva directory. He did not want the trouble that he had had with J.B.Priestley, who had threatened to sue over the first print run of *Stamboul Train*; but Graham did want this name. We will return to it.

Caroline says that Fischer's house was based on a house they all once visited at Mies, near Geneva. The house was owned by Robert Schwab, who owned a chain of shops called Contis. Alfred Jones worked for the great chocolate firm in Vevey. Nestlé, of course: its administrative center is in Vevey. The Swiss ski slopes, "Les Diablerets" and "Les Paccots," were well known to the Greene family. This precision of place is typical of Greene. It is the backcloth of his life. Wherever he went all was relevant. He took note.

Once again we find the old specter and tease of suicide. Mrs. Faverjon, one of the Toads, has committed suicide. She was fond of birds and the Quail Party upset her. Having lost his wife, Jones contemplates how he might most easily commit suicide. He does not have the courage to jump from his office building. Whisky and tablets?—possibly; a car accident would involve others; he has no gun[3]; starvation?—perhaps. . . like the Mayor of Cork in 1920 but that would take too long; drowning?—Lake Léman is nearby, but Jones has a phobia about water; gas?—but he was all electric.[4]

We remember how Graham swam in the school swimming pool, having swallowed, he says, twenty aspirins.[5] Even the Divisionaire makes his contribution to the theme: "When I was a boy, I used to play at Russian roulette with a cap pistol. It was very exciting."[6] We have heard it all before. We turn the pages and there is a sense of déjà vu. The miserable Jones searches for a method, "Without too much pain for myself or too much unpleasantness for others."

Describing Jones's experience in the Blitz, Graham relives his *own* wartime experiences. Jones lost a hand and his parents. He tells the vivid story of fire-fighting near The Bank of England and on the Tottenham Court Road. This was Graham's beat as, first, the bombs in 1940, and, then, the V.1s exploded. Jones, on fire warden duty, was reading an anthology called *The Knapsack*. He recalls the poem that he was reading when the bomb dropped. It was Keats' *Ode to a Grecian Urn*.

---

3 Ibid., 108.
4 Ibid., 109.
5 Greene, Graham. *A Sort of Life*. New York: Simon and Schuster, 1971, 86.
6 Ibid., 126.

Like the Mozart music, the poetry provides a point of reference outside time:

> Bold lover, never, never, canst thou kiss, Though winning near the goal—yet do not grieve: She cannot fade though thou hast not thy bliss . . . " Thy streets for evermore will silent be . . .

Death holds ultimate resolution. There is the sublimation which transcends our mortal anxieties. The clues are there.

Frequently in Greene's writing there are echoes of that other favorite poet, Robert Browning. In this book the nod of recognition might be to *My Last Duchess*. There is a picture on Fischer's stairway of a woman holding a skull. Like the Duke in the poem, Fischer has the same lordly inability to accept it that there can be love between his wife, Anna, and another man—Steiner.

> "She preferred his company to mine." Then all smiles stopped together There she stands As if alive.

There is the echo of furtive shuffling of Secret Service documents, Skoda, arms deals, and financial laundering. Palestine, Iran.[7] In some strangely knotted business on which Kips is engaged, we can detect the scheming of Greene's MI6 days.

And Dreams: Greene recorded all his dreams in four notebooks. In Jones's dream, Fischer is standing, black-suited, beside an empty grave.[8] "Strange how one can be affected all day by a dream" says Jones, says Greene. The sad Fischer of dreams almost takes over from the bloodless manipulator.

Dentists are another theme that recurs. Jones helps in the manufacture of tooth-destroying confectionary; dentists and decay are balanced. Greene was always concerned about his teeth, and teeth are a subject of interest in the novels. Belmont—the name of one of the Toads who is a tax specialist—is also the name of a large Swiss dental business dating from the 1920s that makes equipment and dentist chairs. Belmont can make your tax returns look clean and sparkling—the flashing full set of deception. Graham's sense of humor never deserts him.

In all these allusions it is as if Greene is playing a game. The man who preferred to be private and anonymous is saying "Find me if you can." It is like one of those games that the Greene family played in Old Hall in School House at Christmas time: Catch-as-catch-can or Blindman's Bluff. He enjoys the game; and the reader, once he cottons on, can enjoy it too. Sudden similarities give realism to the apparently insignificant. One little instance is that Fischer, being powerful, can afford to be dismissive of the telephone. "'He very much dislikes the telephone,' says Albert."[9] This was true, too, of Charles Greene, Graham's headmaster father. Both preferred to maintain distance.

Through the book runs the theme of the contrived practical joke, even such a joke as Graham loved to play. The actual Bomb Party is his imaginative triumph as well as Fischer's. We can find in this book all the characteristics of a Greene novel. They are often the playful moments of nostalgia, but they are weighted here with the seriousness of a lifetime's thinking. They serve also to show the integrity of Graham's life from beginning to end.

---

7 Ibid., 76.
8 Ibid., 66.
9 Ibid., 98.

Greene's preoccupation with tax was a more weighty legacy from his past. He settled in Antibes, and in Switzerland because he was a tax exile. His whole life had taken a turn for the worse because of the devious tax laundering of his adviser, Tom Windsor Roe. Greene was always concerned about money. The "Rich" Greenes had so much of it; the "Intellectual" Greenes had too little. Always for Greene it was a matter of maximizing what he could earn. In later life he would ask his accountant what he was worth. Englishmen don't have money, we learn in the novel. He need not have worried. By this time in his life, Greene was very comfortably placed, but tax is nevertheless a theme. Tom Roe was bad news; the Royal Victorian Sausage Company and the Cadco Pig Project were bad news. Roe went to prison. He had mismanaged the affairs also of Charlie Chaplin and Noel Coward, but they already lived abroad, and so were less affected.

*Dr. Fischer*, then, harps on tax avoidance—and on keeping teeth and bank credit white, with a flashing smile. Tax, the fisc, evasion, investments, Switzerland, special cantonal arrangements, War Loans—they pay no English tax. It would be better if the Bomb Party checks were not signed. Mrs. Montgomery and Belmont discuss safe "bonds." Fischer can be aloof from mere worldly tax matters because he has so much that money matters do not trouble him. Lawyers and police are his agents. The theme of manipulating money is an obsession: it runs through the book like an insistent income tax demand. Jones is safe because he is poor. But is he poor enough? Riches and Poverty are another duality.

One other person who had harmed Greene in youthful days was Kenneth Richmond, the psychoanalyst. What started as a benign and liberating influence had turned sour. The bent tax adviser—Tom Roe in real life—becomes Belmont in the book. One might wonder if the name "Richmond" is lurking somewhere in Greene's mind. The names are similar: the characters superimposed. Names were carefully chosen: they had a significance to Greene.

Indirectly, it was because of Roe that *Dr. Fischer* is set in Switzerland. Greene makes Art out of Necessity. It has already been said: our author recycles everything. Everything is reinvested—for the story primarily—but the actual financial investment in a new book was not irrelevant.

On the subject of names, let us round up the field. Jones, as a name, is a favorite with Greene. We have met him before in the *Comedians*. There, Brown and Smith were his companions. Jones in this novel is sometimes miscalled Smith. These are all names to sign furtively in a hotel register. Jones is the ordinary man; and with the Christian name, Alfred, he is on the edge of being ever-so-slightly ludicrous, more so if it had been Aelfred:

The Christian name... belonged exclusively now to the working class and was usually abbreviated to Alf.[10]

Shorn of its "Mr." the name is horribly indeterminate. Jones is a Welsh name but Fischer asks him about porridge!

"I understand that the Welsh—no, no, I remember, Jones—I mean the Scots—consider it a blasphemy to spoil their porridge with sugar."[11]

It is all part of Dr. Fischer's plan to unsettle and humiliate. Mrs. Montgomery gets his

---

10 Ibid., 12.
11 Ibid., 57.

name wrong. The servant, Albert, equally proletarian, forgets Jones's name. That is the final insult.

Jones is a pawn, a mere translator, an earner of only 3,000 francs a month, but capable of love and honor. He is contented and complete in his little world. His father was all right because he was Sir Frederick Jones. He had a handle on his commonplace name, just the same as with Greene who had an uncle, Sir William Graham Greene. Jones, then, has similarities with Greene, and so does Fischer, though the two in many ways seem opposites. Fischer does have that distinctive title: he is "of Geneva." It gives him a handle: Kitchener of Khartoum, Lawrence of Arabia. Big men can use mere surnames with impunity.

We shall consider the name "Fischer" later.

Of the other names there is less to say but always I suspect that Greene had some reason for his choices. Kips, the international lawyer, looks like a figure "7" written in the continental way with a bar across. He looks like his written initial, a capital "K." Spare, gaunt, angle-armed, head down, looking for dropped money: Kips Krupp. Greene associates the names, and he remarks that the latter was as subservient to Hitler as the former is to Fischer.

Divisionaire Krueger is Swiss. The name is Germanic, sounding of militarism and resolution. The name has money associations. But the man is old and his high military rank means little in a determinedly neutral country. He has never heard gunfire, and pathetically shuns risking himself in a bomb explosion. He likes being referred to as "General," although he is not a General.

Had Greene anyone in mind with Richard Deane, the film actor? He knew plenty of failed actors only too willing to boast of their own successes:

"Did you by any chance see me in '*The Beaches of Dunkirk*'? . . . I think it was quite the best film I ever made."

"I will go, sir, if I may go alone."[12]

Deane was proud of that line: he had introduced it himself.

Richard Burton? The drinking would fit. "What about Basil Dean?" suggested Neil Sinyard when I asked him. "He directed the screenplay for *21 Days*; Greene had scant regard for him." What of the premature ejaculation? What does Graham know about someone? He is amusing himself with a private joke.

Montgomery was a name Greene had used before. Here, she is the blue-rinse American. Greene recycles names for reasons that are probably now lost to us. One can never assume that with Greene anything is casual. Everything is weighed, deliberate.

This brings me to Steiner, the stone, the man whom Fischer flung aside, the man who loved both music and Anna. At the very end, standing together in the darkness of a New Year morning are Fischer, Jones, and Steiner. Steiner is the 'hard place' that Fischer cannot penetrate or understand. They stand face to face. In a minute there is a shot, and Fischer is dead. The "stone" remains. Jones remains. Not happy, but the two of them survive to hand on . . . something.

We immediately recognize the Greene polarities, the opposites, and the rivalries

---

12 Ibid., 114.

that are gradually drawn together: strength balanced against weakness; power against ordinariness, poverty against wealth, decay against cleanliness, Chocolates against Dentophil Bouquet, Love against Hate. Eventually it is God matched with Satan, the two sides of the famous green baize door, point—counterpoint. Greene works by sharp oppositions. By indirections he finds directions out, not final answers, but directions. And this is what is so fascinating about this book. Greene never patronizes by telling us "What is" but "What might be."

And along that path we now travel. The central counterpoint is between Fischer and Jones: they are mirror images. Literary critics and moralists come down hard on Fischer. We know better with Graham. Listen to the resonances between the apparently good and the apparently evil:

1) Jones is maimed—he has one hand. Fischer, too, is incomplete. Maybe he lacks heart.
2) One man marries Anna, the other Anna-Luise.
3) Both wives die. One man grieves; the other may grieve. It is open to question.
4) Both men need a confidant, a point of reference. Fischer wants Jones at the next party "as a witness."
5) Suicide is a factor in both men's lives.
6) Both talk about God.
7) Jones humiliates the Toads at the Porridge Party more than Fischer does. His freedom of choice shows them up, and Fischer enjoys it the more because of Jones, and Jones is partially responsible for the conduct of the party. Deane is given the pigskin photograph frame that Jones suggests, and the idea of the checks comes from Jones. Rejected at first, it becomes the final exquisite insult. The Toads are strangely deferential to Jones. They give him Christmas cards.
8) Neither Jones nor Fischer take second helpings of caviar. Both are observers of the scene, detached.

There is enough to make us realize that we must look shrewdly. Let me say that I do not entirely dislike Fischer. I should find him uncomfortable, but that is different. Jones's indifference proves that attendance at the parties is entirely voluntary—and if the Toads are prepared to be humiliated, they have nothing of which to complain. They are as guilty as, and certainly less interesting than, Fischer. They are a captive audience by their own inclination. They are no more obliged to go on with the humiliation than the reader of this chapter has to make the effort to follow the argument.

Of Fischer, then, we rely on Jones and Anna-Luise for our perspectives. We like Jones because we see the story through his eyes. He claims nothing for himself; he is not ambitious; he is not spiteful; he is capable of love; he has enough self-esteem to stand up to Fischer and he will not compromise his own decent standards. He is a decent Greene-ian hero. He is ordinary "Jones," not even "Mr. Jones."

For these reasons he colors our view of the apparently unassailable Fischer. He detested Fischer, not for his money, but for his pride, for his contempt of the world, his cruelty. Fischer loved no one, not even his daughter: "He didn't even bother to oppose our marriage."[13]

He stands outside ordinary life; he is cold and calculating; he cares for no one; he is a recluse in his great white mansion. He hardly ever comes out; from there he is the puppet-master. Albert looks after him;

---
[13] Ibid., 10.

Fischer is ruthless, rude, and impossible to live with. (Greene in self-analysis said similar things about himself to his mistress, Catherine Walston.) Jones predisposes us to loathe Fischer's ritual humiliation of the Toads. Humiliation is Fischer's speciality; his games are imaginative and sophisticated. Kips is made into a Christmas storybook character and sees himself in the bookshop windows. Like a conductor, Fischer has them all under his baton. They perform to his conducting of the *Jupiter Symphony*. Fischer is King of the gods. But he does not—cannot—respond to music. "Music taunted him with his failure to understand."[14] He does not sleep well. He gives no enjoyment in sex: he sees sex as mere "animal impulse." He is humiliated because his wife's lover is so poor. Like everyone in one way or another, he too is maimed.

But watch! Graham, the master of his craft, gives us the earliest possible caveat. Hark to the striking opening sentence.

> I think that I used to detest Doctor Fischer more than any other man I have known, just as I loved his daughter more than any other woman.

Of the second half of that sentence there is no qualification. "I loved his daughter more than any other woman." I shall talk about that later, for this is a love story, as tender as anything I know. But consider the first half of the sentence: "I think that I used to detest Doctor Fischer more than any other man I have known." This implies that detestation becomes modified.

As the story progresses, we find the clues. With power comes loneliness. Power may provide endless opportunities for amusement, but there is no denying the emptiness. The power to bully does not dull his personal honesty, his intellectual precision or his awareness.

Characters whom we view from the outside (like the Toads) we can readily dislike, although, of course, we are cradle-Christians and conditioned to be "nice." Those others whom we struggle to understand—they begin to demand some measure of our sympathy. Any fun, any imagination, any warmth that they show can gain our grudging respect.

> "I think that I used to despise Doctor Fischer..."
> .... But I have come to know him better:

It is as if Jones says that.

Part-answer to Dr Fischer's terrorism is to understand him and stand up to him. Jones calls Fischer's bluff. Jones has nothing to lose, and so terrorism loses its terror.

We must not label Fischer in the simplistic terms of the critics: bully, misanthrope. W. J. West, generally so perceptive, says that he "corrupts."[15] Not true: he may destroy, but most of those with whom he has dealings are already corruptible if not corrupted. He is a study in power. and power has always, inevitably, limitation.

Greene gives us little handles on this cold, distant man. In the early years of his marriage there was love. Jones—here the authentic voice of Greene—says:

> I doubt if one ever ceases to love, but one can cease to be in love as easily as one can outgrow an author one admired as a boy.[16]

---

14 Ibid., 38.
15 West, W.J. The Quest for Graham Greene: A Biography. New York: St. Martin's Press, 1977, 242.
16 Ibid., 12.

Fischer was young once. Mrs. Montgomery suggests that he has not had a happy childhood, and that 'at bottom he is very sensitive.' He was not always rich or powerful: Dentophil Bouquet had yet to be invented. He once was happy; there was an ordinariness in his sex and in the baffled questions he asked, and he had a child. He had women at his table in the early days of his marriage. He does not like to be reminded of those times, but that is not so very odd.

Sauccess only makes us acutely conscious of where we are not successful. Fischer comes up against different dimensions: music, and Mozart and the *Jupiter Symphony.* Jupiter, the King of the Gods versus Fischer of Geneva, of the Empire of Dentophil. He comes up against a hard place: the stone, against Steiner. His wife resorts to Steiner, and the two of them have a shared interest, music. Fischer is hurt because the clandestine meetings show his inadequacy; they were "A region into which he could not follow."[17]

Fischer hates music because he does not understand it. Music is the taunt of his inadequacy. He cannot compete. He is a maimed man. It is a key word and used deliberately. The terrorist who seemed to hold all the cards does not have a full hand. The Duke in *My Last Duchess* feels compromised. "I gave commands, all looks stopped."

None of us likes being made aware of our own limitations. Similarly, Fischer feels humiliated in love. He had been so busy (like Charles Greene, Graham's father) that he had never labored for the tenderness of love. So it is that his wife, Anna, finds love with Steiner–the Stone. Fischer learns too late and is soured: "A woman who betrayed me with a clerk . . . . She preferred his company to mine."[18]

"Despising," says Fischer, "comes from great disappointment." He has lost his hopes of finding a spiritual completeness in the world of his creation. His feelings are bleak; his mind is acute.

He speaks scornfully of Pity, and of being pitied: "Pity. My daughter took after her mother in that. Perhaps she married you out of pity, Jones."[19]

If that were true and Jones is humiliated in the same way, then Fischer need not feel so isolated. Fischer watches Jones's face and almost reaches out for understanding.

Fischer wants to talk. There are hints of his utter emptiness of life: "Nothing is a bit frightening, Jones."[20]

At least he can articulate the problem. So he sets up his diversions, and he tests; and he watches. He is almost grateful to find that the independent Jones can be a confidant. "I have no friends,"[21] he says with a composed arrogance. The Toads are lackeys; they have no independence. They are the free loaders, the gravy train, the addicts of competitions for winning a free holiday, a free car, a free Christmas hamper. He can only despise them—not dislike. He feels drawn towards Jones who has an equality of honesty. Jones is brave enough to call Fischer mad. Fischer respects that and confides in him. He talks about the Toads to him:

"Sometimes I have a desire to talk."[22] It is only to Jones that he can talk. "I owe you

---

[17] Ibid., 39.
[18] Ibid., 105.
[19] Ibid., 115.
[20] Ibid., 137.
[21] Ibid., 102.
[22] Ibid., 104.
[23] Ibid., 102.

something, Jones, and I'm not in the habit of running up debts."[23] Fischer needs Jones. In the monopoly of his power there is a terrible fragility. He is, comments the taxi driver, "un peu farfelu"—a bit scatty.

Fischer hesitates as to how to begin conversation with Jones after the death of Anna-Luise. He is also at a loss with Steiner, whom he has ruined. He looks around for help. He finds in Steiner some incomprehensible resource of love. His own incapacity is an irritation, a disease:

> "It was a disease I caught when you came into my life, Steiner. I should have told Kips to double your salary and I could have presented Anna with all the Mozart records she wanted. I could have bought you and her, like I bought all the others—except you, Jones.[24]

Steiner, realizing that this man is also maimed, cannot at the end spit in his face.

Fischer is not complete, yet he has humor, and a detached and philosophical honesty. And he is brave. Of them all, he is the one person who, without fuss or hesitation, can pull the trigger and end it all. In that one act we find Greene's unequivocal admiration. With one bullet in the revolver, Fischer takes us all by surprise.

We have so far deliberately kept God out of the business, but it will not surprise you that Greene does not do so. Dr. Fischer is constantly spoken of in terms of God and Satan. There is little to choose between them: God and the Devil are the same if you are damned or poor: "To the damned God Almighty looks very like Satan."[25]

The nature of God is an endlessly fascinating speculation. Graham approaches it in his own way, and the novel is a parable, an extended metaphor. "Theology (is) an amusing intellectual game," says Fischer[26]. If Fischer is, as it were, God, then Anna-Luise is his only begotten daughter bringing happiness and love to ordinary mankind: Jones. She died in "the white Christmas sweater stained with blood." We are reminded of Christmas and Easter.

But Greene ventures one stage further and holds God/Fischer up for our consideration. Man is made in God's image, and so it is not unreasonable to suppose that Man can repay the compliment. We come at God, who is ineffable, through Fischer who is explicable. The two are spoken of in similar terms.

> "Thank God for that," says Anna-Luise.
> "Thank Dr. Fisher," Jones replied, "or is it the same thing?"[27]
> Again:
> 'You make him sound like our Father in Heaven,'–says Jones 'his will be done on earth as it is in Heaven.'
> 'That about describes him,' replies Anna Luise.[28]

Fischer talks of his gifts to the Toads as being "given," not "earned." They are like God's Grace. And Fischer likes to think that his greed "is a little more like God's." God wants our love, but his creation fails him: "Perhaps he found that he was a rather bad craftsman and he is disappointed in the result."[29]

---

24 Ibid., 137.
25 Ibid., 32.
26 Ibid., 61.
27 Ibid., 28.
28 Ibid., 23.
29 Ibid., 61

We can easily see God as a kind of eternal Fischer, who behind his great portico, has become profoundly dissatisfied with objects of creation that have, unaccountably, turned out maimed. Bitterness and cynicism may be all that is left for a god who has suffered huge disappointment, and ends by despising. "God's disappointment is that we have turned out like Kips, Belmont, Deane, Mrs. Montgomery: that Dentophil Bouquet cannot keep up with the manufacture of chocolate, with or without whisky. It cannot account for the fact that we are never satisfied, that we are drunk, cowardly, deformed, and greedy. We cannot altogether blame God that we have given him reasons for disappointment."

Worse for God/Fischer is that he finds a galling, insignificant Steiner who hears his heaven in music and shares it with another. God is disappointed, withdraws into his "Pharoah's tomb" of a mansion, and finds more pleasure in our humiliation than in our love. The great experiment has failed. We are maimed, and God—while it is true that he retains power—is more aware of the shortcomings of his created enterprise than of its glory. God is maimed in that he cannot resolve his world. It is imperfect. What is left but an ironic delight in exploiting our incompleteness? Who has cancer of the rectum, a streaming cold, incontinence, premature ejaculation? Let us laugh at the one-handed man trying to engage in love. Who dyes her scant hair? Who resorts to drink in order to blur the recognition of cowardice or creeping age?

God would have the teeth white and healthy, but we all, with the bloody-mindedness of humanity, eat chocolate. Somehow God's intentions twist and turn and get away. A boy falls on a ski slope. We see accident and death: a woman killed because she swerves on the ski slope to avoid that injured boy. The final unsettling joke is that, although Death may provide a respite, a resolution, we are frightened of it. Kips is frightened to pull the cracker. He and the Divisionaire slink out of the experiment with tears of self-disgust.

Only Jones cracks wide the theory of Fischer's disgust. But he does not play fair because he is motivated by the sadness of loss of love. He seeks to end himself in heroic despair. The last three crackers he pulls. The last enemy is not Death, as St. Paul would have us believe; it is Un-Death—not being able to remove ourselves from the nightmare. Jones, with his maimed hand, can open the crackers only with his teeth. He chews at the wrappings desperately, but there is no explosion. For Fischer, Jones is cheating because he wants death: "There is no credit in choosing death if you want to die."[30] "My research must go on to its end. I won't give up now,"[31] says Fischer almost in frustration, but Jones has destroyed Fischer's hypothesis about human littleness of spirit. In all the sadness and unpleasantness, Jones and Anna-Luise stand out with a radiance.

A god of detached cynicism is not distinguishable from the Devil. So runs the equation. Analogies must not be pushed too hard, but they are there, and Greene, we must imagine, enjoys banging them backwards and forwards with Fr. Leopoldo. God and Satan are the two sides of the green baize door. It is Anna-Luise, who has lived with him, who knows her father best. He has become totally disinterested and remote:

"He's hell," said Anna-Luise[32]
"You'll let him take you into a high place

---

[30] Ibid., 125.
[31] Ibid., 59.
[32] Ibid., 18.

and show you all the kingdoms of the world," she taunts. (32)

The thesis is that if you take away love and benevolence then there is nothing to choose between God and Satan. Handy-dandy—it's the same fellow. In naked power terms, they are both pretty nasty; they are antitheses to mercy, pity, and love. If we considered God without being conditioned by our knowledge of Christianity, then we see him as the retributive God of the Old Testament. He is like some unsympathetic Dr. Fischer using us for research. If we look at the world cynically, then we may regard it like Job. God has become an appalling Dr. Mengele who wants to probe how much we can endure, how far we can be pushed.

Is he God? Is he Satan? As ever it is a matter of perception: Pinkie, the Lieutenant in *The Power and the Glory*, Lord Rochester in *Lord Rochester's Monkey*. We must contend with both sides of the equation, and understanding brings with it a greater sympathy than we first thought possible.

Let me turn aside for a moment to a character that no one has considered, Albert, the man-servant. I wonder if Greene created him as an indicator, a fugleman.

On his first appearances, Albert is wearing white. He is, however, loathsome: He insults Jones, forgets his name, shuts the door in his face and threatens him with physical violence. But when Jones goes to see Fischer just before the Bomb Party, Albert is wearing black, the color of the Devil, but also the color of mourning and sympathy. In this guise he behaves with impeccable courtesy and calls Jones "Mr." and "Sir." The black suit seemed to have changed his character for the better.

The Bomb Party is the ultimate reach of Fischer's research, but he fails because Jones spoils the cunning plan. Greed may be a factor, but what else motivates us, or gives us hope? Fr. Leopoldo Duran was adamant about Greene's state of grace because he continued to receive the sacrament. The final efficacy is not power, nor infinite riches, nor Dentophil Bouquet, but a celebration of Love, of sacrifice. Even the Toads turn up to the Christmas service. Jones wonders whether they come to the eternal Birthday of Christ, or to a Toad Party.

If Fischer is like God, then he is like God before the Incarnation and before the first Easter. Here is the moment when he talks to Jones:

"My greed—I told you before—is of a different order. I want . . . ." He raised the Christmas cracker rather as the priest at midnight Mass had raised the Host, as though he intended to make a statement of grave importance to a disciple—"this is my body." He repeated: "I want . . ." and lowered the cracker again.[33]

Fischer cannot understand love without the experience of Love. For him there is no 'salvific incarnation'[34] that places God in the material world. On that analogy, God without Christ would, like Fischer, merely act out a history of unsatisfactory diversions. But there are symbols that catch the eye and give hope. The human love of Anna-Luise and Jones is compressed into the symbol of the skiing sweater. White—it was her Christmas present. Red—it is the color of sacrifice. And Anna-Luise was Fischer's only-begotten child.

---

33 Ibid., 107.
34 Bosco, Mark. *Graham Greene's Catholic Imagination*. New York: Oxford University Press, 2005.
35 Ibid., 139.

At the very end[35] Jones remembers:

> As I boiled myself an egg for my supper, I heard myself repeating a line which I had heard spoken by a priest at the midnight Mass at Saint Maurice: "As often as you do these things you shall do them in memory of me."

The answer is in memory of the love that is spontaneous, generous, unmaimed.

There is infinite longing in this book. Fischer wants, but does not tell us what. Perhaps he hopes for something better than the greed of the Toads but fears that that may be all. Jones wants "le jour le plus long." Graham Greene wants a Faith more satisfactory than mere hope.

There is one last tack. Greene was very concerned to have the name Fischer, the Swiss spelling. His daughter Caroline checked the Geneva telephone book. Why did Graham want the name? He used "Fisher" before, briefly, in *The Honorary Consul*. The name is significant.

The name "Fisher" is important in the medieval Grail stories, and in 1922, the year Graham went up to Oxford, T.S. Eliot had given it a new prominence with his "Fisher King" in the *The Wasteland*. The Fisher King was the guardian of the Grail, and the Grail was the cup of the Eucharist. Symbols merge: grail, redemption, power. But the Fisher King was old and maimed, and his land, like him, had become impotent and infertile. Maiming is again the subject. For there to be hope in the future, right answers must be given and the old King must die, be replaced; the Grail must be found and handed on. Only then will the land flower.

Greene was growing old. All his life he had placed himself in scenarios of absolute power and political futility: Indo-China, Haiti, Mexico. In this fable of *Dr. Fischer* he reflects and leaves us with a counterpoint of love–not of youthful love that sings with the heart, but of love that remembers the past with a sad pleasure. The poetry of Keats and the music of Mozart can still be heard; the Grail can be found, and the sacrament held aloft with priestly assurance.

This novel has the most touching, real portrayal of love. Greene means what he writes. In the context of greed, money-making, and power-games, there is a picture that is truthful, unsentimental, recognizable: human love. Never idealized, but surrounded by domesticity—"the cheerful clangour of human washing-up." Jones is confident that we shall recognize it—"it needs no explanation."

We sense from the first page that the love is doomed. The story is tinged with Jones's sadness. Anna-Luise does not want to live without love. She seeks and takes it where it comes, unexpectedly. In spite of her fathering, she is warm-hearted, intelligent, giving: "We took each other for good and all." Their first meeting was so natural–"the waitress . . . assumed we were together . . . And so, quite suddenly, we actually were." They gave themselves to each other on the very first day of their meeting. You are "the only family I want," she said. Jones comes home to the sound of a voice he loves. Their thirty-year difference in age is immaterial, and so is the maimed hand. "I've never been so happy," says Jones. He cannot think of Anna-Luise without tears coming into his eyes. Their love is referred to as a "near miracle." They look forward to "Le jour le plus long." But Anna-Luise's death is mentioned specifically as early as page 15. Their love is doomed.

The day of Anna-Luise's death is recalled with a breath-taking suspension of time. The signs are there: the omens before the

Porridge Party, the talk of buying skis, of avoiding an accident when pregnant. It is heart-rendingly awful. Every trivial detail makes us catch breath with hope. The film is slowed down and love is caught in little moments of still-life.

On that day when Anna-Luise goes off to ski, they act as loving people do:

They sensibly ring the météo to find about conditions.
Jones gives her a good breakfast: Two eggs.
He puts chains on the car.
He persuades her to go on an easier red piste.
He does not want her to ski alone. "Safety in numbers. Be careful."
He sits at a window where he can watch her return, and reads *The Knapsack*.
An Accident. A boy with a broken ankle. But, reassuringly: "She is a good skier."
The Chinese philosopher's *33 Happy Moments*. Jones adds his 34th happiness.

And then . . . .

". . . I can remember the gist," says Jones, though not the exact words when I laid the book down for ever."
"In battle when men are hit, they never feel the hurt till later."
A woman—on a stretcher.
A different sweater, red not white.
What we shall do when she is better.

It was not to be. Jones at first, like Fischer, thinks in terms of revenge against the indifference of the powers that govern us, but comes to realize that love, though subject to inevitability and chance, is yet not crushed. "*Vulneratus non victus*"—that cry is on a memorial seat at Berkhamsted School. Desperately, Jones wants God to exist because Anna-Luise can exist somewhere, but only if God exists. There is not one orthodox "believer" in the book, yet Anna-Luise makes God a possibility, and she, so strangely, is the child of Fischer. The memory of love and the chance of "le jour le plus long" keep our poor hopes alive.

This novel never ceases to engage me. It possesses the sharp edge of wit and perception. It is closely textured. It is never sentimental, but it has humor and seriousness. Because Greene does not shun the possibility of the empty awfulness, we know that we can trust him. There is the answer of happiness even if the cup is dashed from our lips.

Strangely, the novel has received little attention. One critic has called it "short, slight and trivial." The first adjective I will concede. Norman Sherry[36] mentions it not at all.

I regard it as a bran tub full of goodies with ne'er a bomb to put me off reaching down into the depths again and again, like Jones. Were I to recommend a novel that encapsulated Greene's art and his thinking, I should not hesitate to suggest *Dr. Fischer of Geneva and his Bomb Party*.

---

36 Sherry, Norman. *The Life of Graham Greene, Volume II: 1939-1955*. New York: Viking, 1994. *The Life of Graham Greene, Volume III: 1955-1991*. New York: Viking, 2004.

**David Pearce** gained an MA at Oxford University and worked for 33 years at Berkhamsted School where his responsibilities included Head of English Department and also Housemaster. He was a Founding Trustee of the Graham Greene Birthplace Trust and a Festival Director and speaker on a number of occasions. The text of his 2008 paper, 'Stamboul Train and the Timetable for 1932', was later published in *Dangerous Edges of Graham Greene: Journeys with Saints and Sinners* (2011). A keen thespian, David also co-directed a rehearsed reading of Greene's unpublished play *A House of Reputation* which was presented at the Festival in 2000—a world premiere. Yearly, he delighted festival goers with his highly animated, conducted tours of those parts of Berkhamsted School associated with Graham Greene.

# REVIEW

## Judith Adamson

Jon Wise and Mike Hill, *The Works of Graham Greene, Volume 2: A Guide To The Graham Greene Archives*. London: Bloomsbury, 2015.

ISBN: 978-1-4725-2819-3, 357 pages.

Jon Wise and Mike Hill are too modest when they say their book "is not a biography nor is it a literary criticism" of Graham Greene's work. A literary criticism, maybe not, but it is certainly a biographical bibliography with sometime critical insights—a comprehensive guide to nearly sixty repositories of Greene's papers in Canada, Ireland, the United Kingdom, and the United States. It includes an engaging synopsis of most of their contents; this means that as well as directing readers to the location of his papers, their book reveals a great deal about Greene's life and work. It is elegantly written, easily accessible to general readers and invaluable to literary researchers. For years we have marveled at Greene's productivity; this chronicle adds to the more commonly known list of his archived journals, diaries, notes, correspondence and the innumerable drafts and manuscripts of his published work, many fragments and letters along with abandoned, unpublished or unfinished stories, poems, plays, film scripts, and novels. In an undated typescript at the University of Georgetown, the compulsively self-critical Greene admits to being "an obsessive writer... I cannot support idleness (even these words which I write now are an escape—better than writing nothing)."

Greene began selling off his manuscripts and papers in the early 1960s and did so on a regular basis for the rest of his life, encouraging his family, friends and lovers to do likewise with the letters, manuscripts and inscribed editions he had at one time or another sent them. Papers were sold to university archives and dealers, sometimes with embarrassing results. In May 1964 the *Daily Mail* mocked Greene when the manuscript of *Carving a Statue* was auctioned off by Sotheby's four months before the play was staged. Greene apologized to his agent and subsequently sold other manuscripts prior to publication.

Soon after he appointed Alan Redway as his bibliographer in 1949, Greene learned that Neil Brennan had independently taken up the same work. He told Redway that "bibliography has always had a certain fascination for me;" he introduced the two men and helped them itemize differences between his various editions, bindings and textual changes, reminding them not to forget the blurbs he had written for *A Burnt-Out Case* and *Travels With My Aunt*, among other books. A stickler for detail, he argued that these seemingly insignificant pieces should be listed as part of his work. In those days scholars shared bibliographies they had compiled themselves, and before Redway and Brennan could finish, Roland Wobbe published *Graham Greene: Bibliography and Guide To Research* in 1979, and in 1981 A.F. Cassis followed with *Graham Greene: An Annotated Bibliography of Criticism*. By then Greene's bibliographic interest must have waned: when John Bray, a serious collector of his work, later asked him to send Wobbe a get-well message, Greene declined. Redway died in 1983 and Brennan in 2006, their work unpublished. Quoting Greene, Wise and Hill's epigraph reads: "What a life a bibliographer's must be!"

At Columbia University they have found a cache of one hundred letters, postcards and telegrams between Greene and Mercia Ryhiner Schwob Tinker Harrison (she eventually married Rex Harrison) dating from 1954 to 1990. The letters suggest "an intense passion" not discussed by Norman Sherry or Michael Shelden. The two met in the Far East and were together in Bangkok, Penang, and Singapore. In 1954 Greene wrote that he longed to see her again and that the only two people he loved were "you and Catherine." In the '60s he arranged for her to stay in his villa at Anacapri and offered advice on writing about love after reading a novel she had written: "the colder and the more detached your writing is the more warmth it can convey to a reader."

Wise and Hill's other discoveries are many: probably the only original text of *Stamboul Train*, a 73,000-word manuscript of the 1924 novel, *Prologue To Pilgrimage* (usually called Anthony Sant) about a black boy born to white parents, another unpublished novel of 82,000 words from 1925–6 called *The Episode*, and a novel of 18,000 words titled *Lucius*, which seems to date probably from the 1950s. They found a seven page fragment of another abandoned novel called *Fanatic Arabia*, which they claim was written in 1927–28; a twenty-seven page unpublished piece called *A Man of Extremes*, which appears to feed into *The Comedians*; eight pages of a melodrama in three acts called *The Clever Twist*, which they say was clearly intended to be a significant piece of writing, another untitled piece of eleven pages that may have been intended as a novel; and many abandoned stories.

Of equal interest are the diaries and journals from Greene's travels, which are housed at Georgetown University. As Wise and Hill say, travel was an escape for Greene. In 1938 he went to Mexico, some claim, to avoid attending the libel trial over his *Wee Willie Winkie* review in *Night and Day*; his Mexican diary forms the basis of *The Lawless Roads*. On the first page of his November 1957 Havana Journal he said he was "running from myself, and my chaos and my loss." If Batista's Havana offered louche charms it also gave him the backdrop for *Our Man In Havana*. His travel reports paid his way for the research that informed many of his novels. From his Vietnam trips came *The Quiet American*. A journey on the Orient Express in 1968 served him well in *Travels With My Aunt*. Visits to Argentina and Paraguay provided background detail for *The Honorary Consul*. Two Panama diaries (Greene took six trips to Panama) include notes for a novel he never completed, for *Getting to Know The General*, and his story "On The Way Back."

Then there are the letters. Perhaps most interesting among them are those to Catherine Walston (over 1200 at Georgetown University), to Yvonne Cloetta (these chronicle Greene's travels as well as his love for her), to Leopold Duran (which include discussion about *Monsignor Quixote*), to Gloria Emerson (journalist and author of the novel *Loving Graham Greene*), to John and Gillian Sutro (close friends for 40 years), and to Vivienne Dayrell-Browning before she and Greene were married. Wise and Hill say that with her, Greene "adopted the conventional gender role of that time, that of the strong male caring for the delicate and emotionally fragile female who needed protecting" and that they cannot tell from these letters "if this romantic yet chaste relationship was what the deeply sexually charged Greene really wanted or if he was adopting a role simply designed to please a person he genuinely loved." Here Wise and Hill's sensitive editing begins to explain that doomed marriage.

Given the mass of information they have condensed, it is not surprising that their comments sometimes mislead. Greene was on the Board of The Bodley Head from June 1957 until 1968 when he stepped down to establish beyond question that he was domiciled in France, and his brother, Hugh, soon replaced him. He, nonetheless, remained active in the firm's affairs and his suggestions were almost always taken up. However, in September 1962 Reinhardt did not publish Henry Miller's *Tropic of Cancer* and *Tropic of Capricorn* when Greene thought he should. Wise and Hill say the reasons are "unfortunately... not known." But they are.

Reinhardt and Greene had to intervene many times between September 1957 when they first contacted Charlie Chaplin about his autobiography and 1964 when it was finally published. Getting Chaplin to finish his manuscript was a very delicate task. Early on Greene proposed shortening it by about 15,000 words, cuts Chaplin agreed to, and Greene and Reinhardt made many other suggestions as time passed. Part way through these often difficult Chaplin years, Reinhardt urgently needed a new editorial director; Greene suggested he steal James Michie from Heinemann. Among Michie's desires was the freedom to take on whatever books he liked. When he asked if The Bodley Head would publish *The Tropic of Cancer*, Greene advised Reinhardt not "to discourage [him] at this point and I personally would be all for publishing Henry Miller.... The courageous thing for us to do would be to publish in one volume both 'Tropics'." If you add this publishing information to what Wise and Hill quote of Greene's 12 May 1960 letter to Reinhardt, it becomes clear that while Greene was in favor of publishing Miller's books, the possibility was raised, or temporarily not denied, only to encourage Michie to come to The Bodley Head, which he did and where for years he was a highly valued member of staff.

However, Wise and Hill's editing is almost invariably thorough and helpful. Their book is an invaluable guide to the various Greene archives and it often provides startling insights. It should be used in conjunction with its companion volume *The Works of Graham Greene: A Reader's Bibliography And Guide* (Bloomsbury, 2012), which was so recently published that one is in awe of Wise and Hill's energy.

## THE RITZ

An elegy written on first reading that the Hotel was for sale.

### 1

A bird's been flapping in the chimney
All the long day long.
Smoked salmon instead of eggs for breakfast –
Something must be wrong.
An Egyptian waiter has kissed a girl
In room number four-two-three
(Why the hell did she make such a fuss
Instead of calling for me?)
The Ritz may be falling like London Bridge
And I be a bloody fool,
But in an hotel where Victor ceased to rule
I would not wish to be.

### 2

It's hot as hell and the windows won't open
All the long day long.
It's freezing and the heat is off –
Something must be wrong.
A yank's been phoning all night to New York
In room number four-two-three.
Why the hell won't he wait till morning
Instead of awakening me?

The Ritz is falling like London Bridge,
And I am a bloody fool,
But in the hotel where Victor ceased to rule
I would not wish to be.

3

I wait for breakfast ordered at seven

All the long day long.

Though the "tea" will be black and the toast will be soggy –

Something must be wrong.

They've chilled the claret and bombed the Terrine

Ordered by four-two-three,

And I quite forgot what I ordered them to bring –

It's a far off dream to me.

The Ritz has fallen like London Bridge

And I weep like a bloody fool,

For the hotel where Victor has ceased to rule

It's not the hotel for me.

1976

The poem is published with the permission of the Graham Greene Literary Estate.
A copy of this poem is in the Georgetown University Archives.

# *Graham Greene Studies*

## Call for Papers:

The University of North Georgia Press, in conjunction with The Graham Greene Birthplace Trust, is issuing a Call for Papers for a peer-reviewed journal dedicated to the life and work of the English writer Graham Greene (1904–1991). University academics, independent researchers, and doctoral, post-graduate, graduate, and undergraduate students are invited to submit papers. Suggested topics include, but are not limited to the following:

- Greene's political and theological landscapes
- Greene's depiction of women
- The short fiction
- The early novels
- The plays
- Greene's travels on 'the dangerous edge of things'
- Book and film reviews and other feature articles will also be considered.

Please submit all papers to digitalcommons.northgeorgia.edu/GGS.

All submissions must be original, unpublished work. Papers should be between 2,500 and 10,000 words. Citations must follow *The Chicago Manual of Style*, 16$^{th}$ edition documentation guidelines. All papers should be submitted double-spaced in Word document format. Readers and Graham Greene International Festival goers are encouraged to submit.

Deadline: June 30, 2018

Call for Papers issued by
Joyce Stavick, University of North Georgia
Jon Wise, Graham Greene Birthplace Trust

www.ingramcontent.com/pod-product-compliance
Lightning Source LLC
Chambersburg PA
CBHW080735300426
44114CB00019B/2605